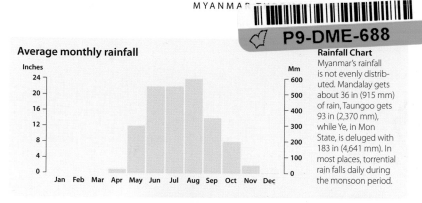

Average monthly rainfall

Rainfall Chart

Myanmar's rainfall is not evenly distributed. Mandalay gets about 36 in (915 mm) of rain, Taungoo gets 93 in (2,370 mm), while Ye, in Mon State, is deluged with 183 in (4,641 mm). In most places, torrential rain falls daily during the monsoon period.

Wet Season

The incidence of showers increases through May, but by June it is time to prepare for the huge monsoon storms that sweep into the country from the southwest. Beach resorts close and travel throughout Myanmar can be difficult from July through September. October sees a second, shorter intensification of rainfall with the northwest monsoon. At times of heavy downpours, roads are frequently blocked by flooding, and by landslides in the hills; flights are also often diverted, causing long delays.

Women weaving robes for Tazaungdaing, Shwedagon Pagoda, Yangon

July

Dhammasetkya *(mid-Jul)*, nationwide. Coinciding with the onset of the heaviest monsoons, the three-month period of Buddhist Lent starts with the full moon of Waso. Laypeople travel to local monasteries to offer new robes, alms, and other essentials to monks.
Waso *Chinlone* Festival *(Jul/Aug)*, Mandalay. Myanmar's most accomplished *chinlone* players come to the Mahamuni Temple for the country's top tournament. More than 1,000 teams take part, as traditional *hsaing waing* orchestras provide musical accompaniment.

August

Brother Lords Festival *(Jul/Aug)*, Taungbyon, near Mandalay. In the most raunchy and lively of Myanmar's numerous *nat* festivals, two gilded wooden deities are processed around the village, watched by over 10,000 worshippers. *Hsaing*

music, gambling, singing, and drunken spirit possession rituals by transvestite oracles are also among the day's events.

September

Manuha Temple Festival *(mid–late Sep)*, Myinkaba, Bagan. Larger than life papier-mâché figures of heroes, celestial creatures, and *nats* (nature spirits) are paraded around the village shrine. Dances and plays are staged through the night.
Golden Bird Festival *(Sep/Oct)*, Inle Lake. Enshrined inside huge *hamsa* bird boats, four of the Phaung Daw U Pagoda's five Buddha statues are ceremonially paddled around the lake by leg rowers. Fairs and boat races are also held during the event.

October

Thadingyut Festival of Lights *(Sep/Oct)*, nationwide. The Buddha's return from heaven to Earth at the end of the Buddhist Lent is celebrated by all manner of colorful illuminations, with homes brightly lit by candles and lanterns.
Dancing Elephants Festival *(mid-Oct)*, Kyaukse, near Mandalay. Life-sized elephants made of colorful cloth and bamboo, and animated by

pairs of men inside, compete in dance competitions.
Tazaungdaing Weaving Festival *(late Oct/early Nov)*, nationwide. Under the full moon, unmarried women work all night to weave new robes on traditional looms. These are presented to the local temple early the next morning.

Public Holidays

Independence Day (Jan 4)
Union Day (Feb 12)
Full Moon Day of Tabaung (Feb/Mar)
Peasants' Day (Mar 2)
Armed Forces Day (Mar 27)
Myanmar New Year (Apr 13–17)
Full Moon Day of Kason (Apr/May)
Workers' Day (May 1)
Full Moon Day of Waso (Jun/Jul)
Martyrs' Day (Jul 19)
Full Moon Day of Thadingyut (Sep/Oct)
Full Moon Day of Tazaungmon (Oct/Nov)
National Day (10th day after full moon of Tazaungmon)
Christmas Day (Dec 25)

THE HISTORY OF MYANMAR

In common with its neighbors, the roots of Myanmar's contemporary culture – and of its ongoing ethnic strife – can be traced back many centuries. Forming a crossroads between India, China, and Thailand, the region attracted invaders who followed, and subsequently settled in, the great river valleys stretching across the country to the sea. The result is a complex cultural checkerboard whose fault lines continue to generate friction, despite the overarching presence of Buddhism. The religion first traveled here from India along ancient trade routes over two millennia ago to become the region's unifying faith, and continues to define the character of both Myanmar's people and its government.

The earliest traces of *Homo sapiens* in the territory now known as Myanmar/Burma span a period from 11,000 to 5,000 BC – the Anyathian Era – when the first roughly polished stone tools were produced along the banks of the Ayeyarwady River and the western edge of the Shan Plateau. Artifacts and paintings found in the remote Padah-Lin Caves, discovered in the 1930s in the hills north of Pindaya near Inle Lake *(see pp166–8)*, include red-ocher images of human hands and hunting scenes.

Knowledge of smelting and copper casting appears to have spread around the region from 1500–1000 BC, along with rice cultivation, which fueled rapid growth in population. By 200 BC, however, the Pyu, Tibeto-Burman-speaking invaders from China's Yunnan region, had begun to move into the area, establishing settlements along the Ayeyarwady Valley. Over time, these coalesced into well-planned city-states governed from walled capitals dotted on the dry plains flanking the rivers

of Upper Burma, where large-scale irrigation networks were established to fuel intensive agriculture. The first and largest of these urban centers was Hanlin, near Shwebo on the Ayeyarwady's west bank, whose economy was dominated by salt production and control of commerce along the river, by now a thriving trade artery connecting China with the Bay of Bengal. At some point in the 7th century AD, however, Sri Ksetra *(see pp98–9)* superseded Hanlin as the region's principal hub.

Heavily influenced through contact with India's Andhra kingdom, the Pyus' religious beliefs, architecture, and art reveal a unique blend of Mahayana Buddhism, Tantricism, Hinduism, and local animist *nat* worship, although by the 5th century BC, Theravada Buddhism had gained dominance. In many respects, Pyu culture provided the blueprint for the Bagan Empire that would supersede it. Some Pyu hallmarks, such as the Burmese script, astrological calendar, and pagoda design, have survived into the present era.

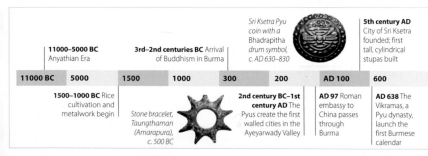

			Sri Ksetra Pyu coin with a Bhadrapitha drum symbol, c. AD 630–830	5th century AD City of Sri Ksetra founded; first tall, cylindrical stupas built
11000–5000 BC Anyathian Era	**3rd–2nd centuries BC** Arrival of Buddhism in Burma			
11000 BC 5000	1500 1000	300 200	AD 100	600
1500–1000 BC Rice cultivation and metalwork begin	Stone bracelet, Taungthaman (Amarapura), c. 500 BC	**2nd century BC–1st century AD** The Pyus create the first walled cities in the Ayeyarwady Valley	**AD 97** Roman embassy to China passes through Burma	**AD 638** The Vikramas, a Pyu dynasty, launch the first Burmese calendar

◀ Detail from a 6th-century stonework relief in the Nyaung Ohak complex, Inthein, Inle Lake

The Rakhine and Mon

Two other groups colonized different parts of the country at around the same time as the Pyu. In the northwest, the Rakhine people lived in similar city-states, with an economy based on rice farming and trade with India. At Wethali and Dhanyawadi, near the medieval city of Mrauk U *(see pp110–14)*, remnants of their ancient walled towns attest to an Indian-influenced Buddhist tradition dating as far back as the 4th century AD.

Golden spire of the Shwezigon Pagoda, begun in Anawrahta's reign

In the southwest, the Mons, originally from western China, are thought to have colonized the flat coastal land around the Gulf of Mottama (Martaban) in the 9th century, founding a capital at Thaton, the largest regional port of its day. Although they were later defeated by the Bamars and absorbed into the Bagan Empire, the Mons developed a highly sophisticated culture that would greatly influence that of their subsequent overlords.

The Bagan Dynasty

By the early 9th century, a new force from the northeast was beginning to make itself felt all along the Ayeyarwady Valley. An offshoot of the Nanzhao kingdom of Yunnan, the Mranma people, or Myamars, launched repeated raids on Pyu cities using hordes of mounted archers, eventually destroying Hanlin in 832 and carrying off 3,000 of its inhabitants into slavery. Sri Ksetra was attacked soon after.

Having subjugated the Pyus, the Mranmas, henceforth known in the Burmese Chronicles as Bamars or Burmans, built a fortified settlement – Bagan – on a bend in the Ayeyarwady River, close to its confluence with its main tributary, the Chindwin. From here, the dynasty carved out a domain extending 200 miles (322 km) from north to south and 80 miles (129 km) across. Gradually, over the next 200 years, the Burmese language became the lingua franca and the separate city-states of the region evolved into a centralized kingdom.

The First Burmese Empire

The Bagan Dynasty's golden age dawned in 1044 with the accession to the throne of a fiercely ambitious, energetic teenager who seized the crown after defeating his cousin in single combat. Anawrahta "The Ungovernable" (1015–78) immediately embarked on a series of military campaigns that would, in less than two decades, unify the four main kingdoms of medieval Burma. The high point was the conquest, in 1057, of the Mon capital, Thaton, from which Anawrahta returned with 30,000 prisoners, among them the Mon royal family and legions of skilled builders and architects. The talents of these enslaved

artisans were put to use during the two remaining decades of Anawrahta's reign, and that of his son and successor Kyanzittha (1030–1112), during which a huge number of monasteries, stupas, temples, and other monuments were erected in the capital, Bagan.

Fueled by wealth from trade and military conquests, the construction boom was coupled with a program of economic, social, and religious reform that would leave an enduring legacy, not least the adoption of Theravada Buddhism by the kingdom. The man credited with originally converting Anawrahta to this relatively austere form of the faith was a monk named Shin Arahan (1034–1115). He had fled his Mon homeland when it was threatened with invasion by the Hindu Khmers from the east, and served as the chief spiritual advisor to four successive Bagan monarchs. During his lifetime, Theravada became the predominant tradition, overlayering the more arcane practices of Mahayana Buddhism, Hinduism, and the animist worship of *nats*, or nature spirits.

By the 13th century, however, the Bagan Empire had gone into sharp decline. Laws exempting land grants and other donations to Buddhist monasteries from tax caused the royal coffers to empty. Without enough funds to maintain a large army, rebellion stirred in the kingdom. Then, in 1277 and

Well-preserved glazed tiles at the base of the Ananda Temple, built by King Kyanzittha

1283, during the reign of Kublai Khan (1215–94), Mongol forces invaded northern Myanmar. In 1287 the Mongols advanced to Bagan, with the resulting instability leading to the ruin of the city and its rulers.

The Post-Bagan Era

The decades following the break up of the Bagan Empire were ones of upheaval and strife as the region's powers struggled for overall supremacy. Eventually four main kingdoms emerged from the melee. In the east, a constellation of petty Shan chiefs, who had come to the region with the Mongols, ruled the hill tracts. In the northwest, the kingdom of Arakan, founded in 1430, became in time one of the wealthiest in Southeast Asia, with a writ extending from the mouth of the Ganges to the Ayeyarwady. In Upper Burma, Inwa (Ava) saw itself as the true successor to the Burmese-Bagan Dynasty, but exhausted its reserves trying to reform the empire. Most formidable among its adversaries was the Mon kingdom of Pegu-Hanthawaddy to the southeast, which emerged victorious from the Forty Years' War against Inwa to prosper on trade. The monuments that survive in modern Bago from the kingdom's heyday between the 1420s and 1530s attest to the town's former splendor and its importance as a great center of Theravada Buddhism.

1105 King Kyanzittha builds the Ananda Temple in Bagan

1290s Marco Polo (1254–1324) becomes the first Westerner to visit and write of Burma (Mien)

Marco Polo, the Venetian merchant traveler

1364 King Thadominbya (1345–67) moves capital from Sagaing to Inwa (Ava)

1150	1250	1350	1450

11th–13th centuries Bagan's golden age of temple building

1287 Collapse of the First Burmese Empire after the Mongol invasion

Kublai Khan, the great Mongol leader and grandson of Genghis Khan

1430 Men Saw Mon (1380–1433), also known as Naramithla, founds new Arakanese capital at Mrauk U

The Taungoo Dynasty (Second Burmese Empire)

Pegu's prosperity was being watched covetously by a power emerging to the north, in the landlocked Sittaung Valley. Following the conquest of Inwa (Ava) by a confederacy of Shan states in 1527, many Bamars had fled Upper Burma and settled in this new dynasty's capital, Taungoo, bolstering the power of its redoubtable king, Tabinshweti (1516–50).

Tabinshweti wanted Taungoo to become the hub of an empire, and to further this aim, he captured the Mon port of Pegu (Bago) in 1539, using its wealth to fund further conquests. By 1545 he controlled all of Upper and Lower Burma, except Arakan. Toward the end of his rule, however, the king succumbed to alcoholism, and by the time of his death (by assassination, on his 34th birthday), most of his territorial gains had been lost.

The job of restoring them fell to his brother-in-law and successor, Bayinnaung (1516–81), regarded as the greatest of all Burma's kings for his audacity, ambition, and military prowess. Over the following three decades, he recaptured all of the lost lands and amassed the largest empire in the history of Southeast Asia, encompassing Upper and Lower Burma, Laos, southern Yunnan, Siam, and Manipur. His most lasting legacy, however, was the pacification of the Shan hill states by means of a tributary system which endured until the British annexation of

Burma in 1885, and which made certain that successive capitals around Mandalay remained free from attack from the east.

European Merchants and Mercenaries

The reign of the last powerful Taungoo king, Anaukpetlun (1578–1628), coincided with the arrival on Burmese shores of a new potential threat. European merchants with powerful backers had been making inroads along the coastline of Southeast Asia since the creation of a Portuguese colony in Goa in 1510. Iberian slave traders and renegades had also become a fixture at local royal courts. Impressed by their weapons and modern military tactics, rulers of all the region's major kingdoms had employed European mercenaries to help fight their wars, and in many cases lived to regret the fact. A case in point was the king of Arakan, who, in the early 17th century, recruited the Portuguese adventurer Filipe de Brito e Nicote. Having been given the governorship of Thanlyin, de Brito soon began to use the port as a base from which to plunder the interior, until he was killed by King Anaukpetlun in 1613 *(see p82)*.

Rise of the Konbaungs and the Third Burmese Empire

Toward the end of Anaukpetlun's reign, rebellions throughout the country gravely weakened Taungoo/Burman rule and in 1740, the capital had to be moved from Pegu to the less vulnerable Inwa. Shortly after, however, the Mons

18th-century illustration of Konbaung nobility in court dress

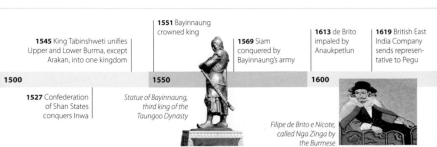

1545 King Tabinshweti unifies Upper and Lower Burma, except Arakan, into one kingdom

1551 Bayinnaung crowned king

1569 Siam conquered by Bayinnaung's army

1613 de Brito impaled by Anaukpetlun

1619 British East India Company sends representative to Pegu

1500

1527 Confederation of Shan States conquers Inwa

Statue of Bayinnaung, third king of the Taungoo Dynasty

1550

1600

Filipe de Brito e Nicote, called Nga Zinga by the Burmese

mounted a successful revolt and sailed up the Ayeyarwady to take the capital in 1752. Watching the Mon advance through his homeland was a young village chief named Aung Zeya who, after a series of daring raids on Mon positions, managed to gather around him a small but highly motivated army. In 1752, at the very moment Pegu's forces were about to breach the defenses of Inwa, Aung Zeya declared himself the new Burman king, taking the honorific title Alaungpaya, the "Embryo Buddha."

It is a name that still stirs great pride among the Burmese, for King Alaungpaya (1714–60) not only managed to expel the Pegu troops left behind to govern his kingdom, but also fended off the inevitable backlash two years later when an army was sent north to retake Inwa. This was followed in 1757 by a counterattack on Pegu itself, at the end of which Alaungpaya slaughtered the city's entire population.

In his short but seminal eight-year reign, Alaungpaya reconquered all of Burma and subdued Manipur and northern Thailand, setting the scene for the third and final Burmese Empire, ruled by the dynasty he founded, the Konbaungs (see pp54–5).

Konbaung Rule

The first major threat to Konbaung rule came in 1767–70, when the Qing Dynasty from Manchuria mounted a series of invasions. Their armies got to within three days' march of Inwa, causing panic in the capital, but were eventually halted by a combination of disease, inclement weather, and dogged resistance from the Burmese themselves. Achieved against all odds, the

Silk painting depicting Konbaung military practice

Konbaung victory conferred a sense of invincibility on the Burmese kings, who thereafter retreated to the cosseted luxury of their palaces on the banks of the Ayeyarwady, and left their generals to do the fighting.

The image of a Konbaung ruler as a sybaritic megalomaniac, a commonplace in the colonial era, first gained currency during the reign of Bodawpaya (1745–1819), Alaungpaya's fourth son, who grabbed the throne after murdering dozens of kinsmen and other potential challengers. Although famous for having 207 queens and concubines and fathering 120 children, Bodawpaya is perhaps best remembered for attempting to construct the world's largest brick stupa at Mingun, and for ordering the audacious attack on Arakan that resulted in the destruction of its capital, Mrauk U. The Burman army returned home from the campaign in triumph, bearing the most sacred of all Arakanese Buddhas, Mahamuni, which was carried over the Rakhine-Yoma Hills to Mandalay city, where it still rests.

Burmese war elephants on a 19th-century temple mural

1666 Mughal Empire defeats Arakan

1688 French East India Company opens branch at Syriam

550

1700

Alaungpaya, founder of the Konbaung Dynasty

1740 Mon capital moved from Pegu to Inwa

1752 Konbaung Dynasty established

1750

1767 Burmese army attacks Siamese capital Ayutthaya

1784 Bodawpaya invades Arakan

The Konbaung Dynasty

The Konbaungs, who dominated Burma from 1752 until the British invasion of 1885, were the country's last independent rulers. Founded by the legendary Alaungpaya, the dynasty had humble beginnings but went on to create an empire stretching from the borders of India to the Gulf of Thailand, even conquering Siam in 1767. The courtly culture and, later, reforms promoted by the Konbaungs have left a lasting effect on Myanmar's government, traditional arts, and sense of national identity.

Bhamarasana, the Bee Throne, was where the king sat during the nomination ceremony of the chief queen

The Court of the Konbaungs

The court was where the king demonstrated his absolute power, embodied most dramatically in the gilded Sihasana, *literally "Lion Throne," before which other royals, the nobility, and courtiers would have prostrated themselves. The ultimate symbol of Burmese sovereignty, the Lion Throne once formed the focal point of the Great Audience Hall of Mandalay Palace (see pp144–5).*

Nine Noble Gems adorned the Lion Throne, each representing a particular attribute or virtue.

The Celestial King represented the monarch's role as protector of the Buddhist faith and the highest judge of his people.

Niches in the doors behind the Lion Throne hold figurines of Kinnara and Kinnari, the bird-humans.

Thibaw and Supayalat
King Thibaw (1859–1916) and his queen are seen as the Lord and Lady Macbeth of Southeast Asian history for their massacre of their royal relatives to consolidate their power.

The base, in the form of two lotus blooms, is carved from yamanay wood *(Gmelina arborea)*, which is light but strong.

Auspicious earth from sacred sites around the kingdom is packed into the base.

Konbaung Art and Architecture

As well as being the kingdom's political hub, the court was also a crucible for the traditional arts, from dance-drama, music, and song to puppetry, poetry, and calligraphy. Burma's finest architects and craftsmen created and embellished wondrous teak buildings in Mandalay's walled city, of which only a few fragments still survive.

Tapestry
Kalagas, velvet panels embroidered with mythological scenes, are still crafted, carrying on a tradition that flourished in the Konbaung era.

Shwenandaw Monastery
This exquisite teak monastery was once part of the palace, and gives a vivid impression of how the vanished city would have looked in its prime.

Carvings
Although most of the elaborately worked teak buildings created by Konbaung artisans have disappeared, the Shwenandaw carvings and the religious images that survive are reminders of their masterly skills.

Konbaung Wars

In common with most Burmese rulers, the Konbaungs were an expansionist dynasty. While its founding father Alaungpaya pushed his kingdom's borders to the limits of modern Myanmar, his successors extended them into India and Siam. Only with the arrival of the British were their territorial ambitions thwarted.

The Burma-Siam War and the Anglo-Burmese Wars
The conquest of Siam in 1767 brought great treasure to the Konbaung court, as well as skilled artists who left a lasting mark on classical Burmese culture. In stark contrast, the 19th-century Anglo-Burmese Wars, and the subsequent punitive reparations forced on the Burmese, crippled Konbaung power forever.

King Thibaw's Exile

To ensure that he never became a martyr in the eyes of his former subjects, Thibaw was exiled by the British following the Third Anglo-Burmese War. An unseasonal rain shower had just ended when, on November 28, 1885, the royals made their way from the palace, past weeping crowds, to the wharf to begin their journey to Ratnagiri, India, where the king eventually died, depressed and penniless. After their departure, Mandalay Palace was comprehensively looted, and the royal apartments commandeered as barracks.

Painting c. 1900 showing British troops escorting the Konbaungs from the palace

Storming of a stockade during the First Anglo-Burmese War

First and Second Anglo-Burmese Wars

Bagyidaw (1784–1846), Bodawpaya's grandson, pursued an equally aggressive policy of expansion, targeting Manipur and Assam in India. The British East India Company regarded these states as a buffer against Burmese invasion of their empire in the subcontinent and reacted by sending troops to support the Assamese and Manipuris. But it was only when the Burmese targeted the hill state of Cacher that direct conflict became inevitable.

Declared in 1824, the First Anglo-Burmese War lasted two years and was a catastrophe for both sides: 15,000 British-Indian troops and many more Burmese perished. The bill, which ran to over £5 million (US$19 billion in modern money), nearly ruined the East India Company before its forces prevailed and the Treaty of Yandabo brought the bloodshed to a close. The treaty's terms were punitive: huge swaths of Burmese territory were lost (including all of Arakan) and massive indemnities set, crippling the Konbaung economy for generations.

Heavy-handed gunboat diplomacy was to blame for the Second Anglo-Burmese War of 1852, which erupted after the Burmese governor of Rangoon fined two British captains for customs violations. The ensuing conflict dragged on for a year and only ended when a coup in the Burmese capital, Amarapura, brought to power King Mindon (1808–78), by which time the whole of Lower Burma had been annexed by the British. A devout, scholarly Buddhist, Mindon is most remembered for the splendid monasteries and pagodas he founded in his new capital, Mandalay. He was also a determined modernizer, implementing a program of forward-looking reforms. The changes, however, were to prove powerless in the face of the cataclysmic events about to unfold.

Third Anglo-Burmese War

Mindon died in 1878 without naming a successor. After months of intrigue, the throne went to Thibaw (1859–1916), a prince chosen for his perceived pliability, and because he had fallen in love with Supayalat, the daughter of Mindon's most senior and influential queen. However, the new king and queen proved far from biddable. Shortly after their coronation, to eliminate any potential threat to their rule, the couple oversaw the killing of scores of young royals in a massacre that outraged world opinion. The British called for regime change, but finally it was a dispute over timber taxes on Scottish teak importers that ignited the third, and decisive, Anglo-Burmese war of 1885. This time, the Konbaung king offered no more

British soldiers at the Shwedagon Pagoda, First Anglo-Burmese War

Bahadur Shah Zafar, India's last Mughal emperor

1862 Exiled emperor Bahadur Shah Zafar dies in Rangoon

1800	1825	1850	
	1824 First Anglo-Burmese War	**1826** Treaty of Yandabo between the British East India Company and the king of Inwa (Ava)	**1852** Second Anglo-Burmese War; British seize and expand Rangoon	**1859** Mindon moves capital to Mandalay

than token resistance to the army that steamed up the Ayeyarwady. Without a single shot being fired, General Henry Prendergast accepted Thibaw's surrender in Mandalay. As the royal family sailed to exile in India, looters plundered the palace and the country descended into anarchy.

Colonial Rule

Burma was now officially part of British India, ruled by a government from Calcutta which, to keep the Burmese majority in check, deployed similar divide and rule tactics to those used in the subcontinent – a ploy that would have a dramatic effect over the coming century.

Meanwhile, the economy had begun to revive. The Ayeyarwady Delta region was developed, and waves of Indian immigrants poured in to take advantage of the boom. By 1927, Indians were in the majority while the Burmese, denied administrative posts by the British, suffered mounting poverty and unemployment. The consequent growth of Burmese opposition to British rule was spearheaded initially by radical Buddhist monks, and later by groups from Yangon University. Among the latter was an association called the 30 Comrades, led by the young socialist Aung San, future leader of the country and father of Aung San Suu Kyi. Rejecting Gandhian-style nonviolence in favor of military action, they turned to the Japanese for support.

World War II

The main goal of the Japanese invasion of Burma in December 1941 was to close off the "Burma Road," the supply line from Assam to Yunnan by means of which the Allies were able to re-provision Chinese forces. The north of the country was also regarded as a potential back door to British India and total domination of Asia.

As the Japanese forces pressed north, British and Indian soldiers were pushed back 930 miles (1,500 km) to the jungles and mountains of the Indian border. They were accompanied by hundreds of thousands of Indian refugees who were harassed and murdered by the Burmese as they struggled to regain their homeland. Around 12,000 troops and over 30,000 civilians perished in the mass retreat – one of the forgotten disasters of World War II.

Once the Japanese army had been halted at Kohima in northeast India, the Allies were reinvigorated by improved air support and forced the Japanese back across the Chindwin, while deep-penetration units, such as Orde Wingate's Chindits and their American counterparts, Merrill's Marauders, attacked them from behind their own lines. The battle then spilled across the central plains of Burma before the Japanese finally surrendered on August 28, 1945.

A convoy of military trucks on the Burma Road around 1945

1878 King Mindon dies of dysentery

1879 First massacre of royals by Thibaw

British troops entering Mandalay in 1885

1937 Burma granted its own Legislative Council by the British

1941 Japanese invasion

75

1900

1925

1885 Third Anglo-Burmese War and the British pacification of Burma

1884 About 400 members of the royal family killed in jail by Thibaw

The Burmese Army under British command in 1940

1944 Operation Capital: Allies recapture Burma

1945 Japanese surrender

Independence

During the Japanese occupation, Burma had become a de facto puppet state, with leaders of the former Burmese Liberation Army nominally at the helm. But in March 1945, Aung San switched allegiances, placing his troops at the disposal of the Allies during the final stages of the campaign. After the war, Burma pressed for full independence. Talks were concluded in January 1947, with Britain agreeing to grant Burma its freedom the next year.

Three months later, Aung San's party won the general election, but the celebrations were shortlived: on July 19 gunmen shot dead Aung San and six of his ministers. U Nu, a friend of Aung San's since their student days, took over to become independent Burma's first prime minister. However, the country descended into civil war almost immediately as conflicts erupted between the army and various regional forces, from communists and Chinese Kuomintang rebels to former resistance fighters and ethnic minorities such as the Shan, Kachin, and Chin, who had been promised full autonomy but now saw the government dominated by Burmese.

U Nu, friend of Aung San and first prime minister of independent Burma

Military Rule and the 8888 Uprising

Meanwhile, the economy went into rapid decline as rice exports plummeted and expenditure on arms rose. U Nu handed over control in 1958 to a temporary military government under General Ne Win, a move widely welcomed at the time, leading to considerable improvement in Burma's chaotic political situation.

In elections two years later, U Nu was restored to power, but regional calls for autonomy were threatening to drag the country into civil war, so Ne Win and the army stepped in again. The 1962 coup marked the start of radical military dictatorship under the Burma Socialist Programme Party. Private property was confiscated by the state; businesses, agriculture, and the media were nationalized; and foreign aid groups and opposition parties were banned. As a result, Burma became one of the poorest nations in the world. In July 1988 Ne Win resigned after a spate of public protests started by students and monks in Yangon. By August, the demonstrations had spread nationwide, leading to the declaration of martial law. Aung San's daughter, Aung San Suu Kyi, emerged as the popular leader of what became known as the 8888 Uprising (after the date of the strike). In the ensuing crackdown, thousands of protesters were imprisoned, killed, or forced to flee abroad.

SLORC

In September 1988, another army coup brought the hard-line State Law and Order Restoration Council (SLORC) to power under General Saw Maung. The following year, SLORC changed the country's official English name to Myanmar.

1947 Aung San assassinated

1948 Burma gains independence from Britain

1958–60 General Ne Win's caretaker government

General Ne Win, military commander and founder of the Burma Socialist Programme Party

1945   1955   1965   1975

1962 Prime Minister U Nu ousted in military coup

1974 New constitution transfers power to army

U Thant, UN Secretary-General, 1961–71

General Aung San

In 1990, confident that it had the support of the people, and having confined members of the opposition parties under house arrest during the campaign, the military government held free elections, only to lose by a crushing margin, with Aung San Suu Kyi's National League of Democracy (NLD) polling 60 per cent of the votes. Instead of respecting the results, the regime rounded up dissidents and NLD activists: many were sent to forced labor camps or "disappeared." Aung San Suu Kyi spent most of the 1990s imprisoned in her own home, as Myanmar became ever more distanced from the outside world.

General Than Shwe dominated politics in the 2000s, and promised a transition to democracy, but is best known for his multi-billion-dollar military and trade deals with the Russians and Chinese, and for moving the capital from Yangon to Naypyitaw.

The Saffron Revolution and Road to Democracy

A dramatic rise in gas and fuel prices in 2007 sparked a popular uprising which, because it was led by monks, was dubbed the Saffron Revolution. Protests were held across Myanmar before the army launched a brutal clampdown in which 31 people were killed and thousands arrested.

A Constitutional Referendum was held in 2008, and although opposition groups condemned the result as a sham, this historic poll paved the way for major political reforms. These included the release of Aung San Suu Kyi in 2010, amnesties for political prisoners, new labor laws, and a relaxation of press censorship. The

Aung San Suu Kyi, leader of the National League of Democracy

international community was quick to respond to the changes: Hillary Clinton and Barack Obama visited for talks, and Myanmar saw a huge surge in foreign tourism. Aung San Suu Kyi entered parliament in 2012 for the first time after by-elections. The same year, ceasefire agreements with several minority groups fighting for autonomy also brought peace.

However, the country has continued to see sporadic eruptions of communal strife. In Rakhine State in 2012, thousands of Rohingya Muslims were displaced by rioting and scores left dead.

Despite these outbreaks of sectarian violence, international pressure and a need for foreign investment has maintained the reforming momentum. In 2015 Myanmar held a general election which saw sweeping victories for Aung San Suu Kyi's NLD, and though the military retains considerable influence, there seems to be a genuine push for improved human rights and greater transparency. Whether this new openness will survive the challenges posed by greater freedom of speech remains to be seen, but for the time being the spirit in Myanmar is one of optimism for the future.

1989 SLORC declares martial law

1991 Aung San Suu Kyi awarded Nobel Peace Prize

2005 Naypyitaw announced as new capital

2011 Thein Sein elected president

2012 NLD win seats in elections; government signs peace accord with Karen rebel army

2015 General election sees NLD become the main elected party

85
1995
2005
2015

1988 8888 Uprising; Aung San Suu Kyi speaks at the Shwedagon

Rioting in Yangon during the 8888 Uprising

2008 Cyclone Nargis devastates the Delta region

President Thein Sein

2013 Communal disturbances in Meiktila; Thein Sein announces release of political prisoners

MYANMAR AREA BY AREA

Myanmar at a Glance

Myanmar stretches from the Himalayas in the north to the intensely tropical regions of the south. Between the two, the mighty Sittaung and Ayeyarwady rivers drain across vast arid valleys bounded by jungle-clad hills, while in the east, the Thanlwin cuts through the Shan Plateau, dividing China from the Andaman Sea. The rivers meet the ocean at deltas where patchworks of paddy are interlaced by winding canals and rivulets, but where devastating cyclones also regularly wreak havoc. A storehouse of art and culture, Myanmar offers sights ranging from the ethereal ruins of Bagan to the faded structures of colonial Yangon, and rich traditions of music and dance nurtured in the conservatories and theaters of Mandalay.

Hkakabo Razi (see p185), lying at the head of remote river valleys, is Myanmar's highest mountain and perfect for adventure trekking.

Bagan (see pp116–35), on the banks of the Ayeyarwady River, is one of Southeast Asia's greatest archeological treasures. Dotted across sandy plains, these exquisite remnants of the medieval Bagan Empire's lost city remain, despite natural disasters and neglect, an unforgettable sight.

Hakha

WESTERN MYANM. (see pp100–

Mrauk U

Sittwe (Aykab)

Mrauk U (see pp110–14), set deep amid the hills of Rakhine State, holds the evocative remains of the medieval kingdom of Arakan, once famed across Asia for its riches of its kings and the splendor of its palaces and temples. Today only a few ruined stupas and ordination halls remain.

The Shwedagon Pagoda (see pp74–7), Myanmar's most venerated Buddhist shrine, soars above Yangon's skyline from a complex of shining gold and marble. Despite being vandalized by colonial invaders and suffering earthquake damage, it has been beautifully restored and looks resplendent today.

◀ View of the sunset over the Ayeyarwady and the stupas of Mandalay city from Mandalay Hill

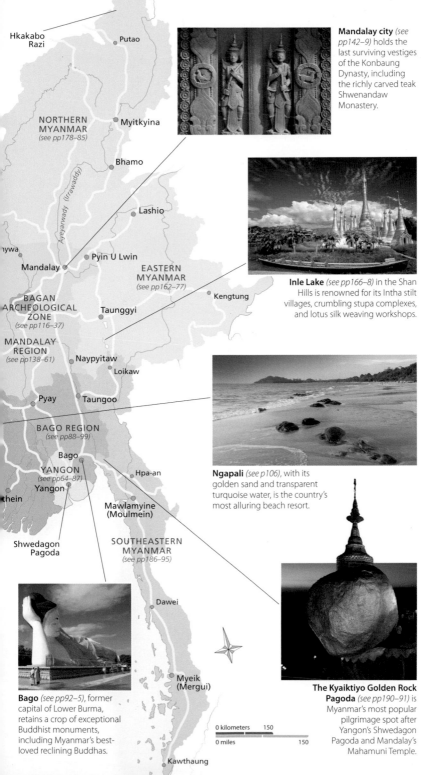

Mandalay city (*see pp142–9*) holds the last surviving vestiges of the Konbaung Dynasty, including the richly carved teak Shwenandaw Monastery.

Hkakabo Razi

Putao

NORTHERN MYANMAR
(*see pp178–85*)

Myitkyina

Bhamo

Lashio

yywa

Pyin U Lwin

Mandalay

EASTERN MYANMAR
(*see pp162–77*)

Kengtung

BAGAN ARCHEOLOGICAL ZONE
(*see pp116–37*)

Taunggyi

MANDALAY REGION
(*see pp138–61*)

Naypyitaw

Loikaw

Pyay

Taungoo

Inle Lake (*see pp166–8*) in the Shan Hills is renowned for its Intha stilt villages, crumbling stupa complexes, and lotus silk weaving workshops.

BAGO REGION
(*see pp88–99*)

Bago

YANGON
(*see pp64–87*)

Yangon

Hpa-an

hein

Mawlamyine
(Moulmein)

Shwedagon Pagoda

SOUTHEASTERN MYANMAR
(*see pp186–95*)

Ngapali (*see p106*), with its golden sand and transparent turquoise water, is the country's most alluring beach resort.

Dawei

Myeik
(Mergui)

Bago (*see pp92–5*), former capital of Lower Burma, retains a crop of exceptional Buddhist monuments, including Myanmar's best-loved reclining Buddhas.

Kawthaung

0 kilometers   150
0 miles   150

The Kyaiktiyo Golden Rock Pagoda (*see pp190–91*) is Myanmar's most popular pilgrimage spot after Yangon's Shwedagon Pagoda and Mandalay's Mahamuni Temple.

YANGON

Although it was superseded by Naypyitaw as the official capital in 2005, Yangon, overlooking the confluence of the Hlaing and Bago rivers, remains Myanmar's largest and most populous city, as well as its diplomatic, economic, and cultural hub. The city has retained a great deal of its colonial charm, but with its chic five-star hotels, restaurants, car showrooms, and air-conditioned shopping malls, Yangon is also where Myanmar's reentry into the mainstream of modern Asian life is most clearly discernible.

Until the British invasion of 1852, the city was a ramshackle port of only 20,000 people, distinguished less by its flagging maritime trade than by the presence of the Shwedagon Pagoda, Myanmar's principal religious monument. However, both trade and the population expanded rapidly in the wake of the British annexation, bolstered by waves of immigration from India. The new rulers called the town Rangoon, an anglicized version of the Burmese Yangon (literally "End of Strife"), the name chosen by Alaungpaya following his devastating conquest of Lower Burma between 1755 and 1757. By the early 1900s, it had become one of Asia's richest and most cosmopolitan capitals.

A grid plan of grand municipal buildings and multistory tenements was laid out on land close to the riverfront, where the colonial-era British authors Rudyard Kipling and Somerset Maugham sojourned en route to more far-flung postings in the empire. The Japanese bombings of World War II, and seven decades of neglect since, have taken their toll on the architecture, but the flaking, mildewed façades create a charismatic backdrop for the busy street life of the modern city, where commuters breakfast on bowls of steaming *mohinga* (noodle soup) at sidewalk stalls, and new hatchbacks vie for space with old-style trishaws.

Close to the waterfront, the Botataung and Sule pagodas are worth visiting, perhaps combined with trips to the traditional markets. North of downtown, the soaring golden Shwedagon Pagoda is deservedly the city's main visitor attraction; farther north, the broad, park-lined avenues and lakes of the suburbs provide welcome respite from the heat and traffic.

Monks taking a *Tipitaka* examination in the Mahapasana Guha at the Kaba Aye Pagoda, Yangon

◀ The Middle Terrace of the Shwedagon Pagoda, with a host of ornately decorated subsidiary shrines surrounding the main stupa

Exploring Yangon

Yangon's principal sights are mostly concentrated in the south of the city, between the river and the Shwedagon Pagoda. Apart from the colonial quarter and the stretch of Bogyoke Aung San Road from the Sule Pagoda to the market area, both of which make for interesting walks, the downtown area is too congested and spread out to be easily covered on foot. A quick taxi ride, however, will access the sights around the Shwedagon. It is best to leave the pagoda itself until sunset, when it looks most spectacular. The walkway around Kandawgyi Lake, whose waters reflect the great gilded stupa, is good for an evening stroll. The Kyauk Htat Gyi and Nga Htat Gyi pagodas are midtown highlights, while toward the airport, the Kabe Aye Pagoda and Lawka Chantha Abhaya Labha Muni are worth visiting.

The colossal reclining Buddha statue at the Kyauk Htat Gyi Pagoda

Getting Around

Taxis are inexpensive and only difficult to come by during rush hour. Trishaws are still common, though losing ground to motorcycle taxis. Buses cover all of Yangon, but for non-Burmese speakers they are not an easy option – there are no route maps; numbers and destinations are written in Burmese; and while cheap, services are usually very crowded. Given the heat, traffic, and distances, walking can be tiring, except in the markets and colonial district, which are best explored on foot.

Sights at a Glance

Temples, Pagodas, and Tombs

1 Sule Pagoda
5 Botataung Pagoda
7 Bahadur Shah Zafar's Dargah
8 Maha Wizaya Pagoda
9 *Shwedagon Pagoda pp74–7*
11 Nga Htat Gyi Pagoda
12 Kyauk Htat Gyi Pagoda
14 Koe Htat Gyi Pagoda
16 Kaba Aye Pagoda
17 Lawka Chantha Abhaya Labha Muni

Towns

19 Thanlyin
20 Kyauktan

Museums and Historic Sights and Buildings

2 City Hall
4 Strand Hotel
6 National Museum
10 Martyrs' Mausoleum
21 Taukkyan War Cemetery

Parks and Lakes

3 Mahabandula Garden
13 Kandawgyi Lake
15 Inya Lake
18 Hsin Hpyu Daw
22 Hlawga National Park

Worshippers praying under the vividly painted ceiling of the Maha Wizaya Pagoda

For hotels and restaurants in this region see p202 and pp210–11

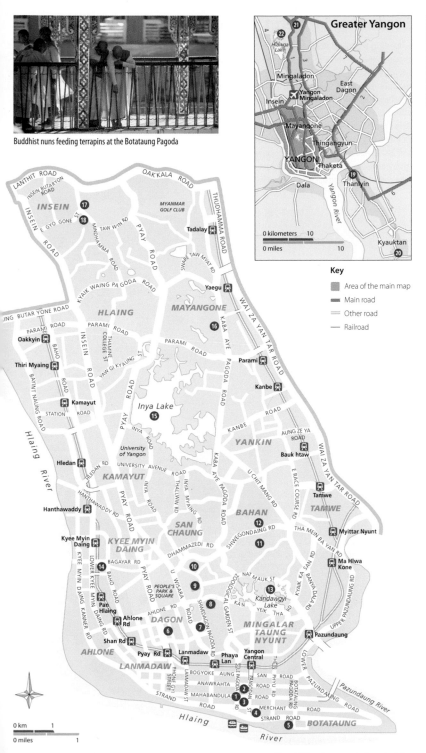

Buddhist nuns feeding terrapins at the Botataung Pagoda

Greater Yangon

Hlawga Lake

Mingaladon

Insein

Yangon Mingaladon

East Dagon

Mayangone

Thingangyun

YANGON

Thaketa

Dala

Thanlyin

Yangon River

Kyauktan

0 kilometers   10

0 miles   10

Key

- Area of the main map
- Main road
- Other road
- Railroad

LANTHIT ROAD
OAK KALA ROAD
INSEIN BUTARYON ROAD
INSEIN
E GYO GONE ST
MINDHAMMA ROAD
THUDHAMMA ROAD
TAW WIN RD
PYAY ROAD
MYANMAR GOLF CLUB
Tadalay
SWE TAW MYAT RD
KYAIK WAING PA GODA ROAD
HLAING
Yaegu
MAYANGONE
WAI ZA YAN TAR ROAD
ING BUTAR YONE ROAD
PARAMI ROAD
THAMINE COLLEGE ST
PARAMI ROAD
KABA AYE
PAGODA ROAD
Parami
Oakkyin
BAHO ROAD
INSEIN ROAD
YAW GI KYAUNG
PARAMI ROAD
Kanbe
Thiri Myaing
BAYINT NAUNG ROAD
Kamayut
STATION ROAD
INYA ROAD
PYAY ROAD
Inya Lake
KANBE ROAD
YANKIN
AUNG ZE YA ROAD
WAI ZA YAN TAR ROAD
Hlaing River
Hledan
HLEDAN RD
University of Yangon
UNIVERSITY AVENUE ROAD
KABA AYE PAGODA ROAD
Bauk htaw
KAMAYUT
HANTHAWADDY RD
PYAY ROAD
INYA ROAD
INYA MYAING RD
THANLWIN RD
U CHIT MANG RD
E RACE COURSE RD
Hanthawaddy
SAN CHAUNG
BAHAN
Tamwe
TAMWE
Kyee Myin Daing
KYEE MYIN DAING
DHAMMAZEDI RD
SHWEGONDAING RD
THA MEIN BA YAN RD
Myittar Nyunt
BAGAYAR RD
BAHO ROAD
U WISARA ROAD
NAT MAUK ST
ZOOLOGICAL GARDEN ST
KYAIK KA SAN RD
BANYA DALA RD
UPPER PAZUNDAUNG RD
Ma Hlwa Kone
LOWER KYEE MYIN DAING KANNER RD
PEOPLE'S PARK & SQUARE
SHWEDAGON PAGODA ROAD
Kandawgyi Lake
YEIK THA
Pan Hlaing
Ahlone Rd
AHLONE RD
DAGON
MINGALAR TAUNG NYUNT
Pazundaung
Shan Rd
AHLONE
Pyay Rd
Lanmadaw
Phaya Lan
Yangon Central
THEIN PHYU ROAD
LOWER PAZUNDAUNG RD
LANMADAW
BOGYOKE AUNG ROAD
THONE GYI STREET
LANMADAW ROAD
ANAWRAHTA ROAD
SAN PYA ROAD
PAZUNDAUNG ROAD
Pazundaung River
MAHABANDULA ROAD
SULE PAGODA RD
BOTATAUNG PAGODA RD
MERCHANT ROAD
STRAND ROAD
BOTATAUNG
Hlaing River

17
18
22
21
19
20
16
15
14
13
12
11
10
9
8
7
6
5
4
3
2
1

0 km   1

0 miles   1

For additional map symbols *see back flap*

Street by Street: the Colonial Quarter

Following the Third Anglo-Burmese War of 1885, the colonial capital on the banks of the Yangon River witnessed a dramatic building boom, with the Sule Pagoda its centerpiece and the riverfront its grandiloquent gateway. Today, this group of late-19th- and early-20th-century buildings in downtown Yangon is the largest of its kind in the world, a miraculous vestige of the era when old Rangoon was one of Asia's most affluent, cosmopolitan cities. However, after decades of neglect, several of the once grand edifices have become derelict, and the 2011 move of the Myanmar government to Naypyitaw has left many of them empty. In recent years, dozens of century-old structures have also been demolished to make way for modern concrete blocks.

Mohinga stalls

Shwedagon Pagoda & train station

❶ ★ Sule Pagoda
The gilded linchpin of Yangon cuts a striking silhouette in the center of a busy intersection. Uniquely, the stupa's octagonal layers extend to the bell section, which is normally smoothly curved.

SULE PAGODA ROAD

BANK ST

MAHABANDULA GARDEN

MERC

❸ ★ Mahabandula Garden
Originally called Fytche Square after Lieutenant-General Albert Fytche, a 19th-century Chief Commissioner of Burma, this memorial park near the Sule Pagoda forms a peaceful enclave in the heart of downtown.

Yangon Division Court

Customs House

STRAND ROAD

Colonial buildings
Many of Yangon's once grand colonial buildings are now dilapidated, with weed-choked flaking façades, while squatters occupy former department stores, banks, and government offices.

Key

— Suggested route

Hlaing River

Pansodan Jetty

❷ ★ City Hall
This was among the first large civic buildings in the former capital designed by a Burmese architect, and the style is noticeably more vernacular than that of earlier British-era landmarks.

Samosa stalls

Myanmar Travels and Tours (MTT)

0 meters 100
0 yards 100

PANSODAN STREET

MAHABANDULA ROAD

38TH STREET

SEIKKANTHA STREET

39TH ST

BO AUNG KYAW ST

British Embassy

Australian Embassy

Botataung Pagoda

Immanuel Baptist Church
This 1830 church is one of Yangon's oldest. The Baptist faith was brought to Burma by American missionaries in 1812 and still has a fervent following among the Karen.

★ High Court
The Queen Anne-style building, formerly the High Court, was completed in 1911, and with its municipal redbrick façade and lofty clock tower epitomizes the pomposity of the Raj at its height.

❹ ★ Strand Hotel
After years of neglect during the post-colonial period, Yangon's most prestigious hotel was restored to an immaculate state by Burmese and Indonesian entrepreneurs.

❶ Sule Pagoda

City Map D5. Junction of Sule Pagoda
Rd and Mahabandula Rd.
🚉 Yangon Central Train Station.
🚌 Mahabandula Park Terminus.
Open 5am–9pm daily. 🅿

Hundreds, and possibly
thousands, of years before the
British set out their orderly trellis
of streets around it, the Sule
Pagoda served as an important
place of pilgrimage and worship. Buddhist legend asserts
that its central stupa encloses
a sacred hair of the historic
Buddha, Gautama, and that it
was founded in 230 BC by Sona
and Uttara, a pair of missionary
monks dispatched from India
to the court of nearby Thaton.
The pagoda's name, however,
most likely derives from that of
Sulerata, the guardian spirit of
the site, who is said to have
guided the monks to nearby
Singuttara Hill, where three
other hairs of the Buddha were
enshrined and which is now the
site of the Shwedagon Pagoda.
 Whatever the actual origins of
the monument, it was certainly
reconstructed several times
before the Mon Queen Shin
Sawbu of Pegu-Hanthawaddy
(1394–1471) had the central

zedi (stupa) enlarged to its
present height of 144 ft (44 m).
The stupa is unusual for the fact
that its octagonal layers encompass the normally smoothly
curved bell section.
 The pagoda's central position,
at the hub of Lt. Alexander
Fraser's colonial-era street
layout, make it the city's most
prominent landmark after the
Shwedagon Pagoda *(see pp74–
7)*, which explains why it has
played such an important role
in Myanmar's political life.
During the pro-democracy
demonstrations of 1988 and
2007, the intersection that
surrounds it was the scene of
bloody encounters between
scores of unarmed protesters
and the Tatmadaw (military).
 Dwarfed by the phalanx
of skyscrapers surrounding it,
the pagoda is ringed by Internet
cafés, print studios, and dozens
of shops; the four entrances lie
at the cardinal points, aligned
with the main streets. The best
vantage point overlooking the
pagoda is the Sky Bar at the top
of the Sakura Tower, located a
few blocks north on Sule
Pagoda Road, from where the
view of the *zedi* is particularly
striking after dark.

The massive City Hall, built in a fusion of
British and Burmese styles

❷ City Hall

City Map D5. Mahabandula Rd.
🚌 Mahabandula Park Terminus.
Closed to the public.

Located to the northeast of the
Sule Pagoda, City Hall dates
from the 1920s and ranks
among the more grandiose
edifices erected by the British.
Its design, by the Burmese
architect U Tin, incorporates
traditional Myanmar motifs,
such as multitiered roof
pagodas *(pyatthats)*, peacocks,
lotus flowers, and serpents,
while somehow retaining the
stolid appearance of a typical
British municipal building. The
focus of many mass demon-
strations since the 1960s, it has
in recent years been the target
of a succession of bomb attacks.

The richly gilded Sule Pagoda rising from a busy intersection at the heart of Yangon

The elegant lobby of the colonial-style Strand Hotel

❸ Mahabandula Garden

City Map D5. Sule Pagoda Rd.
Mahabandula Park Terminus.
Open daily.

Facing the City Hall is a small park named after the hero of the First Anglo-Burmese War, General Mahabandula, who masterminded a valiant, but ultimately unsuccessful, resistance to the British invasion of 1824. The defense ended after the general was killed by a mortar shell while parading around the front line dressed in full regalia under a gilded parasol to boost the morale of his men. The obelisk at the center of the park is a memorial to those who died in Burma's 20th-century independence struggle. Early morning is the best time to visit, when the neatly cropped, flower-lined lawns are sprinkled with serene Tai Chi practitioners.

Mahabandula Garden, offering a pleasant respite from the city's bustle

❹ Strand Hotel

City Map E5. 92 Strand Rd.
Tel (01) 243377. Bogalay Zay,
650 ft (200 m) SE.
W hotelthestrand.com

Since its gala opening in 1901, the Strand has served as the city's most prestigious hotel – frequently mentioned in the same breath as the Taj Mahal Palace in Mumbai, Raffles of Singapore, and the Eastern & Oriental in Penang – although one with a checkered history. It was originally the creation of the famed Sarkies brothers, Armenian entrepreneurs who were the first to recognize the need for luxury accommodations in Rangoon after the opening of the Suez Canal. During its colonial heyday, the Strand was visited by and immortalized in the writings of Somerset Maugham, Rudyard Kipling, and George Orwell. The hotel went into sharp decline following Burmese independence in 1948, and was only restored in the mid-1990s.

Elegant teak and marble floors, mahogany and rattan furniture, paddle fans, and the absence of a swimming pool or a modern wing preserve the Raj-era ambience and charm. It is worth sampling the hotel's timeless atmosphere over high tea in the famous Strand Café, accompanied by the soothing strains of the *saung gauk* (the traditional Burmese harp) and the xylophone.

❺ Botataung Pagoda

City Map F5. Strand Rd, 10 min walk E of the Strand Hotel. Botataung Pagoda stop. **Open** 6am–9:30pm daily. Nov/Dec: annual pagoda festival in the month of Nadaw.

The beautiful Botataung Pagoda is revered by Buddhists as the resting place of some of the country's most sacred relics. Two millennia ago, all eight of the Buddha's hairs said to have been brought to Burma from India during his lifetime were kept here, protected by a 1,000-strong armed guard – in old Mon, *bo* means "soldier," and *tataung* "one thousand." Only one hair remained which, alongside many other precious objects, was secreted inside the stupa until the building was hit by a bomb during World War II. Reconstruction work revealed precious reliquaries, with one containing pieces of bone and a single strand of hair. These are now installed in the golden *zedi*'s hollow interior.

Built in classic Mon style, the new 131-ft- (40-m-) high bell-shaped stupa has a shining coat of gold leaf. Planetary shrines mark the cardinal points, while a side hall houses a gilded bronze Konbaung-era Buddha, which originally sat inside Mandalay's famous Glass Palace. Carried off to London after the British invasion of 1885, it was returned to Burma in 1951.

Gilded Buddha at the Botataung Pagoda, one of Yangon's main pagodas

Statue of King Bayinnaung of the Taungoo Dynasty outside Yangon's National Museum

Ksetra *(see pp98–9)*, including silver reliquaries, carved votive tablets, and a group of exquisite bronze figurines of musicians, dancers, and clowns, rare survivors from the Pyu civilization (1st century BC–9th century AD). The third floor has traditional puppets and musical instruments, including a magnificent *hsaing waing* ensemble and a couple of superbly decorated *saung gauk*, or Burmese harps. The fourth floor holds a dimly lit but fine collection of ancient gold and silver jewelry, while the uppermost floor has a collection of Buddha images spanning 1,500 years of Burmese history, along with costumes from Myanmar's ethnic minorities.

❻ National Museum

City Map C3. 66/74 Pyay Rd, Dagon Township. **Tel** (01) 2825634. 🚍 Pegu Club stop. **Open** 10am–4pm daily. 📷 ♿ 📷

A short taxi ride north of Yangon's downtown area, the National Museum is an essential stop on any city tour. Despite the poor lighting and labeling, it is worth visiting just to see the resplendent *Sihasana*, or Lion Throne, of the Konbaung Dynasty, housed in a gallery on the first floor. Less a seat than a raised ceremonial doorway on which Mindon and Thibaw used to preside over audiences with their courtiers and ministers at Mandalay Palace *(see pp144–5)*, the sumptuously gilded and richly carved object is topped with flaring ornaments inspired by the shape of ox horns. Divine

beings, astrological symbols, floral motifs, glass mosaic, and the eponymous lions feature in the elaborate decoration, which was intended to express the links between the monarch and the heavenly realm of Thagyamin, the king of the *nats* (nature spirits). Sealed in glass cases around the edges of the gallery are miniature reproductions of the other thrones that once adorned the halls of Mandalay Palace.

Displays of jewel-encrusted courtly regalia in an adjacent gallery underline just how ornate and refined Konbaung culture was at the twilight of the Yadanabon era in late-19th-century Mandalay.

Standout exhibits in the Prehistory Hall on the second floor include treasures found at the archeological site of Sri

❼ Bahadur Shah Zafar's Dargah

City Map D3. Zi Wa Ka St, off U Wisara Rd. 🚍 No. 43 from Sule Pagoda to the Shwedagon Pagoda South Gate stop. **Open** 8am–8pm daily.

Tucked away down a residential side street is the final resting place of Bahadur Shah Zafar II, the last Mughal emperor of India, whom the British deposed and exiled to Rangoon following the great Indian uprising of 1857. Held under house arrest with his wife, Begum Zeenat Mahal, and other family members, the former ruler survived only four years of imprisonment.

Upon his death in 1862, his body was hastily interred in an unmarked grave in the garden, a move which the British

Bahadur Shah Zafar's mausoleum, a place of pilgrimage for Myanmar's Indian Muslims

officials at the time vainly hoped would discourage pilgrims. A *dargah* (mausoleum) was eventually constructed on the site of the old house, but the location of the grave remained unknown. It was only in 1991, when workers were digging trenches for a new building on the site, that a brick structure was found 3.5 ft (1 m) below the surface containing the graves of Bahadur Shah and his wife and grandson. The spot has since been enshrined in a style more befitting a monarch renowned to this day as a polymath, fine calligrapher, inspired poet, and Sufi mystic: with a covering of gilt-edged silk and a scattering of fragrant rose petals.

Sufi musicians performing at the *dargah* of Bahadur Shah Zafar II in Yangon

The exterior of the Maha Wizaya Pagoda, with its 11-tiered *hti* (finial)

❽ Maha Wizaya Pagoda

City Map D3. opposite Shwedagon Pagoda's south entrance. 🚌 No. 43 from Sule Pagoda to the Shwedagon Pagoda South Gate stop. **Open** daily.

This plain, though finely proportioned, modern stupa, located opposite the southern stairway of the Shwedagon Pagoda on the other side of U Htaung Bo Road, was built in 1980 using public donations. It celebrated the unification of all of the country's Theravada Buddhist monastic orders under one supervisory body.

The king and queen of Nepal donated sacred relics from their personal collection for the relic chamber. They also gifted the main image for the circular central shrine inside the main stupa. The rotunda's domed ceiling has vivid murals and painted stuccowork depicting episodes from the life and enlightenment of the Buddha.

The splendid *hti* (finial) that crowns the structure consists of 11 tiers – two more than the nearby Shwedagon Pagoda – and was gifted to the stupa by Burma's former military dictator, General Ne Win.

India's Last Mughal

An undistinguished wooden house on the northern fringes of Rangoon is a far cry from the splendor of Delhi's Red Fort. But this is where the deposed Mughal emperor of India, Bahadur Shah Zafar II, spent the last few years of his life, stripped of his riches and privileges, without even a pen to write his beloved Urdu poetry. The indignity was his punishment for his role in the events of 1857, when a force of *sepoys* (Indian soldiers) rose up against their British overlords. By the time the rebellion was suppressed, hundreds of thousands had lost their lives and the magnificent Mughal capital, with its refined Sufi-inspired culture, had been reduced to ruins. Recounted in William Dalrymple's *The Last Mughal*, the role Bahadur Shah actually played was more of a bewildered,

reluctant puppet than a steely warlord. Manipulated into supporting a war for which he had no stomach by an army who had no respect for his rule, the emperor looked on powerlessly as the terrible events of 1857 unfolded, and paid a high price for his acquiescence. At his trial, British prosecutors implicated him in the events of what was called the Indian Mutiny by some historians and the First War of Independence by others. Bahadur Shah's sentence was exile, and he was sent to Rangoon with the surviving members of his family. There, attended by his wife Zeenat Mahal, he spent his last days writing despairing verses on the walls of his prison with lumps of charcoal. Since his death, his *dargah* has become a place of pilgrimage for Myanmar's Indian Muslims, while his poetry continues to be read across South Asia.

Portrait of the Mughal emperor Bahadur Shah Zafar II, c. 1838

❾ Shwedagon Pagoda

The chimeric Shwedagon Pagoda is Myanmar's most sacred Buddhist shrine. At 325 ft (99 m), the stupa dominates Yangon's skyline, and looms even larger in the consciousness of the country's Buddhists. No site is more revered, nor visited in such numbers. Legend says that the shrine encloses the relics of four Buddhas, including eight hairs of Gautama believed to have been brought here during his lifetime. Successive rulers enlarged and embellished the complex, adding countless shrines, halls, and lesser stupas. Despite earthquake damage and several acts of vandalism by colonial invaders, it has been lovingly restored several times and today looks resplendent.

The Shwedagon Pagoda at dusk, with its gently glowing gilded surfaces

Eastern Devotional Hall holding a Kakusandha Buddha statue

★ **Maha Tissada Bell**
King Tharrawaddy (1787–1846) had this 80,000-lb (36,000-kg) bell cast in 1841. The ceiling of its pavilion is made of superb lacquerwork that is inlaid with glass mosaic.

KEY

① **The Naungdawgyi Pagoda** was built where the Buddha's hairs were kept before being placed in the stupa.

② **The Mahabodhi Pagoda**, a replica of its namesake in Bodh Gaya, India, where the Buddha achieved enlightenment, is noticeably different in style from the other structures.

③ **The Bo Bo Aung shrine** is believed to have been created by a wizard with miraculous powers.

④ **The ruby-eyed Tawa Gu Buddha** is one of the nine miracle-working wonders of the pagoda.

⑤ **The banana bud** is covered with more than 13,000 solid gold plates, unlike the lower parts of the stupa, which are covered in gold leaf.

⑥ **The octagonal upper terrraces** are only open to monks.

⑦ **64 pagodas** encircle the stupa, eight for each *bo bo gyi*, or planetary post *(see p33)*.

⑧ **The Maha Gandha Bell**, cast in 1779, was raised in 1825 from the Yangon River, into which it had fallen during a British attempt to steal it.

Northern Devotional Hall
A statue of the historical Buddha, Gautama, is enshrined in the northern devotional hall, which is flanked by the planetary posts for Venus.

★ Southern Entrance and Devotional Hall

This chamber is centered on a statue of Konagamana, second of the five Buddhas of the present era. Its roof has some exceptional iron tracery work.

Memorial honoring the 1920 student uprising that led to the Independence struggle

Rakhine Tazaung

Commissioned by two wealthy Arakanese traders, this hall has some wonderfully intricate woodcarving on its eaves and a large reclining Buddha inside.

Western Devotional Hall featuring a statue of the Kassapa Buddha

The *Sein Bu*

The topmost point of the Shwedagon Pagoda, the *sein bu* or "diamond bud" crowning the tip of the spire, is set with a priceless 76-carat diamond. The gem refracts the sun's rays into rainbow colors on the terrace below that change as the viewer steps forward and back at a certain spot of about 6.5 ft (2 m) in length, which local guides and monks identify for visitors.

0 meters 50
0 yards 50

Mahabodhi Tree, grown from a cutting of the original banyan in Bodh Gaya, India

★ Wish Fulfilling Place

Devotees kneel and pray facing the great stupa at this star-shaped open space in the belief their wishes will be granted. The view of the stupa from here is the finest in the complex.

Exploring the Shwedagon Pagoda

Thousands of visitors stream through the Shwedagon Pagoda every day to pray at the shrines clustered around its base. Approaching from one of the four principal stairways, the majority proceed in a clockwise direction, pausing to make offerings at various landmarks along the way, or to savor the spectacle of the great stupa from the shaded comfort of the covered halls encircling the marble-lined middle terrace. The atmosphere is especially intense at dusk, when the crowds peak, red-robed monks encircle the upper tiers of the golden spire, the air is filled with the scent of incense and candles, and the gilded *zedi* glows an ethereal color. Dress codes apply (no shorts, miniskirts, or plunging necklines), but otherwise the mood is surprisingly relaxed and inclusive for a place of such religious significance – a testament to the tolerant, hospitable nature of the Burmese.

The Mahabodhi Tree, grown from a cutting of the tree under which the Buddha sat

🪟 The *Zaungdan*

The great stupa and its surrounding terrace may be approached via four different covered stairways, or *zaungdan*, aligned with the cardinal points. Each is lined with stalls selling religious paraphernalia, floral offerings, incense, Buddhas, colored flags, streamers, souvenirs, and other curios, but they all have a slightly different feel. Damaged by fire in 1931, the western stairway leading from the People's Park is the most modern, with new escalators and a pair of giant shiny *chinthe*, or leogryphs. The northern approach dates from 1460 and has 128 steps, while the eastern one, a continuation of Bahan Bazaar, has the most traditional ambience, due to the elaborate woodcarving and paintwork of its pillars and roofs. This entrance has an elevator. The southern stairway, leading up from the city side of the monument, also has an elevator and tends to be the busiest of all, especially in the evenings and on weekends.

🏛 The Middle Terrace

Emerging for the first time from the entrance halls to the glare of white marble and gold of Shwedagon's Middle Terrace is an experience few visitors forget. The principal monument, towering ahead, is surrounded by a forest of elaborately gilded and decorated subsidiary stupas, shrines, and pavilions (*tazaung*), ranged around a processional walkway built in the 15th century by the Mon kings, who leveled the top of Singuttara Hill for the purpose. Worshippers generally proceed in an auspicious clockwise direction *(let ya yit)*, replicating the movement of the heavens.

The first stop is usually the *bo bo gyi* or planetary post corresponding to the day of their birth *(see p33)*. Eight in total – Burmese astrology recognizes eight days, with Wednesday divided into two – these take the form of little white Buddha statues to which devotees offer water, flowers, and paper umbrellas. Each day is associated with a different animal, represented beneath the statue: a winged gryphon for Sunday, tiger for Monday, lion for Tuesday, tusked

One of the Shwedagon Pagoda's four massive stairways, or *zaungdan*, lined with a variety of shops and stalls

The Shwedagon Pagoda's Middle Terrace, with elaborately decorated subsidiary shrines

elephant for Wednesday morning, tuskless elephant for Wednesday afternoon, mouse for Thursday, guinea pig for Friday, and mythical dragon-serpent for Saturday. The larger statues behind are the planetary posts' guardian spirits, or *nats*.

Other popular sites around the Middle Terrace are the Nine Wonders of the Shwedagon: mostly miracle-working statues of Buddhas, saints, wizards, and necromancers believed to be capable of creating beneficial, or counteracting malevolent, spells. In the evening, hundreds of people file between them, then kneel at the open court to the northwest of the enclosure, known as the Wish Fulfilling Place, to murmur prayers and prostrate themselves before the stupa. Often there are also large family groups attending their children's *shin pyu* or coming-of-age ceremony, the children dressed in white silk suits and wearing elaborately sequined hats on their heads, and their elders sporting the finest silk *longyis* and *htameins*.

As the stupa's floodlights are illuminated after sunset, thousands of candles and bundles of incense are lit at the table lining the base of the monument, filling the air with fragrant smoke.

🔋 The Great Stupa

Originally built to enshrine eight hairs of the Buddha, along with other precious relics, the great stupa is believed by Myanmar Buddhists to be 2,500 years old,

although archeologists maintain that it more probably dates from the Mon era of the 4th–9th centuries AD. Earthquakes and fires have toppled the mighty tower on several occasions, leading to ever larger and more beautiful reconstructions. Queen Shin Sawbu of Pegu-Hanthawaddy (1394–1471) first covered the stupa in gold leaf, donating her own body weight in gold for the purpose. She was later outdone by her son-in-law, King Dhammazedi, who gave four times his weight, plus that of his wife, to re-clad the stupa. Its present imposing height of 325 ft (99 m), though, was achieved only in 1769.

The pagoda's design follows a standard Burmese archetype (*see pp32–3*), which has since been often copied throughout the country, most recently in

Naypyitaw, where the ruling generals built an exact replica on the outskirts of the capital.

The arresting spectacle of the golden tower soaring from the summit of Singuttara Hill astonished the British troops who used the complex as a cannon emplacement in the Anglo-Burmese Wars of 1824 and 1852, although this didn't stop them from pillaging the shrines in search of treasure and attempting (unsuccessfully) to carry off the great Maha Gandha bell to be melted down for cannonballs.

In modern times, the pagoda has served as a rallying point for the pro-democracy struggle. Aung San Suu Kyi addressed a massive crowd here in 1988 during the uprising of that year, and in 2007 the stupa was occupied by protesting monks during the Saffron Revolution.

The beautifully illuminated *zedi* (stupa) of the Shwedagon Pagoda

The Legend of the Shwedagon Pagoda

A much-loved Burmese legend attributes the foundation of the stupa to the brothers Pu and Tapaw, also known as Tapusa and Hpalika, who were once sent to India by their father, a rich merchant, to buy rice for famine victims in Bengal. While traveling along the Ganges, they were taken to meet the Buddha and became his disciples. On hearing the brothers were from Okkalapa (west of Yangon), the Buddha asked them to take back eight hairs from his head and bury them with relics of his predecessors secreted under a tree at Singuttara Hill. The 27-ft- (8-m-) tall *zedi* they built on the hilltop to encase the relics is recorded in ancient inscriptions as dating from 588 BC. It is quite possible that the hairs, the gold casket holding them, and the original stupa lie below the present structure, but no one is ever likely to find out, there being a strict taboo against excavation work on the site.

Gilded Buddha

❿ Martyrs' Mausoleum

City Map C2. Arzani St, near North Gate of Shwedagon Pagoda.
No. 43 from Sule Pagoda to Shwedagon Pagoda North Gate.
Open 9am–4pm Tue–Sun.

In a wooded park just north of the Shwedagon Pagoda, on the far side of Arzani Street, stands the Martyrs' Mausoleum. It was erected in honor of General Aung San, the first leader of independent Burma, and six of his ministerial colleagues, who were assassinated while holding a cabinet meeting of the interim government in 1947. Each year on July 19, the anniversary of the attack, the country's leaders gather in the park to lay wreaths at the curved red wall on its southern side. General Aung San's daughter, pro-democracy leader and Nobel laureate Aung San Suu Kyi, has attended the ceremony since her release from house arrest in 2010. She was only two years old at the time of her father's death; he was 32. The gunmen, along with U Saw, the rival politician who allegedly masterminded the killings, were captured and hanged the following year. Other than the iconic red wall, set on a raised marble terrace amid manicured lawns and landscaped grounds, there is little to see here, although the site is an atmospheric one.

Nga Htat Gyi Pagoda's Buddha, seated against a grand carved wood backdrop

⓫ Nga Htat Gyi Pagoda

City Map E1. Shwegondaing Rd.
Bandarpin stop, Shwegondaing Rd. **Open** 7am–10pm daily.

One of Myanmar's most imposing seated Buddhas resides in a temple crowning a low hill a short taxi ride to the northeast of the Shwedagon Pagoda. Sometimes called the "Five-Story Buddha," the pale-faced statue dates from 1558, although the polished hall in which he rests was built only in the 1930s. As well as his richly bejeweled crown and intricately carved golden robes, the figure is famous for the ornate, flame-like armor that emanates from his body, and the sumptuous carved wood backdrop against which he sits. Glass windows set in the raised ceiling above his head illuminate the Buddha to superb effect.

⓬ Kyauk Htat Gyi Pagoda

City Map E1. Shwegondaing Rd.
Kyauk Htat Gyi (or Chauk Htat Gyi) stop, Shwegondaing Rd.
Open 7am–8pm daily.

A bit farther up Shwegondaing Road is a less well known temple housing a colossal reclining Buddha. Constructed in 1966 using funds donated by a wealthy local businessman, the 230-ft- (70-m-) tall figure rests in a vast hangar made of red corrugated iron and steel girders. A stepped platform at its northern end provides a useful vantage point from which to view the Buddha's giant feet, divided into squares and inscribed with 108 auspicious symbols. The adjoining monastic complex is home to around 500 monks and also holds a renowned Vipassana meditation center.

Martyrs' Mausoleum, commemorating the deaths of seven independence heroes including General Aung San

For hotels and restaurants in this region see p202 and pp210–11

⑬ Kandawgyi Lake

City Map E3. Kan Yeik Tha Rd/Bahan Rd, Dagon Tsp. 🚌 3 St on Bahan Rd. **Open** daily. 🏵 Nov: annual regatta.

Convoluted Kandawgyi Lake forms a refreshing oasis in the heart of the city. It is a 20-minute walk east of the Shwedagon Pagoda, whose gilded profile is reflected to dramatic effect in its shimmering waters. Created by the British as a source of clean water for Yangon, it is fed by Inya Lake *(see p80)* to the north and is only a few feet deep. Kandawgyi means "Royal Lake," and its elegant wooden walkways and bridges resting on stilts in the water are popular places for an evening stroll. In November, leg rowers from across the country descend on the lake to race in the annual regatta, sponsored by the government. The road skirting the southern shore of the lake, site of a luxury hotel, also hosts large, decorated pavilions during the Thingyan water festival celebrations in April. In 2010, ahead of the national elections, the festivities here were marred by a triple bomb attack in which nine people lost their lives and more than 60 were injured.

The leafiest area of Kandawgyi Lake is along its northern shore, encompassed by the **Bogyoke Aung San Park**. This public garden is laid out around the two-story former home of General Aung San and his wife Daw Khin Kyi; it now holds a small museum dedicated to the memory of the man who was the architect of Burmese

The iconic Karaweik Palace, modeled on the royal barges of the Konbaung kings

independence. A bronze statue of Aung San stands at the entrance to the gardens.

The lake's southeastern shore is the site of the **Kandawgyi Nature Park**, a massive sprawl of woodland encompassing walkways, children's play enclosures, picnic areas, a mini zoo, and cafés. Crowded with young families during the daytime, it becomes a party zone during the evening, where the city's young, hip, and rich come to eat, drink, and relax with the rippling reflection of the floodlit Shwedagon as a backdrop.

Inside the nature park, the most iconic landmark on the lake is the somewhat surreal **Karaweik Palace**, a giant, bird-shaped edifice seemingly afloat on the water. It was built by the government in the 1970s to resemble the royal barges on which the Konbaung kings used to travel on the Ayeyarwady River, complete with multitiered

roof and mythic Hindu *karaweik* birds. The sumptuous interior holds a restaurant, handicrafts emporia, and a performance space where shows of traditional Burmese music and dance are staged most nights for visiting tour groups.

🌳 **Bogyoke Aung San Park**
15, Bogyoke Museum Lane, Natmauk Rd, Bahan Township. **Open** 9am–5pm daily. 🚻 ♿ 🖥

🌳 **Kandawgyi Nature Park**
Kan Yeik Tha Rd, Bahan Tsp. **Open** 6am–10pm daily. 🚻 ♿ 🍴 🖥

🏛 **Karaweik Palace**
Kandawgyi Nature Park, Kandawgyi Lake. **Open** noon–10pm daily. 🚻 ♿ 🍴 🌐 karaweikpalace.com

⑭ Koe Htat Gyi Pagoda

City Map A2. Bagayar Rd.
🚌 Koe Htat Gyi stop on Bagayar Rd. **Open** 6am–8pm daily.

Famed for his eerily lifelike eyes, the huge Koe Htat Gyi – which translates literally as "Nine-Story Buddha" – sits within an airy corrugated-iron structure with a traditional nine-tiered roof on Bagayar Road, not far from the east bank of the Hlaing River in central Yangon. The Buddha, dating from 1905, measures 72 ft (22 m) from head to toe. His famous eyes, made from blown glass, gaze impassively into space from beneath a beautifully decorated gold and black ceiling.

The leafy shores of Yangon's serene Kandawgyi Lake

The tree-lined shores of Inya Lake, a popular spot with residents of Yangon

⓯ Inya Lake

West Yankin/Sin Way Tin/Lava Hill Tsp. Kaba Aye Pagoda Rd stop. **Open** daily. ♿ 🚻 🅿️ 📷 Nov: Irrawaddy Literary Festival, Inya Lake Hotel.

The main source of water for the city of Yangon, Inya Lake is a sprawling reservoir originally laid out by the British in 1882 beyond what was then the northern edge of the city, but which has long since been subsumed by residential neighborhoods. Lying approximately 6 miles (10 km) from the downtown area, Inya Lake is the site of the city's university campus, the US Embassy, and a string of exclusive waterfront properties. Among the last are the residence of General Ne Win and the much-photographed home of Aung San Suu Kyi, where she spent many years under house arrest prior to her release in 2010. Her residence was one of many built to accommodate high-ranking British officials in the colonial era, and which now constitute some of Southeast Asia's most valuable real estate.

Yangon University's campus once held classes for all categories of students, although it is almost empty today. Only graduate studies are conducted here, with undergraduates having been dispersed in the 1990s to newer institutions on the fringes of the city to disrupt possible student activism.

Lining the southern shore of the lake near the university is the 37-acre (15-ha) **Inya Lake Park** with floral displays set out on sloping embankments. Featured in countless Burmese movies, the location is a favorite with young couples and has long been emblematic of love and romance in the popular imagination. In stark contrast, the **White Bridge** (Tada Phyu), abutting the western shore of the lake, is synonymous with the brutality of the military government. In March 1988, hundreds of student protesters were gunned down or drowned by security police after being trapped between barbed wire barricades, the lake, and nearby houses. This incident fueled support for nationwide demonstrations and the start of the 8888 Uprising a few months later (so named because it took place on August 8, 1988). The tragedy is commemorated by Burmese dissidents as Red Bridge Day, referring to the blood which is said to have stained the walkway.

⓰ Kaba Aye Pagoda

Kaba Aye Pagoda Rd, Chawdwingone District. Kaba Aye stop, Kaba Aye Pagoda Rd. **Open** 6am–8pm daily. 📷 Jun: Kaba Aye scripture recitation.

This unusual pagoda northeast of Inya Lake was built by U Nu, the first prime minister of independent Burma, in the 1950s ahead of the Sixth Buddhist Synod. Enshrined inside its main temple are the relics of two of the Buddha's principal disciples, presented to the Myanmar government by the British Museum, where they had been deposited in 1854 as war plunder. Around 1,100 lb (500 kg) of silver was used in the creation

Entrance to the Yangon University campus at Inya Lake

Buddha statues seated against the great hollow central pillar of the Kaba Aye Pagoda

of the central image in the inner shrine. Dozens more statues adorn the rest of the complex.

In the pagoda's grounds, and also built for the Sixth Synod of 1954, is the **Mahapasana Guha**, a cavernous structure intended to resemble the cave in India where the First Buddhist Synod was convened shortly after the death of the historic Buddha, Gautama. It holds an enormous assembly hall capable of accommodating 10,000 worshippers and is said to have been built by volunteers in only three days and nights.

⑰ Lawka Chantha Abhaya Labha Muni

Mindhamma Rd, Insein Township. 🚉 Insein Station, Yangon Circular Railway. 🚌 Sawbwar Gyi Kone stop, Pyay Rd. **Open** 6am–9pm daily.

Throughout history, Burmese kings have considered boulders of flawless white marble particularly auspicious material from which to sculpt monumental Buddhas. In 1998, when an exceptionally large one came to light at the Sangyin quarry, 21 miles (34 km) north of Mandalay, the government lost no time in commissioning the country's most acclaimed religious sculptor, U Taw Taw, to produce a statue. It took the artist over a year to complete the Buddha, which measures 37 ft (11 m) from head to toe and weighs 600 tons.

The colossal Lawka Chantha Abhaya Labha Muni is now housed in a glass-sided shrine atop Mindhamma Hill in the northern suburbs. Painted panels inside the temple recount the extraordinary events surrounding the transportation of the huge statue from the workshop near Mandalay where it was carved to the then capital, Yangon. To ship the figure, a special eight-rail track had to be laid from the Sangyin quarry to the Ayeyarwady River. A ceremonial golden barge with *karaweik* heads was used to carry it south, watched by vast crowds of excited onlookers from the riverbank. The barge stopped at one town every day on its 12-day journey to allow public obeisance. Yet another specially built rail line took the statue from the docks to the 37-acre (15-ha) garden site at the top of

Mindhamma Hill, where it now stands as one of the city's best loved religious destinations. The statue can easily be visited en route to or from the nearby Mingaladon International Airport, or from guesthouses or hotels in the north of the city.

⑱ Hsin Hpyu Daw

Mindhamma Rd, opposite the Lawka Chantha Abhaya Labha Muni, Insein Township. 🚉 Insein Station, Yangon Circular Railway. 🚌 Sawbwar Gyi Kone stop on Pyay Rd. **Open** 9am–5pm daily.

White elephants are considered auspicious in Southeast Asian tradition, and for centuries the region's rulers have prized albino pachyderms, which are believed to confer good luck, prosperity, and a long reign for Burmese kings (*see p107*). The custom has endured into the modern era. In a small temple set in a park in the north of the city, out toward the airport, Myanmar's former Tatmadaw (military) rulers have housed three white elephants that were discovered in the forests of Rakhine. The trio, not so much white as reddish-brown, have a specially built waterfall in which to bathe and a shaded enclosure to protect their albino skin from the sun. However, many people – encouraged to visit by the city's tour guides – find the sight of these large animals kept hobbled in chains an unedifying experience.

White elephants, thought to bring luck and prosperity

Farther Afield

A handful of sights dotted on the flat, riverine countryside around Yangon offer a number of pleasant escapes from the city. The most popular is the trip across the river to Thanlyin and Kyauktan, where an ancient hilltop stupa and island temple can be visited in an easy half-day excursion. To the north, the journey to Bago or Kyaiktiyo may be broken at the Taukkyan War Cemetery, the final resting place of thousands of Commonwealth soldiers who died in Burma during World War II, or at the nearby Hlawga National Park, a rare pocket of undeveloped, forested land on the fringes of the city.

Subsidiary stupas encircling the terrace of Thanlyin's Kyaik Khauk Pagoda

⑲ Thanlyin

10 miles (17 km) SE of Yangon.
🏠 181,000. ✈ Yangon Mingaladon.
🚉 Oak Pho Su Station. 🚌 No. 173 or 189 from Sule Pagoda.

Archeological remains dating from the Andhran period of the 2nd century BC have been unearthed at Thanlyin (formerly known as Syriam), across the river from Yangon, but it wasn't until the appearance in the 16th century of Portuguese adventurer Filipe de Brito e Nicote that the port flourished as a city in its own right. He had traveled east from Lisbon as a cabin boy, taking advantage of the wave of Portuguese expansion from Goa to the Moluccas (Spice Islands) before arriving in Arakan when it was at the height of its powers. De Brito established a fort at Syriam, ostensibly on behalf of the Arakanese king, but in fact to carve out a kingdom of his own.

From here he made pillaging raids inland and controlled shipping in the area, amassing a fortune in the process. However, his force of 3,000 mercenaries, drawn from Europe, Asia, and Africa, was no match for the great flotilla of 4,000 vessels dispatched in 1613 by King Anaukpetlun to destroy Syriam and its impudent Portuguese overlord. After a bloody, protracted siege, the port was captured and its ruler impaled.

The tumbledown ruins of a solitary Catholic church, half a mile (0.8 km) southeast of the river in an overgrown, weed-choked plot off Kyaikalot Pagoda Road, are all that remain of this brief period of European rule on the coast of Burma.

Thanlyin's renaissance came about in the 1980s after the construction of an iron bridge connecting it to Yangon. Since then, its modern container port at **Thilawa** has become the

busiest in the country, handling the bulk of Myanmar's maritime trade. However, apart from the ruined church, this bustling town of broad, leafy streets and low-rise concrete houses has little to detain travelers.

Environs
Crowning a low hill called Hlaing Pote Kone on the southern edge of Thanlyin is **Kyaik Khauk Pagoda**, an 800-year-old Mon stupa which resembles Yangon's Shwedagon Pagoda. The shrine is believed to contain hairs of the Buddha, originally enshrined here in the 3rd century BC by King Sulathrima of Thaton. Now beautifully gilded, the stupa has been rebuilt five times after being destroyed by earthquakes. Its terrace, ringed by smaller *zedis*, offers a spectacular view over the surrounding fields, stretching to the east bank of the Yangon River.

Buddha statues at the 800-year-old Kyaik Khauk Pagoda in Thanlyin, near Yangon

Kyauktan's "floating" Ye Le Pagoda, built on a small island in the Hwaw Wun Creek

⑳ Kyauktan

13 miles (20 km) S of Thanlyin.
🏙 108,000. ✈ Yangon Mingaladon.

On the banks of Hwaw Wun Creek, a tributary of the Yangon River, Kyauktan is best known for its uniquely situated temple, the "floating" **Ye Le Pagoda**, which rests on a tiny islet midstream. Beautifully decorated in traditional style, with gold paint and multitiered roofs, the shrine is a popular half-day excursion from Yangon, a couple of hours away by road. A special launch is on hand to ferry visitors across to the temple (Myanmar nationals can take the cheaper local boats). The complex also has a small pond teeming with catfish, which worshippers feed with little bags of puffed rice that are on sale nearby.

🔖 Ye Le Pagoda
Open 7am–9pm daily. 🛶

㉑ Taukkyan War Cemetery

21 miles (35 km) N of Yangon on the Yangon–Bago Rd. 🚌 No. 9 from Aung Mingalar Bus Terminal.
Open 7–11am, 1–4:30pm daily. ♿

This immaculately maintained cemetery on the northern outskirts of Yangon holds the graves of 6,374 servicemen who lost their lives during World War II, along with memorials to the 27,000 others whose remains were never reclaimed, the majority of them from the Indian subcontinent and Africa. Set amid lawned gardens, the rows of polished stones are a moving tribute to the fallen, most of whom perished in unimaginably harsh conditions fighting the Japanese in the early 1940s. Lying just off the highway, it makes a worthwhile stop on the journey to Bago, Mawlamyine, or Kyaiktiyo.

A memorial to the fallen of World War II at the Taukkyan War Cemetery

㉒ Hlawga National Park

Yangon–Bago Rd. ✈ Yangon Mingaladon. 🚌 No. 9 from Aung Mingalar Bus Terminal.
Open 8am–6pm daily. 🛶 💻 🏠

Encompassing just over 1,500 acres (6 sq km) of wetland, semi-evergreen, and mixed deciduous forest on the northern fringes of Yangon, Hlawga National Park was created in 1982 to preserve the green belt around the Kokanabe and Hlawga lakes, the city's principal water supply. The national park offers a pleasant escape from the nearby city, although wildlife is thin on the ground – the only animals that can reliably be seen are monkeys, various species of common deer, including sambar and barking deer, and occasionally the odd pangolin. The park is also home to a variety of reptiles, from monitor lizards and pythons to kraits and cobras.

A network of hiking trails provides access to the forest, and short elephant rides are offered, as well as boat trips on the lake. A play area for children, with a large model dinosaur, will appeal to visitors with young families. The national park tends to be particularly busy on weekends, when Yangon residents drive out on National Highway 1 (the main road to Bago and Kyaiktiyo) for family picnics.

Children playing on a model dinosaur at the Hlawga National Park outside Yangon

YANGON STREET FINDER

Navigating Yangon can be a challenge. The lack of standard Burmese transliteration means that street names appear with different spellings even on the same maps, and may not always correspond to those in this guide. Some roads are also known by more than one name, having been renamed after Independence. Except in the downtown area, street numbers are not often displayed, and those that are tend to be in Burmese script.

The map references given for all hotels, restaurants, shops, and sights in this guide refer to the Street Finder maps on the following pages. The letter and number in the map reference give the grid reference on the main map. The key map below shows the area covered by the main map. Symbols used on the map are given in the key below. The opposite page has an index of street names and places of interest marked on the Street Finder map.

The golden *zedi* of Yangon's Sule Pagoda at night

Key

- ▢ Major sight
- ▢ Other sight
- ▢ Other building
- 🚉 Train station
- ⛴ Ferry jetty
- ⛴ Riverboat jetty
- 🛈 Visitor information
- 🚓 Police station
- ✚ Hospital
- 📖 Buddhist pagoda
- 🛕 Buddhist temple
- 🛕 Hindu temple
- ☪ Mosque
- ✝ Church
- ✡ Synagogue
- ═ Railroad

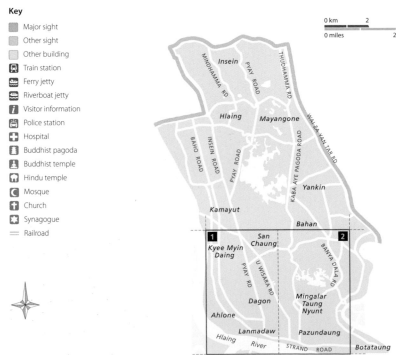

Scale of Maps 1–2

| 0 meters | 500 |
| 0 yards | 500 |

Street Finder Index

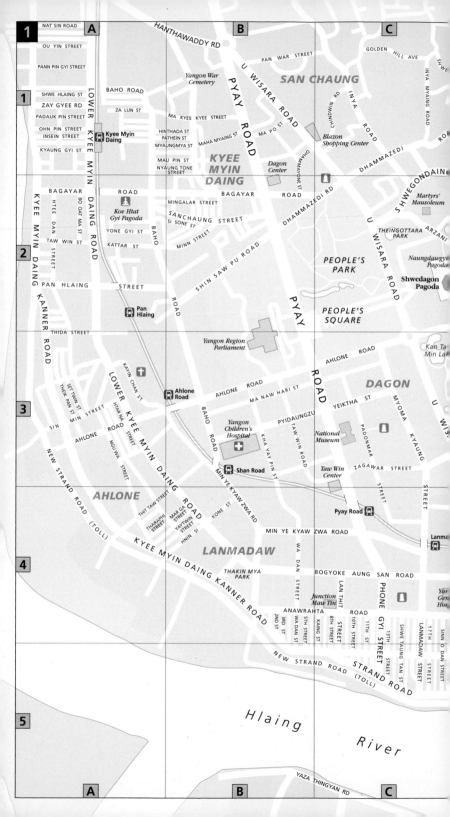

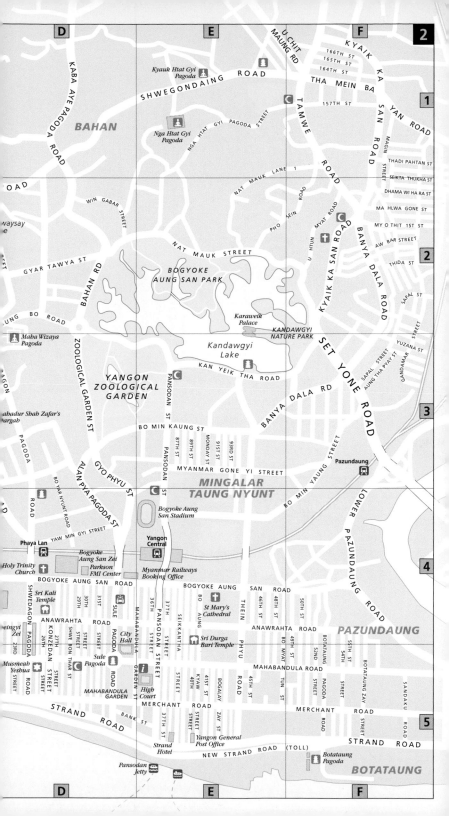

BAGO REGION

Bago Region's vast stretches of alluvial plain and jungle were the setting for one of Southeast Asia's most splendid cities, the port of Bago (Pegu), before successive invasions and the shifting of the Sittaung River sent the settlement into decline. Although little more than a scruffy market town today, Bago boasts a spectacular crop of monuments spanning more than 1,400 years of history. They include several remnants from its medieval heyday, among them the magnificent Shwemawdaw Pagoda, a stupa even larger than Yangon's Shwedagon.

Legend has it that the city was founded in AD 573 by a pair of Mon princes after they spotted a female *hamsa* bird resting on the back of its mate on an islet *(see p92)*. The capital they built on the spot, Hanthawaddy, later rose to become the hub of a far-reaching Mon empire whose riches proved too strong a temptation for the Burmese kingdom in Taungoo, farther north. In 1539, the Taungoo king Tabinshweti invaded the city, by then known to European traders as Pegu, and his successor, Bayinnaung, made it the capital of the Second Burmese Empire.

The Mon briefly reoccupied Bago in 1740, but the city was again brutally sacked 17 years later, this time by the redoubtable King Alaungpaya, who massacred the entire population. The ensuing decline only accelerated once the Sittaung shifted course in the 1790s, leaving Bago a day's journey inland from the sea and cut off from the maritime trade that had always been its lifeblood. Today Bago makes a rewarding day trip from Yangon, or a stopover on longer journeys up the Sittaung Valley.

Taungoo holds a few impressive remnants of Tabinshweti's reign, but given its location at the foot of the Bago-Yoma Hills, the town serves primarily as a springboard for forays into what remains of the once vast teak forest that cloaked the region's hills. Purpose-built and working timber camps provide accommodations in the thick of the jungle, where elephants can be seen at work. Access is via a poorly maintained road that winds west across the hills to Pyay, on the Ayeyarwady River, where the enigmatic ruins of ancient Sri Ksetra, strewn across expanses of mustard fields and scrubland, are the principal attraction.

A row of statues depicting the Buddha's disciples at Shwedaung's Shwemyetman Pagoda

◀ Detail of a brightly colored *chinthe* (leogryph) at the spectacular Shwesandaw Pagoda in Pyay (Prome)

Exploring Bago Region

Bago city is a 90-minute drive northeast of Yangon, making it an easy day trip. To reach Taungoo, there is either the old Mandalay road, National Highway 1, passing through a string of Burmese market towns, or the new concrete expressway, more direct but with little of interest along the way. Running west of Taungoo, the infamous Oktwin–Paukkhaung logging road is a fragile artery through the Bago-Yoma Hills to Pyay. In the rainy season it is all but impassable, but can be tackled in chartered 4WDs the rest of the year. The main incentive to brave the trip is for the chance to overnight in forest camps, watching elephants extracting timber. Pyay is a popular starting point for river cruises but few visitors use it as a waystage on longer journeys north via Bagan, as onward transport is scarce. Apart from its splendid Shwesandaw Pagoda, the key attraction is ancient Sri Ksetra, centuries older than Bagan.

The Payama Pagoda in Sri Ksetra, one of the major sights near Pyay

Getting Around

A fleet of beaten-up local buses and faster luxury buses run along the four-lane Yangon–Bago Highway, although most visitors based in Yangon hire taxis for the day trip. Buses run north up the Sittaung Valley to Mandalay, pausing at Taungoo. For anyone not traveling in their own chartered vehicle, transport across the Bago-Yoma Hills is sporadic and rough, limited to local trucks that depart only when full. Pyay, on the Ayeyarwady, can be reached by bus, government ferry, or train; private operators also run cruises from here.

Statue of the Buddha under a serpent's hood at the Nawdawgyi Myathalyaung Buddha, Bago

For hotels and restaurants in this region see p203 and p211

Giant *chinthe* at the entrance to the pavilion housing the massive Shwetalyaung Buddha, Bago

Sights at a Glance

1. *Bago pp92–5*
2. Taungoo
3. Pyay (Prome)
4. *Sri Ksetra (Thayekhittaya) pp98–9*
5. Shwedaung
6. Akauk Taung

View from the terrace of Bago's Mahazedi Pagoda

Key

- Highway
- Main road
- Other road
- Railroad
- Regional border
- △ Peak

0 kilometers   30

0 miles   30

For additional map symbols *see back flap*

❶ Bago

Former capital of the Mon kingdom and the Second Burmese Empire, Bago (Pegu) had its golden age between the 1420s and 1530s when its treasuries were filled with gold amassed from trade in silk, spices, and slaves across the Indian Ocean. With close trading links to India and Sri Lanka (Ceylon), the city also became an important center for Theravada Buddhism. Spectacular religious monuments are scattered across the modern town, all of them in pristine condition, having been upgraded in typically contemporary Burmese style with layers of gilt and vibrant gloss paint which belie their considerable antiquity. The sights are concentrated in two main groups: one in the grid-planned old quarter to the east, the other farther west across the creek.

The mighty golden pinnacle of the Shwemawdaw Pagoda in Bago

🔒 Shwemawdaw Pagoda

Pagoda Rd. **Open** 7am–9pm daily. 🎟 day ticket.

No monument in the region conveys the power and wealth of the lost kingdom of the Mons as dramatically as the Shwemawdaw Pagoda, whose gilded pinnacle soars 374 ft (114 m) above Bago's old palace quarter. It was built to enshrine relics of the Buddha, including two hairs said to have been gifted by Gautama himself during his lifetime. The original structure erected here has been rebuilt or enlarged on several occasions, both by the city's own Mon rulers in times of prosperity, and by repentant Bamar monarchs as atonement for the loss of life incurred by their conquests. Bayinnaung even donated his crown jewels to make a new *hti*, or finial, in

the 1550s. Several devastating earthquakes and storms in the early 20th century nearly destroyed the pagoda, before it was overhauled by public subscription in 1947. It is now officially Myanmar's tallest *zedi* (stupa). Four covered *zaungdan*, or stairways, lead to the main terrace, where a small museum houses antique Buddhas recovered from the rubble after a strong earthquake in 1930. Remnants of the old banana bud, which also fell during that temblor, can be seen near the eastern approach. As the area's most important religious site, Shwemawdaw is visited in great numbers year around, but deluged during April when thousands of local farmers take advantage of the pre-monsoon lull in the rice calendar to attend the pagoda's annual festival.

🔒 Hintha Gon

Hintha Gon Paya Rd. **Open** 7am–9pm daily. 🎟 day ticket.

The top of a low hillock next to the Shwemawdaw is believed to be the spot where the *hamsa* birds of Bago's origin myth landed. Statues of the pair stand at the entrance to the Hintha Gon, a temple built to mark the auspicious event. It can be reached via a staircase at the east side of the Shwemawdaw. The summit is a great place from which to admire the sun setting over the golden stupa to the west. The temple is also an important center for *nat* (nature spirit) worship and the venue of a lively *nat pwe* festival, when transvestite dancers perform spirit possession rituals to raucous musical accompaniment.

🏛 Kanbawzathadi Palace

Myin Taw Tar Rd. **Open** 9am–6pm daily. 🎟 day ticket.

No sign of the original Mon palace has been found at Bago, but in 1990, traces of huge post holes and brick foundations were discovered in parkland just south of the Shwemawdaw. Archeologists identified this area as the site of Bayinnaung's royal palace. One of the most powerful kings of Burma, Bayinnaung (1516–81) took the great city in 1551 with a combined force of his own elephant corps and Iberian mercenaries. Court chronicles record that in a last bid to save his capital, the Mon ruler, Smim

The *Hamsa* Bird

Legend has it that the site of Bago was chosen by two Mon princes after a pair of golden-necked *hamsa* birds landed on an islet which was so small that the female had to rest on the back of her mate. The *hamsa* – or *hintha* in Burmese – is an aquatic bird that crops up throughout the folklore and mythology of South Asia. It seems to have symbolized virility, strength, purity, divine knowledge, and spiritual accomplishment since Vedic times. Widely depicted in ancient Buddhist art, it is often featured on reliquaries found inside stupas. No one is sure why, but it is likely that the bird – whose Latin name *hansar* is the root of the German *gans* and English *goose* – is revered for being equally at home in the three elements of water, air, and earth.

Antique Burmese *hamsa* opium weight c. 1900

The gates to the Kanbawzathadi Palace, ornately decorated with stuccowork

Htaw (r. 1550–52), challenged his Burmese adversary to single combat on elephant back, a duel that Bayinnaung is said to have won with ease.

Among the travelers dazzled by the splendor of the palace built in the wake of this victory was the Englishman Ralph Fitch, who visited in 1586 and spoke of sumptuously gilded wooden buildings of great workmanship. The somewhat gaudy, fanciful reconstruction of the palace installed by the Tatmadaw government probably bears little resemblance to the original, but it does convey a sense of the scale of the lost buildings.

🐍 Snake Monastery

Bandula Rd. **Open** 8am–8pm daily.
A popular diversion for both local Buddhist pilgrims and foreign visitors is the Thatana Lin Yaungshwe, or Snake Monastery, which is located near the Hmorkan Tank, a couple of blocks southwest of the Kanbawzathadi Palace area. Its pride and joy is a 30-ft (9-m) python that is believed to be the reincarnation of a famous abbot from the Shan Hills. Streams of devotees come every day to pay their respects to it by leaving cash donations or food, particularly during the period of Buddhist Lent. Five monks are required to carry the snake between enclosures. Visitors are sometimes allowed to touch the reptile, which is said to be around 110 years old, except during the Burmese month of Waso (June-July), when it is said to be fasting.

The python at Bago's Snake Monastery, believed to be a reincarnated abbot

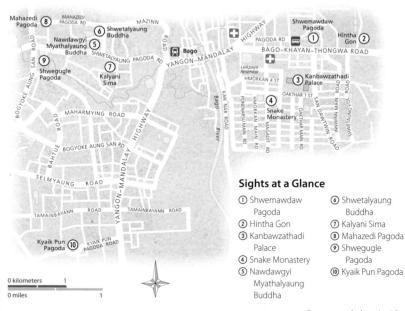

Sights at a Glance

① Shwemawdaw Pagoda
② Hintha Gon
③ Kanbawzathadi Palace
④ Snake Monastery
⑤ Nawdawgyi Myathalyaung Buddha
⑥ Shwetalyaung Buddha
⑦ Kalyani Sima
⑧ Mahazedi Pagoda
⑨ Shwegugle Pagoda
⑩ Kyaik Pun Pagoda

0 kilometers 1
0 miles 1

For map symbols *see back flap*

Nawdawgyi Myathalyaung, Bago's largest reclining Buddha statue

🏛 Nawdawgyi Myathalyaung Buddha

Shwetalyaung Rd. **Open** 7am–8pm daily. 🎫 day ticket.

On the west side of town is a monumental Buddha, the Nawdawgyi Myathalyaung, oriented east to west facing a rectangular tank. Built only in 2002, it is even longer (250 ft/ 76 m) than its better-known neighbor, the Shwetalyaung Buddha, although it receives a lot less attention. The figure makes for a great photo opportunity in the early morning, when it is reflected in the glassy waters of the adjacent reservoir.

🏛 Shwetalyaung Buddha

Pagoda Rd. **Open** 7am–8pm daily. 🎫 day ticket.

Immediately north of the Nawdawgyi Myathalyaung Buddha is Shwetalyaung, Bago's superb reclining Buddha, the star attraction among the monuments on the west side of town. Measuring 180 ft

(55 m) from head to toe and 52 ft (16 m) in height, the figure is thought to have been built in 994, although by the time of Alaungpaya's sack of 1757, it lay wreathed in jungle and all but forgotten. It was only in the 1880s, after a British survey team spotted the head of the statue protruding from the foliage below, that the Buddha was renovated. A corrugated-iron *tazaung* (pavilion) was erected over it soon after to protect the paintwork, which has since been maintained in pristine condition. The mosaic pillow is a 19th-century addition. While this is not the largest reclining Buddha in the country – that honor goes to the one near Mawlamyine *(see p193)* – it is the best loved, thanks to its particularly serene expression. The statue's countenance is meant to convey to worshippers the joy the Buddha experienced on his deathbed at the moment of entering *parinirvana*, as well

as the meaning of his final words to his assembled disciples: "All living things are subject to decay; strive with diligence for your liberation."

🏛 Kalyani Sima

Kalyani Sima Rd. **Open** 7am–8pm daily. 🎫 day ticket.

As part of a wider effort to revive the monkhood following the demise of the First Burmese Empire, King Dhammazedi (1412–92) constructed this grand ordination hall close to the Shwetalyaung Buddha. Its name derives from the Kalyani River in Sri Lanka, site of a famous Mahavira monastery, to which a mission of 22 monks was dispatched by the king to be reordained. Dhammazedi's reasons for wishing to do this are set out on a series of 10 inscription stones erected to the west of the hall, dominated by expressions of dismay at the sectarianism that had taken hold of the faith in the late 15th century. Some of the stones were damaged in attacks by de Brito in 1599 *(see p52)* and others during the sack of Bago by Alaungpaya in 1757 *(see p53)*, when the hall was totally destroyed. The tablets, written in Pali and Mon, are of value primarily as a testament to the close links between Burma and Ceylon in medieval times.

The hall itself, used as a model for over 400 similar structures erected by Dhammazedi across his kingdom, was rebuilt after

The 10th-century Shwetalyaung, Bago's serene-faced reclining Buddha

collapsing in the earthquake of 1930, and now has a modern appearance, with gleaming marble floor tiles and glass mosaic adorning the main chamber. Mirror-encrusted *nat* figures stand beneath the pillared arches lining the side walls. The Kalyani Sima remains in use for twice-monthly confessional assemblies, in which monks are publicly asked whether they have committed any offences against the strictures of their monastic order. Elaborate instructions for the rituals carried out on these occasions are contained in the Dhammazedi inscriptions.

Mahazedi Pagoda, which once held the fake tooth relic brought from Sri Lanka

🏛 Mahazedi Pagoda

Mahazedi Rd. **Open** 7am–9pm daily. 🎟 day ticket.

Less than a mile (1.6 km) west of the Shwetalyaung Buddha stands the whitewashed Mahazedi stupa in which King Bayinnaung famously interred the gold and diamond-encrusted relic he had been tricked by the Ceylonese into believing was the tooth of the Buddha. King Anaukpetlun removed the tooth in 1599, and in later centuries the stupa was destroyed both by Alaungpaya's attack and the great earthquake of 1930. Mahazedi was restored to its former glory, along with Bayinnaung's Victory Ground and the miniature Bagan-style Ananda Temple, also in the complex. The former features vibrantly painted statues of

The massive seated Buddhas at the Kyaik Pun Pagoda

Bamar troops posing in full battle dress with an auspicious white elephant (writing in 1586, the English traveler Ralph Fitch reported seeing four albino pachyderms in the compound of King Bayinnaung's palace).

🏛 Shwegugle Pagoda

Shwegugle Pagoda Rd. **Open** 8am–9pm daily. 🎟 day ticket.

This less-visited stupa, a short distance south of the Mahazedi Pagoda, is noteworthy for the vaulted chamber encircling the base of the monument in which 64 seated Buddhas were installed. The building was constructed in 1494 during the reign of King Byinnya Ran II (r. 1491–1526).

🏛 Kyaik Pun Pagoda

Kayik Pun Pagoda Rd, around 3 miles (4.5 km) S of the train station, just off the main Yangon–Bago Highway. **Open** 8am–9pm daily. 🎟 day ticket.

The Kyaik Pun Pagoda – literally "Four Figures" pagoda – rises from the scrubby southern outskirts of Bago. Built by King Migadippa in the 7th century AD and restored in 1476 by King Dhammazedi, it consists of four colossal seated Buddhas. Placed back to back facing the cardinal points around a square central pillar, they are said to represent Kakusandha, Konagamana, Kassapa, and the historical Buddha, Gautama. The figures measure an impressive 90 ft (27 m) from head to toe.

The Fake Tooth Relic

Bayinnaung was the despotic, expansionist king who created the Second Burmese Empire in the mid-16th century. An acquisitive megalomaniac, he was obsessed with symbols of power, and for Theravadans none was more potent than the tooth relic of Sri Lanka. The king was so keen to bring home the prized object that when, in 1560, he heard that the Portuguese had carried it off, he sent a ship full of gold and precious stones to the Portuguese colony of Goa to buy it. Low on funds at the time, the Portuguese viceroy, Constantino da Bragança, couldn't believe his luck when the Burmese arrived. But Goa's religious authorities ruled that such a sale would be idolatrous. Rather than risk the wrath of the Inquisition, the viceroy had the tooth destroyed. However, Bayinnaung's dismay faded when he learned the stolen tooth was a decoy. He later bought the original from the Ceylonese and had it interred in Bago's Mahazedi Pagoda. Alas, this one too turned out to be a fake (along with the princess he bought as part of the deal). The king refused to accept the fact, attributing all kinds of magical powers to it. Stolen by Anaukpetlun in 1599, it is now in Sagaing (see p153).

Bayinnaung, National Museum, Yangon

Taungoo's richly gilded 16th-century Shwesandaw Pagoda and its subsidiary shrines

❷ Taungoo

Road Map D4. 177 miles (286 km) N of Yangon. 🚉 66,000. ✈ Naypyitaw, 55 miles (90 km) north. 🚌 🚍

Nestled amid the teak and bamboo forests along the foothills of the Shan Plateau, Taungoo is the largest town in the lower Sittaung Valley. However, since the founding of Naypyitaw farther north, it has rather lost its importance as a stopover on the long haul between Yangon and Mandalay. The few visitors who pause here do so to admire the scant remains of a powerful post-Bagan dynasty whose capital this was 500 years ago.

Founded in 1280, Taungoo had its heyday during the reign of Tabinshweti (1516–50), the ruler who masterminded the unification of Burma's kingdoms and principalities, beginning with the sea port of Bago (Pegu), which he made his capital in 1539. Few remnants of medieval Taungoo survive intact, but it is possible to gain a sense of the town's former prominence from the extent of the square moat and fragments of wall running around it, and the ornamental Kandawgyi Lake on the southwest edge of its old quarter.

Far and away the most impressive monument, however, is the late-16th-century **Shwesandaw Pagoda**, in the center. Believed to hold sacred hair relics of the Buddha, it is richly gilded and rises from a precinct at the end of whose covered northern entrance stand statues of the region's seven dynastic rulers. Side halls house various large Buddhas, including a 12-ft- (3.5-m-) high seated statue cast in bronze and silver in 1912.

A couple of blocks southeast of the Shwesandaw stands the 19th-century **Myasigon Pagoda**, with a gilded stupa atop a brick *pahto* (temple) that features glass mosaic arches and a seated Buddha circled by *bo bo gyi*. Statues displayed in subsidiary shrines include Chinese goddesses gifted by a visiting German Buddhist in 1901. Taking pride of place in the pagoda's small museum are a bronze image of Erawan, the three-headed elephant who is the mount of Indra, and a standing Buddha plundered by Bayinnaung during his attack on the Siamese capital, Ayutthaya.

🔰 **Shwesandaw Pagoda**
Pagoda Rd. **Open** 5am–9pm daily. 📷

🔰 **Myasigon Pagoda**
Near Taungoo Train Station.
Open 5am–9pm daily.

Environs

Taungoo today serves as a springboard for trips into the wooded hills to its northwest, to government-owned forest camps and Karen villages where it is possible to watch domesticated working elephants and their *oozies* (mahouts) extracting teak in time-honored tradition. Despite decades of sanctions, Myanmar's timber industry continues to thrive, not least thanks to the contribution of the tuskers, who are able to work in terrain inaccessible to machines *(see p107)*.

Visitors may travel out to the camps for the day or stay overnight. Among the purpose-built camps is the 20-acre (8-ha) **Pho Kyar Forest Resort**. Guests can take elephant rides into the bush, watch the animals at work, and help bathe the calves. Visits to working **timber camps** deeper in the forest, which move around following the logging, are also available.

🏠 **Pho Kyar Forest Resort**
31 miles (50 km) NW of Taungoo, 10 miles (16 km) E of Thargaya, near Thaing Creek, Swa Forest Reserve.
📷 💳 ⚕ 🛏 🏠

🏠 **Timber camps**
Various in the hills around Taungoo. ℹ Dr Chan Aye, Myanmar Beauty Hotel, 7/134 Bo Hmu Po Kun St, Taungoo. 📷 💳 ⚕ 🛏 🏠
Tel (054) 25073

Domesticated working elephants in Myanmar's Bago-Yoma Hills

For hotels and restaurants in this region see p203 and p211

❸ Pyay (Prome)

Road Map C4. 173 miles (280 km) N of Yangon. 🚶 135,000. ✈ Yangon Mingaladon. 🚌 🚐 🚢 ⛴
🎏 Nov: Shwesandaw pagoda festival.

In the late 19th century, Prome, on the Ayeyarwady's east bank, was founded as the headquarters of the Irrawaddy Flotilla Company, whose paddle steamers served as the main link between Yangon and Mandalay from 1865 to the 1940s. Today known as Pyay, the town is a bit of a backwater, and the trickle of foreign travelers who stop off each year usually do so en route to other destinations along the river. However, the place is full of Burmese atmosphere, with a lively riverside market and one of the country's most spectacular stupas.

The magnificent gilded **Shwesandaw Pagoda** crowns a low hill on the southeast side of town. Said to be a full meter taller than Yangon's Shwedagon Pagoda, the stupa looks especially dramatic around sunset, when its gilded surfaces glow beautifully against the backdrop of the distant Ayeyarwady. A series of inscriptions housed inside a brick *tazaung* in the pagoda complex record that the *zedi* (stupa) was originally sited here in 589 BC, but substantially enlarged during the reign of Kyanzittha of Bagan in 1083. However, it was King Alaungpaya, founder of the Konbaung Dynasty, who gilded the monument and added its distinctive double *hti*, or finial, which he intended as a symbol of Burmese unity after his bloody military campaigns of the mid-18th century.

One of the best views of the Shwesandaw Pagoda is to be had from the terrace encircling the giant **Sehtatgyi Buddha** (literally "Ten-Story Buddha"), a short walk to the east, whose head rises above the treeline to almost the same height. Access to the statue is via a covered walkway on its western side.

The ruins of the ancient city of Sri Ksetra *(see pp98–9)*, capital of the Pyu kings, lie about 5 miles

The bespectacled Buddha at the Shwemyetman Pagoda in Shwedaung

(8 km) to the east of Pyay and, by staying overnight in the town, it is possible to explore them on a day trip.

🏛 **Shwesandaw Pagoda**
Pagoda St. **Open** 7am–9pm daily.

🧘 **Sehtatgyi Buddha**
Pagoda St. **Open** 7am–9pm daily.

View of the Sehtatgyi Buddha from the Shwesandaw Pagoda in Pyay

❹ Sri Ksetra (Thayekhittaya)

See pp98–9.

❺ Shwedaung

Road Map C4. 9 miles (14 km) S of Pyay. 🚶 21,000. 🚌

In a land of countless Buddhas, the figure enshrined at the **Shwemyetman Pagoda** in the town of Shwedaung stands out,

thanks to its pair of enormous gold-rimmed spectacles. The first set is said to have been gifted during the Konbaung era. They were stolen shortly after, and since then the statue has had a series of replacements (thieves keep stealing them). The Shwemyetman Buddha is believed to have the power to cure ailments related to the eyes, and the temple is a popular pilgrimage destination for Myanmar's visually impaired.

🧘 **Shwemyetman Pagoda**
Shwedaung, Pyay Township. **Open** daily.

❻ Akauk Taung

Road Map C4. Near Hton Bo (Tonbo) village. 🚌 by car 36 miles (58 km) south from Pyay to Hton Bo village, then by local riverboat for the remaining 45-minute trip by water.

Another popular excursion out of Pyay is the day trip to Akauk Taung, a sandstone cliff on the Ayeyarwady where hundreds of Buddhas have been carved into niches in the rock. The figures were the handiwork of long-distance boatmen, who used to pause here to pay tolls, or to wait for whirlpools in the river to abate. Viewed from the water, the shrines, with their whitewashed surrounds and fringe of tropical foliage straggling above them, rank among the most photogenic sights on the Ayeyarwady River.

④ Sri Ksetra (Thayekhittaya)

The distinctively shaped stupas, dried-up moats, and earthworks in the fields a few miles east of the Ayeyarwady River at Pyay are all that remains of what was, 1,200 years ago, one of Asia's grandest fortified settlements. Capital of the Pyu kings, Sri Ksetra ("City of Splendor"), also known as Thayekhittaya, grew wealthy by controlling trade down the river and across the Bay of Bengal to India. Between the 4th and 9th centuries, the walled town was known to travelers from as far afield as eastern China and India, and is thought to have been the largest in the country, supporting a population of thousands. No one is sure why Sri Ksetra went into decline (invasion by the Mon is the current theory) but by the 10th century it had been squarely eclipsed by Bagan. Today its ruins lie all but forgotten, visited by only a handful of foreigners each year.

Pyu-era terra-cotta Buddha amulet, c. 8th–9th centuries

0 kilometers 1
0 miles 1

KEY

① **The Payagyi Pagoda** dates from around the 5th century. This large brick stupa is surrounded by three ambulatory terraces, of which the uppermost is only open to men.

② **The Nat Bauk Gate** is the main entrance into Sri Ksetra. The road from Pyay passes through it.

③ **Archeology Field School**

④ **Old canal**

⑤ **The railroad line to Yangon** cuts through the middle of Sri Ksetra.

⑥ **The small museum** displays Buddha statues, beads, and other artifacts uncovered at the site.

⑦ **Throne stone**

⑧ **A large cluster of ruins** have been excavated near the south gate.

⑨ **The Lemyethna Temple** contains four original Buddha reliefs.

⑩ **The "royal cemetery"** is where a concentration of large funerary urns and coins have been unearthed.

⑪ **The 11th-century Rahanta Pagoda** holds a handful of Bagan-era Buddhas, facing the palace area. The Rahanta Gate nearby has been excavated and partially rebuilt.

★ **Bawbawgyi Pagoda**
This late-4th-century cylindrical-sided, elongated stupa is the site's largest and most striking. It served as a prototype for Bagan's earliest pagodas (see pp120–21).

★**Payama Pagoda**
A survivor from the 4th–5th centuries AD, this stupa is one of the oldest monuments in the country and has been well restored.

The royal palace complex
At the center of the city stood the royal palace complex. Recently excavated brick foundations reveal its impressive scale. Sri Ksetra has been put forward by the Myanmar government to UNESCO as a potential World Heritage Site.

The Khin Ba stupa mound, dating from the 5th–6th centuries AD, is the oldest undisturbed Buddhist relic chamber in Southeast Asia and has yielded several precious objects, including this silver Pyu coin.

Yangon

Bei Bei Pagoda
Mounted on a raised plinth, the hollow Bei Bei shrine dates from the early 10th century, when the ancient city was already in decline.

WESTERN MYANMAR

Western Myanmar encompasses two very different regions, each with its own distinctive geography and culture. The Delta, immediately west of Yangon, has since British times served as the country's rice bowl – a vast patchwork of green paddy fields crisscrossed by canals fed by the silty waters of the Ayeyarwady as it splits into a myriad tributaries on its way to the ocean. Farther north, a spine of jungle-covered hills separates the Delta region from the narrow coastal strip of Rakhine State, heartland of the former kingdom of Arakan.

In the Delta, travel traditionally meant long boat journeys. These days the road network has improved, but it's still worth making the overnight river trip from Yangon to the region's capital, Pathein, by ferry. Apart from the chance to sample the atmosphere of the coastal wetlands, the main incentives are Ngwe Saung and Chaungtha, a pair of low-key beaches on the Bay of Bengal, the nearest seaside resorts to the city of Yangon. The fertile Delta region was the area that, in May 2008, bore the brunt of Cyclone Nargis, the worst tropical storm to have hit Myanmar in living memory. It caused catastrophic damage and left more than 138,000 people dead.

Rakhine State, in the far northwest corner of the country, has always maintained an uneasy relationship with the Burmese population of the central plains.

The region remains one of the least developed parts of Myanmar, despite the fact that it holds two of the country's prime visitor attractions: the evocative archeological site of Mrauk U, and Ngapali beach, whose vivid turquoise water and gleaming white sand eclipse every other coastal resort in the area.

Ngapali's relaxed feel can make it hard to believe that towns farther north have seen outbreaks of communal violence in recent years. In 2012, attacks on Rakhine Muslims, known as Rohingyas, left scores of people dead and forced thousands to flee their villages; clashes in 2013 spread as far south as Thandwe. This has led to curfews and occasional travel restrictions in the Rakhine capital, Sittwe (Aykab). At the time of writing, however, no permits were required to visit Mrauk U, a day's journey up the Kaladan River from Sittwe.

Fields of golden rice stubble spread below the misty blue ridges separating Mrauk U and the Lemro River

◀ The clear blue waters of the Bay of Bengal at the exquisite Ngapali beach near Thandwe

Exploring Western Myanmar

Exquisite Ngapali beach is what tempts most travelers across the Rakhine-Yoma Hills to this little-visited, far northwest corner of the country, although few venture to make the trip overland – the road is impassable for much of the year. Taking a flight from Yangon is the best approach to Thandwe, the jumping-off spot for Ngapali. All of this area's visitor facilities are strewn in the coconut groves immediately behind the beach, which serves as a springboard for snorkeling and diving trips to offshore islets. Flying is also the easiest way to reach Sittwe, at the mouth of the Kaladan River, the most popular access point for the ruined medieval city of Mrauk U.

Maungd

■ Area illustrated

Getting Around

Delta towns are accessible by road. There is also a slow overnight ferry from Yangon to Pathein. Flights from Yangon to Sittwe and Thandwe operate daily, year round, but tend to be overbooked December to February. Boats from Taungup (north of Thandwe) to Sittwe do the nine-hour journey five times a week. Ferries and boats leave Sittwe each morning for Mrauk U; the journey takes five to seven hours, depending on the vessel. Taxis make the same trip, but are more expensive. Mrauk U can also be reached on a grueling overland bus journey from Yangon or Bagan via Magway.

The stone entrance of Sittwe's Lokhananda Pagoda

Sunrise viewed from the Shwetaung Pagoda in the ancient ruined city of Mrauk U

For hotels and restaurants in this region see p203 and pp211–12

Fishing boats moored at Ngapali in Western Myanmar

Buddha statue at the top of the hill in Mya Pyin village, Ngapali

Sights at a Glance

1. Twante
2. Pathein
3. Chaungtha
4. Ngwe Saung
5. Thandwe
6. Ngapali
7. Sittwe (Aykab)
8. *Mrauk U pp110–14*
9. Wethali
10. Dhanyawadi

Key

— Main road
— Other road
— Railroad
▬ International border
▬ Regional border
△ Peak

0 kilometers   50
0 miles   50

For additional map symbols *see back flap*

The gilded, bell-shaped *zedi* of Pathein's Shwemokhtaw Pagoda, surrounded by dozens of subsidiary stupas

❶ Twante

Road Map C5. 28 miles (46 km) W of Yangon, an hour by road via the Hlaing River bridge, or 30 mins from the Dalah ferry dock. 🏔 42,000. ✈ Yangon Mingaladon. 🚌

A typical small Ayeyarwady Delta town known primarily for its pottery, Twante is an easy day trip from Yangon and makes a good introduction to the region. Buses and Jeeps leave for the town at regular intervals from Dalah, on the south bank of the Yangon River, which may be crossed by a short but enjoyable ferry ride from the Pansodan Jetty on Strand Road.

Stacked with a range of goods in various stages of completion, the pottery workshops lining Twante's canals are hard to miss, and their staff delight in guiding visitors through the

manufacturing process. The town's other main sight is the 11th-century **Shwesandaw Pagoda** on its southern outskirts. The stupa is said to enshrine hairs of the Buddha. Although Twante was one of the worst-hit areas during Cyclone Nargis in May 2008, the pagoda came through the violent storm unscathed, unlike many of the other religious monuments in the town.

❷ Pathein

Road Map C5. 🏔 237,000. ✈ Yangon Mingaladon. 🛫 Pathein Airport, on the northeast edge of town near the university. 🚌 🚢

Also known as Bassein, Pathein is the capital of the Delta region and one of Myanmar's most populous cities. Its

enduring prosperity comes from the flat expanses of green paddy fields spread across the surrounding wetlands. In the British era, hundreds of thousands of acres of jungle, swamp, and marsh in the area were cleared to create cultivable land. As rice became Burma's main cash crop, people poured in from across India and the rest of the country to cash in on the bonanza. Exports from the Delta supplied Europe during the American Civil War and fueled the growth of Calcutta and Straits Settlements plantations in what was then Malaya. By the 1930s, half of the country's rice was sold overseas. However, rice production has plummeted since Independence due to antiquated agricultural practices, impoverished soil, and the vulnerability of local farmers to periods of drought and also flooding.

Pathein's pride and joy is the 153-ft (47-m) **Shwemokhtaw Pagoda**, whose golden, bell-shaped *zedi* (stupa) soars above the bend in the river at the center of town. Believed to have been founded in the 3rd century BC, it has since been enlarged many times, notably by the peripatetic king of Bagan, Alaungsithu (1089–1168), who sponsored the

A range of goods on display at a pottery workshop in Twante

For hotels and restaurants in this region see p203 and pp211–12

construction of many major temples, ordination halls, forts, and reservoirs across his domain. Shwemokhtaw's crowning glory is a particularly resplendent *hti* (finial) made of three layers: the first layer is made of bronze; the second of silver; and the third layer consists of solid gold weighing 3.9 lb (6.3 kg), with 843 rubies, 829 diamonds, and 1,588 semi-precious stones.

The nearby waterfront is a good spot for a leisurely stroll. Dotted with Chinese and Burmese temples, its banks are lined with wooden boats used to transport pottery and other goods and merchandise around the Delta and to and from the city market.

Also worth a visit is the **Settayaw Pagoda**, on the northeast edge of town, where a Konbaung-style Buddha image cast in bronze presides over a footprint of the historical Buddha, Gautama. The temple can be reached via a pretty red-and-white bridge, which is also a favorite backdrop for local wedding photographs.

🛕 Shwemokhtaw Pagoda
Shwezedi Rd. **Open** 6am–8pm daily.
♿ partial access via the south entrance.

🛕 Settayaw Pagoda
Mahabandula Rd.
Open 8am–9pm daily.

Trishaw carrying a monk in Pathein, capital of the Ayeyarwady Delta region

Pathein Parasols

A traditional Delta industry that has witnessed a sharp decline elsewhere in Myanmar, parasol making still thrives in Pathein thanks to the recent revival of tourism. Several workshops around the city make umbrellas in the traditional way, using bamboo, paper, waxed cotton, and silk. Renowned for their striking colors and delicately painted decoration, the parasols, known as *Pathein hti*, became desirable fashion accessories among the Victorian and Edwardian British aristocracy, and were exported in huge numbers from Burma. Many of the parasol workshops welcome visitors. Over green tea and nibbles, the artisans demonstrate the various stages of the production process, from carving the bamboo spokes and carefully blending the natural pigments used to color the parasols, to embellishing them with traditional floral patterns and bird designs.

Colorful parasols decorated with traditional designs

❸ Chaungtha

Road Map C5. 25 miles (40 km) W of Pathein. 🚹 900. 🚌

Ox-cart rides, picnics, and copious seafood lunches, rather than sunbathing and swimming, are what tend to occupy the droves of Yangonites who descend on Chaungtha beach on sunny weekends. From Monday to Friday, however, the few foreign tourists who take the winding road west of Pathein can expect to have the mile- (1.6 km-) long stretch of golden sand largely to themselves. Accommodations are offered in a string of lackluster, mostly mid-scale hotels behind the beach, whose most distinctive landmark is a small pagoda crowning a plant-covered rock in the middle of the bay.

The islet just off the headland to the southwest – Chaungtha Kyun, dubbed "White Sand Island" – can be explored in a day trip. The water around it is clearer and better for snorkeling, and local fishermen run trips to it every hour or so.

❹ Ngwe Saung

Road Map C5. 29 miles (48 km) W of Pathein. 🚹 4,000. 🚌

Located a couple of bays south of Chaungtha, Ngwe Saung has marginally whiter sand and bluer water than its near neighbor, and although neither are on a par with the beach at Ngapali *(see p106)*, in distant Rakhine, the resort makes for a pleasant stop. The area was closed for a few years after 2008's devastating Cyclone Nargis, which, together with the long journey time from Yangon, has slowed the pace of development. Confined to the north end of the 6-mile (10-km) beach, resort complexes are still few in number; more low-key hotels and budget guest-houses cluster in the south. Various small islands offshore and a more distant cove to the south beyond Sinma village are offered as day trips by local boatmen. The water becomes clearer away from the coast and most of the hotels offer masks and snorkels to rent.

Sandoway Resort, located on the beautiful beachfront at Ngapali

❺ Thandwe

Road Map C4. 231 miles (372 km) NW of Yangon. 🏯 113,000. ✈ Yangon Mingaladon. ✈ Thandwe Airport, 3 miles (5 km) W on the coast. 🚌 daily except public holidays.

The thousands of visitors who stream through Thandwe (formerly known as Sandoway) each winter en route to Ngapali rarely see more of the town than its airport. But it is well worth jumping in a taxi or pick-up truck for the 45-minute drive from Ngapali to visit Thandwe's bustling **market**, located in a former British jail. People from the surrounding villages pack the covered area from around 7am to shop for fresh produce, textiles, and a typically Burmese array of hardware. Souvenirs are also on sale.

On the surrounding hilltops are three gilded stupas offering great views over the town and nearby coast. A brisk 20-minute walk west of the market, the largest, **Nandaw Pagoda**, dates from the late 8th century and is said to have been erected by King Minbra to enshrine a bone relic of the Buddha. **Sandaw Pagoda** is believed to house a hair of the Buddha, and **Andaw Pagoda** a tooth relic.

In October 2013, communal violence from farther north in Rakhine State spread as far south as Thandwe, but the area has stabilized and there are currently no travel restrictions.

❻ Ngapali

Road Map C4. 4 miles (6 km) SW of Thandwe. ✈ Yangon Mingaladon. ✈ Thandwe Airport. 🚌

With its translucent turquoise water, white sand, and backdrop of gently inclined palm trees, Ngapali is one of the country's most stunning beaches, which is why Myanmar's Tatmadaw (military) government earmarked it for high-end development back in the 1990s. As a result, the accommodations here are a bit more chic than at resorts on the Delta coast. Tariffs are sky high by Southeast Asian standards, and infinity pools, stylish teak-built chalets, and sun terraces with uninterrupted sea views are the norm.

For the time being, villagers from the fishing settlement of Gyeiktaw, around the headland to the south of Ngapali's 3-mile (5-km) stretch of sand, still outnumber foreign visitors, even during the peak season. However, this looks set to change when a crop of larger resort complexes currently being built are completed.

Beachside cafés and restaurants at Ngapali beach

❼ Sittwe (Aykab)

Road Map B4. 553 miles (890 km) NW of Yangon. ⓘ 181,000. ✈ Yangon Mingaladon. ✈ Sittwe Airport, 2.5 miles (4 km) SW of the center. 🚌 from Taungup. 🚌 to Mrauk U 🚢 Mon–Sat.

The gilded interiors of the Lokhananda Pagoda in Sittwe

The Rakhine capital, Sittwe (also known as Aykab, its Bengali name), occupies a strategic location at the mouth of the Kaladan River, in the far northwest of the country. The British developed the town as a port and trade hub in the 19th century, but since Myanmar gained independence, political friction between the Arakanese and Burmese has marginalized the region, which now ranks among the most impoverished in the country.

A major setback to the town's economic prospects was the spate of communal clashes between Buddhists and the local Muslim Rohingya minority in 2012 and 2013, following which the government temporarily suspended all travel to the area. Hundreds died in the violence, and many thousands were forced into makeshift camps in safe havens, or across the border in Bangladesh. The situation has stabilized since, and a permit is no longer required to visit Sittwe.

For passing time between boat connections, visitors can explore the huge fish market at the east end of town, where some exotic merchandise is on sale from first light, or try the View Point, a mile (1.6 km) south, which is a popular spot for a breezy sunset stroll and a cold beer.

Less inspiring is the lackluster collection of inscriptions and other minor archeological finds in the **Rakhine State Cultural Museum**. Sittwe's principal stupa is the gigantic, gilded **Lokhananda Pagoda** on the southern edge of town, commissioned by General Than Shwe in 1997. An ordination hall on its northern side houses an intriguing bronze and brass Buddha thought to date from 24 BC, which local fishermen hauled out of the Kaladan.

🏛 Rakhine State Cultural Museum
Main Rd. **Open** 9:30am–4:30pm Tue–Sat. 🚫 🚷

🛕 Lokhananda Pagoda
Ball Lone Quin Quarter, near airport. **Open** 6am–9pm daily. ♿

Myanmar's Elephants

The vast teak forests of Myanmar have always been prime elephant territory, and the animal features prominently in the country's folklore and mythology. Used to represent the Buddha on ancient stupas, tuskers traditionally symbolized spiritual power and vitality. Particularly prized were white (albino) animals, which kings throughout history have gone to great lengths to acquire. Their presence in royal palaces was supposed to assure long and fruitful reigns for their owners, a belief that continues to this day – Myanmar's former military leaders collected white elephants which are now kept in special enclosures in Yangon and Naypyitaw.

From an estimated peak of around 10,000 in the last century, the numbers of wild elephants have plummeted to around 2,000. Poaching for ivory and habitat loss due to mining, hydroelectric schemes, and deforestation have played their part, but research has revealed that the main culprit is the country's state-owned timber industry.

Around 4,750 elephants presently work in Myanmar's forests. However, reproduction rates among domesticated animals are very low, and the working population has to be

A domesticated working elephant

supplemented with captured animals. Between 50 and 100 elephants are currently caught each year using tranquilizer darts, and this is having a damaging impact on the viability of the wild population. Once trapped, elephants suffer a traumatic regime to break them in, involving food and sleep deprivation, physical restraint, and beatings. The training process can last as long as 20 years. Several camps offer visitors the chance to see domesticated elephants at work, but sightings of wild ones are rare, as areas where they survive in healthy numbers are remote and inaccessible to casual visitors.

Sunrise over the mist-shrouded stupas and shrines of the ancient ruined city of Mrauk U ▶

❽ Mrauk U

Occupying a sliver of lush coastal land, Arakan – precursor of modern Rakhine State – was in the 16th century the hub of a trade network in spices and slaves that extended from south India to Indonesia, and brought fabulous riches to the Arakanese kings. The grandeur of their capital, Mrauk U, was renowned across Asia. Merchants from Persia, Afghanistan, Abyssinia, China, Japan, Portugal, and Holland settled here. The arts flourished, and the markets were full of precious stones and perfumes. However, after the Burmese sacked the city in 1784, the population of 16,000 fled and it fell into ruins. Now only a scattering of stupas and temples remain, rising from a carpet of bleached grass and scrub – a sight that is especially beautiful in the mist of early morning.

Lemyethna Temple
Men Saw Mon, the first king of the Mrauk U Dynasty, built this temple in 1430, and lived only just long enough to see it completed.

★ Dukkan Thein
Built in 1571 by King Minphalaung, this ordination hall has an upper terrace accessed by three monumental stairways. The eastern entrance leads to a spiral passageway lined with some of Mrauk U's finest stone carvings.

↖ Dhanyawadi & Wethali *(see p115)*

KEY

① **Bandula Kyaung** is a shrine housing the precious Sanda Muni statue, which was hidden inside a cement block for centuries.

② **The palace museum** has a modest collection comprising Buddha images, stone inscriptions, coins, and a scale model of the site.

③ **The royal palace** of Mrauk U was among Asia's most magnificent royal abodes, but only a few wall fragments remain.

④ **Andaw Thein** was renovated in the 1530s by King Minbin, then enlarged into a temple by King Min Razagyi (1557–1612) in 1596 to house a tooth relic of the Buddha.

⑤ **Ratanamanaung Pagoda**

⑥ **Sakyamanaung Pagoda**

⑦ **Peisi Daung Pagoda**

⑧ **The Shwetaung Pagoda** is a stupa site on a hilltop to the south, reached via a winding path. One of the finest views of Mrauk U is to be had from here at dawn.

★ Sittaung Temple
The highlight of Minbin's temple lies hidden deep inside its walls, where stone passages are lined with splendid bas reliefs and Buddhas.

Wa Ze Creek

Let Se Kan

Anuma Moat

Ratanabon Pagoda
Centered on an elegantly curved stupa, Ratanabon resembles a huge bell. Its name suggests it was originally designed to house treasures that may have been looted when the Burmese sacked the city in 1784.

★ Koethaung Temple
This impressive 16th-century pagoda on the site's eastern fringes is said to have had 90,000 Buddha statues placed within it. It is also the largest building in all of Mrauk U.

City of the Monkey Egg

Mrauk U is often translated as "Monkey Egg," a curious name attributed to the site's mythical origins when a monkey and a peacock are said to have mated on the banks of the Lemro River. In fact, the name derives from the Burmese tendency to mispronounce Mrauk U as "Myauk U," which does indeed mean "Monkey Egg." The original Arakanese, however, means "Holy City of the North," an altogether more plausible moniker.

Mandalay's Mahamuni, originally from Mrauk U

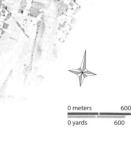

0 meters 600
0 yards 600

Exploring Mrauk U

The remains of the former Arakan capital, Mrauk U, straddle the Lemro River – a tributary of the broader Kaladan – amid an area of low, scrub-covered hills. Connected by sandy tracks, the principal monuments lie close enough together to be explored on foot or by horse cart, although the heat tends to limit serious sightseeing to the mornings and early evenings. Entry tickets can be paid for in US dollars or kyat, either on arrival at the boat jetty or at the Sittaung Temple.

The entrance to the palace museum, which displays artifacts found in Mrauk U

Monk walking down a path next to the walls of the royal palace at Mrauk U

🏛 Royal Palace and Museum

The royal palace at the center of Mrauk U was constructed by the founder of the Mrauk U Dynasty, Men Saw Mon (1380–1433), also known as Naramithla. Built in 1430, it was once the city's most spectacular edifice – a huge, ornately decorated wooden structure set on three receding levels and surrounded by three interlocking walls. Only parts of the outermost rampart remain, along with fragments of a gateway and central platform, but several contemporary descriptions survive, including one by Augustinian monk Sebastian Manrique, who lived in the capital for eight years from 1629. Manrique wrote of the vast gilded pillars inside, and rooms "made of odiferous woods ... which thus gratify the sense of smell by their own natural fragrance. There was one room known as the 'House of Gold' for being entirely ornamented from top to bottom in that metal."

On display at the palace museum inside the western walls is a collection of Buddha statues, inscriptions, and coins – many of them reproductions – found during archeological excavations across the site.

🏛 Sittaung Temple

Some of Mrauk U's most impressive monuments are concentrated in the area immediately north of the palace ruins, at the foot of the ridge of hills running north from the site. Connected by broad dirt tracks, they are all easily reachable on foot.

The standout building in this northern group is the Sittaung Temple, built in 1535 by King Minbin (1493–1554) to mark his victorious Bengal campaign. Its suitably triumphant centerpiece is a grand, bell-shaped stupa surrounded by scores of subsidiary *zedis*. Inside, the central ambulatory passage around the main shrine is lined with thousands of carved stone Buddhas and bas-reliefs of the *Jatakas*, showing scenes from the Buddha's life, which have been heavily restored and are now floodlit. The latter draw much of their inspiration from contemporary life in the Arakan capital, and are a priceless window on this lost medieval world. The profusion of sculpture has earned the building the

The bell-shaped stupa of the Sittaung Temple, surrounded by subsidiary shrines

Painted Buddha statues in the central shrine of the Andaw Thein ordination hall

nickname "Temple of 80,000 Buddhas." At the main entrance, a 10-ft- (3-m-) tall inscribed pillar, originally from the settlementat Wethali (see p115), recounts in Pali the dynastic history of the rulers of Arakan between the 5th and 8th centuries AD.

Andaw Thein

A short distance northeast of Sittaung, the slightly older, smaller Andaw Thein (literally "Tooth Shrine") has a very similar layout to its neighbor, with a central stupa encircled by 16 smaller ones rising from an octagonal base. This gem of a temple dates from the 1520s and was originally built as a monastic ordination hall; it was later enlarged by King Min Razagyi to house a tooth relic of the Buddha brought back from a pilgrimage to Ceylon.

Ratanabon Pagoda

The third structure in this sequence, the Ratanabon Pagoda, a short way farther north, dates from 1612 and is the most picturesque of the trio. Its elegantly curved central stupa was destroyed by a Japanese bomb in World War II but has since been restored.

Dukkan Thein

Farther west stands the impressive Dukkan Thein (or Htukkanthein) ordination hall, whose distinctive stupa, topped by a mushroom-shaped finial, rests on two imposing, fortress-like terraces atop a low hillock. A flight of steps on its east side leads inside to three vaulted chambers connected by a pas-sageway lined with 179 Buddha statues in niches. Flanking these are carved figures thought to be

depictions of the Arakanese donors and their wives who sponsored the construction of the temple, each with a different hairstyle. The main Buddha figure in the central shrine is illuminated at dawn by light filtering through a square window in the dome above.

Lemyethna Temple

The final monument of note in this northern group is the Lemyethna Temple, in which eight Buddhas are seated on thrones around the base of an octagonal column. Facing them are empty niches where another 20 figures formerly sat. Square in plan, with four projecting vaulted porches in the style of classical Bagan, the temple dates from the reign of Men Saw Mon and is one of the oldest on the site.

The Chin Villages

A popular half-day excursion from Mrauk U is the two-hour boat ride north up the Lemro River to a cluster of settlements inhabited by Chin minority people. Until the practice was banned by the government in the 1960s, Chin women used to tattoo their faces with intricate spiderweb designs. One popular hypothesis suggests they did so as a form of disfig-urement to avoid being kidnapped into slavery or concubi-nage, while another says the tattoos were a mark of beauty. A few elderly women in these villages retain the markings, allowing visitors to photograph them in exchange for dona-tions. Discouraged by Baptist missionaries after World War II, facial tattoos have become rare, even in the Chin heartland near the Bangladesh border, where an ongoing insurgency has led to the displacement of thousands of Chin. The group living near Mrauk U are among these refugees and welcome the money received from visitors to supplement the meager income they derive from fishing and subsistence farming.

Chin woman with tattooed face, Kyi Chaung village

A panoramic view of the massive Koethaung Temple, Mrauk U's largest structure

🅐 Koethaung Temple

The cluster of monuments scattered across the low hills, rice paddies, and marshes at the eastern end of Mrauk U are dominated by the iconic Koethaung Temple, the largest on the site. Given the dearth of shade along the lanes leading to this group, it makes sense to start sightseeing early in the morning, or hire a horse cart, tuktuk, or Jeep for the trip.

Oriented toward the east, Koethaung is square in plan with an exterior composed of five receding terraces, each holding rows of small stupas. It was built by Minbin's son, Mintikka (r. 1554–6), who attempted to outdo his father by building a larger temple with an even greater number of

Animal statues around the "bell" of Koethaung

Buddhas – there are allegedly 10,000 more here than at the Sittaung Temple, hence its name, which means "90,000."

🅑 Peisi Daung Pagoda

One of the best views of the eastern group of monuments, and Koethaung in particular, is to be had from the unexcavated pagoda crowning the hilltop immediately to the south. Five Buddhas are enshrined at the dusty Peisi Daung Pagoda (four facing the cardinal points and one on top), each depicted with large white eyes. Some effort is required to push through the undergrowth shrouding the hill to reach the monument, but the views over the surrounding banana groves and rice fields are well worth

Buddha statues at the unexcavated Peisi Daung Pagoda

For hotels and restaurants in this region see p203 and pp211–12

the effort. Traces of the third, outermost belt of city walls are also visible from this splendid vantage point.

🅒 Ratanamanaung Pagoda

Located around half a mile (0.8 km) northeast of the palace site, Ratanamanaung was built by King Sandathudam Raza in 1652. The pagoda is a solid stone structure – plain and octagonal in shape from the base to the tip of its spire. Brightly painted planetary figures astride elephants and mythical creatures are installed at intervals on the ambulatory path surrounding the monument. On the northwest side of the stupa stand the remains of a hall known as the Gupru, or "White Cave," where in 1696 a resident monk, Marone Pyi Ya, was ritually crowned as the symbolic ruler of Mrauk U, a title he retained for a full year.

The unusual geometric tiers of the Sakyamanaung Pagoda

🅓 Sakyamanaung Pagoda

Thanks to its lofty spire and finial, which peak at 280 ft (82 m), the other prominent landmark in this eastern area is the Sakyamanaung Pagoda, which stands roughly midway between the palace and the Koethaung Temple. Attributed to King Thiri Thudhamma (r. 1622–38), Sakyamanaung was one of the last major projects undertaken at Mrauk U and is unusual for being made up of a mixture of circular and octagonal tiers. The overall effect is one of elegant symmetry, although its graceful appearance is somewhat at odds with the grinning, sword-wielding ogres guarding the entrance.

The Great Payagyi Buddha statue, one of the main sights in Wethali

❾ Wethali

Road Map B3. 6 miles (10 km) N of Mrauk U. ✈ Yangon Mingaladon. ✈ Sittwe Airport. 🚌 Sittwe to Mrauk U, then by hired Jeep.

Faint traces of one of Mrauk U's forerunners litter the fields 6 miles (10 km) north of the archeological site, where sections of ancient walls and the foundations of partly excavated monasteries and temples are all that is left of ancient Wethali. Founded in AD 327 by King Devan Sanda, the settlement is thought to have been occupied for around 700 years and bears close similarities to the contemporaneous Pyu cities of the Ayeyarwady Valley. Most of the key finds unearthed here have been removed. They included a famous inscribed obelisk, which now stands at the entrance to Mrauk U's Sittaung Temple *(see p112)*, and a handful of coins and sculpture pieces on display at Mrauk U's palace museum *(see p112)*. But one note-worthy object remains in situ: a 17-ft (5-m) seated Buddha hewn from a single block of stone, known locally as the **Great Wethali Payagyi**. It is believed to be one of Myanmar's oldest sur-viving Buddhas.

Silver coin of King Chandra Surya

❿ Dhanyawadi

Road Map B3. 20 miles (32 km) N of Wethali. ✈ Yangon Mingaladon. ✈ Sittwe Airport. 🚌 Sittwe to Mrauk U, then by hired Jeep.

Another 20 miles (32 km) to the north, Dhanyawadi is the site of a second lost city, which local legend asserts was visited by the Buddha in 554 BC. The event, which took place during the reign of King Chandra Surya, is believed to have been marked by the casting of a huge bronze Buddha statue – the illustrious Mahamuni. The figure was enshrined inside the **Mahamuni Temple** here until Bodawpaya's invading army carried it over the Rakhine-Yoma Hills to Mandalay in 1784 *(see p142)*. Its presiding image may have gone, but the temple, now thoroughly modernized and housing three fine Buddhas, still attracts pilgrims from all over the country. A little museum near the southern walls of the shrine displays fragments of pottery and Pali inscriptions attesting to the antiquity of Dhanyawadi, which archeol-ogists believe reached its peak between the 4th and 6th centuries AD.

The faint outlines of oval perimeter walls, similar to those of the Pyu cities, and a square palace are invisible to visitors at ground level but may clearly be seen on satellite images.

The Lost Kingdom of Arakan

Although virtually forgotten by the rest of the world today, Arakan at its height ranked among Asia's most illustrious kingdoms, with a seaborne empire that stretched from the Ganges to the Ayeyarwady. The key to its wealth lay in trade, particularly in slaves, bought from Portuguese slavers preying on Bengal's coastal settlements and sold in prodigious numbers to the Dutch colony of Batavia (now Jakarta), along with shiploads of rice. Tax revenue from territorial conquests also helped fill Mrauk U's coffers.

Fortune seekers from across Asia and Europe traveled to the city during its heyday, when its pop-ulation peaked at around 160,000. They discovered a sophisticated, refined culture blending Islamic influences from northern India with indigenous Buddhist tradition. This syncretic style was a legacy of the 25-year exile of the dynasty's founder, Men Saw Mon, in the court of the Sultan of Bengal. The prince had fled there to escape repeated attacks by the Burmese, and during his enforced stay became fluent in Persian and a connoisseur of the region's Afghan-influenced Indo-Islamic culture, particularly its poetry, music, and architecture. On his return to Mrauk U, Bengali artists became a prominent feature

The ruins of Mrauk U, capital city of the Arakan kingdom

of his own court, founded in 1430, where the royal attire had more in common with Mughal fashions than the Thai-influenced styles of Burmese kings in Inwa (Ava). Sadly, precious few artifacts survive from what was undoubtedly one of Southeast Asia's great cultural flowerings, other than the exquisite Mahamuni Buddha image, which Bodawpaya's army carried off in 1784 and is now in Mandalay.

BAGAN ARCHEOLOGICAL ZONE

Lost cities abound in Myanmar, but none approach the splendor of Bagan. Scattered across an arid plain in a bend of the Ayeyarwady are the ruins of around 2,000 monasteries, temples, shrines, and stupas – remnants of an imperial capital that reached its peak between the 11th and 13th centuries. Viewed at sunrise or sunset, with the warm light intensifying the red-brown hues of their brickwork, the hundreds of tapering, elegantly symmetrical towers and finials rising from the dusty sand flats create a superb spectacle.

Once a thriving metropolis of between 50,000 and 200,000 people, Bagan dazzled Marco Polo, who described its gilded skyline as "one of the finest sights in the world." Monks and scholars from across Asia came here to study philosophy, law, grammar, astrology, and medicine, and religion permeated every aspect of life. Under the influence of Shin Arahan *(see p51)*, Bagan's kings gradually began to favor and promote Theravada Buddhism. But the faith overlayered a complex blend of arcane beliefs rooted in the Tibetan-influenced Mahayana tradition and Hindu cults of Shiva and Vishnu, as well as in the worship of local nature spirits, or *nats*.

It is possible to chart this cultural shift in Bagan's religious architecture, where small, dark shrines swirling with Tantric murals were, over time, superseded by towering temples and giant, bell-shaped stupas. While a handful of these remain active places of worship, visited in great numbers by Burmese pilgrims, many more stand all but forgotten in the scrub. Virtually none, however, remain in a ruinous state. Since the 1990s, the government has pursued a massive renovation program, restoring even smaller, off-track monuments. Local villages have been forcibly relocated, an unsightly viewing tower set up, and ruins rebuilt, often from scratch and with little regard for original appearances, much to the dismay of UNESCO, which has denied Bagan coveted World Heritage Site status. The heavy-handed government control of the site, however, is effortlessly eclipsed by the phenomenal beauty of the monuments themselves, described as one of the true wonders of the medieval world.

Villagers herding goats through the fields surrounding the ancient temples and stupas of Bagan

◀ Detail of one of the Buddhas at the Htilominlo Temple, one of the greatest of Bagan's shrines

Exploring the Bagan Archeological Zone

Bagan's 2,000 or so surviving monuments are spread over a 26-sq-mile (50-sq-km) area called the Bagan Archeological Zone. Entry tickets to the site can be bought on arrival at the airport or jetty, or at some of the larger temples, and must be paid for in US dollars. Nyaung U village, the main market and transport hub, has most of the budget and mid-scale accommodations. Overlooking the bend in the river and connected via surfaced roads, Old Bagan has restaurants and a handful of mostly high-end hotels, while New Bagan is where most of the tour groups stay. Although major monuments are open from dawn to dusk, less-frequented ones may be locked. Key keepers usually live nearby and will unlock the gates when tourists appear – a service for which they'll expect a small tip.

Mural at the refined Sulamani Pagoda showing a scene from the Buddha's life

Sights at a Glance

Getting Around

To get around Bagan, Chinese-made gearless bicycles may be rented from most hotels, although they puncture easily and can be hard work in the heat. A more relaxing option is to hire a horse cart for the day. Drivers know the zone well and provide a commentary on the monuments, although their English may not be fluent. Taxis can also be hired for the day. Electric bikes (e-bikes) are a popular option, but you have to pedal if they run out of power midway. Pickup trucks run a regular route between Nyaung U, Old Bagan, Myinkaba, and New Bagan. For Popa Taung Kalat, taxis are the most convenient option. Alternatively, pickup trucks leave from Nyaung U market, but some only go as far as Kyaukpadaung, where you have to change for Popa. All travel agents sell tickets for the Malikha 2, Nmai Hka, and Myanmar Golden River Group ferries to Mandalay. Departures are from the Nyaung U jetty, or the Old Bagan jetty in the dry season. The slower IWT ferries leave twice weekly; tickets are sold from their office near the Nyaung U jetty, and by all travel agents.

For hotels and restaurants in this region see pp203–4 and p212

Souvenirs for sale and exhibits at the small Thanaka Museum in Nyaung U

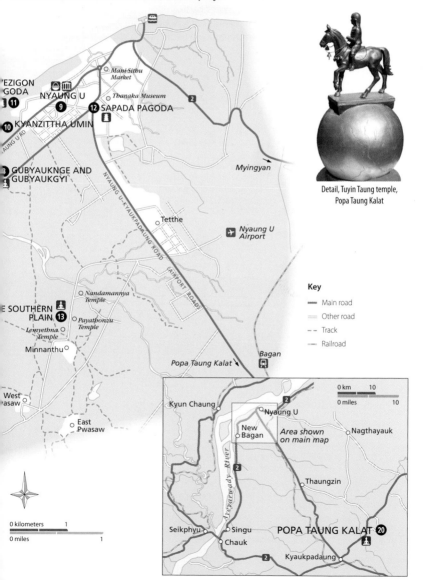

Detail, Tuyin Taung temple,
Popa Taung Kalat

Key

━━━ Main road

═══ Other road

--- Track

━━━ Railroad

The Sacred Architecture of Bagan

Bagan's golden era of sacred building spanned 250 years, during which time architectural styles evolved in a dramatic fashion. Initially imitating the cylindrical structures of the ancient Pyu city of Sri Ksetra, Bagan's stupas gradually grew more slender and bell-shaped, culminating in the elaborately embellished, tapering spire that remains the classical Burmese archetype today. Temples changed from simple replicas of wooden shrines to soaring masterpieces with entrances on four sides, cavernous interiors, and spectacular roof finials – innovations enabled by the emergence of the pointed arch in Bagan. Charting this stylistic metamorphosis and piecing together the historical shifts it represents is one of the great pleasures of a visit to the site.

Fresco at the Sulamani Temple, Bagan Archeological Zone

Bagan's Stupas

Myanmar's oldest surviving stupas are those at the city of Sri Ksetra (see pp98–9). Their cylindrical, elongated shapes influenced the forms of Bagan's first pagodas. These slowly became more bell-like, with squat middle sections and tapering spires, and grew larger and higher, set on grand stepped terraces (see pp32–3).

Bupaya
Early gourd-shaped stupas such as Bagan's Bupaya had gently swelling sides and tapering spires.

Lawkananda
The design gradually evolved to have straight flanks and rounded tops, a bit like the early Pyu stupas.

Sapada
Some of Bagan's pagodas showed Sinhalese influence in the design of the square relic chamber above the bell.

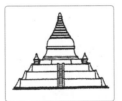

Shwezigon
The scale of the pagodas gradually became grander. Stupas had broad bells and were set on high bases.

Mingalazedi
With the majestic stupas of the 13th century, the Burmese pagoda reached its most colossal, imposing form.

Painting and Stucco

Bagan's brick monasteries and temples were originally encased in a shell of stucco which was applied wet, molded, and allowed to dry. Patches on surviving structures reveal how sophisticated this plasterwork was, combining figurative forms of mythical creatures and saints with floral borders and geometric shapes. Mural fragments also adorn temple interiors; the oldest of them date from the 10th century, when Tantricism and Hinduism greatly influenced Burmese Buddhist iconography. New paintings in a more graphic, folk-art style were also added to several shrines by the Konbaungs.

Detail of stuccowork at the Upali Thein ordination hall

Bagan's Temples

Taking their cue originally from Indian architecture, Bagan's temples grew slowly more imposing, ethereal, and distinctively Burmese over time, culminating in the giant, double-storied shrines that tower above the northern plain to this day.

Pointed arch and door guardians, Nagayon

Floor plan of Nagayon

Mon: Nagayon Temple

Dating from the reign of King Kyanzittha (1030–1112), the earliest temples in Bagan are in Mon style, with a single entrance opening onto a vestibule and a central inner sanctum which contains a Buddha image.

Transitional: Ananda Temple

Kyanzittha's masterpiece still shows Mon influence, but is in the form of a perfect Greek cross, with four entrances and projecting porticoes. Vaulted concentric corridors encircle the inner shrines.

Floor plan showing the Greek cross layout of the Ananda Temple

The graceful exterior of the Ananda Temple

Late Transitional: Thatbyinnyu Temple

Taller, more slender, and lighter inside thanks to the addition of larger doors and windows, the refined Bamar style of the 12th century introduced the concept of "hollow" or *gu*-style cubes placed on top of each other.

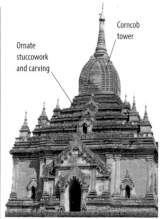

Corncob tower

Ornate stuccowork and carving

Late Bagan: Htilominlo Temple

The last of the great temples erected in Bagan in the 13th century, such as Htilominlo, take the *gu* principle and embellish it with more complex roofs, ornate decor, and elongated towers.

❶ Old Bagan

The area of sandy scrub beside the bend in the river, known as Old Bagan, formed the hub of the medieval city. Traces of the fortified walls and gateways that once encircled it on the landward side are still visible in many places, but it is the great concentration of temples and stupas dating from Bagan's heyday – including two of the site's giants, the Gawdawpalin and Thatbyinnyu temples – that make this a particularly rewarding area to explore on foot or by bicycle. In 1998, the villagers who lived among the ruins were forcibly relocated south in New Bagan, so there are few opportunities for refreshment between the monuments. The nearest stalls cluster along the main road east of the Tharabar Gate.

View over the temples of Bagan with the Rakhine-Yoma Hills in the distance

★ **Gawdawpalin Temple**
Built by King Narapatisithu (1138–1211), Gawdawpalin is one of Bagan's largest and most ethereal temples. It is of the "hollow," or *gu*, type, with porticoes on four sides and a vaulted inner corridor.

Lacquerware Museum

KEY

① **The Bagan Golden Palace** is a reconstruction of the original.

② **The diminutive Pitakat Taik** once held Anawrahta's library, a collection of Buddhist scriptures looted after the attack on Thaton. It reportedly took 30 elephants to carry the books back to Bagan.

③ **The 20-ft (6-m) Thandawgya Buddha** sits in *bhumisparsha* mudra.

④ **Ngakywenadaung Pagoda**, a small bulbous structure, is similar to the early Pyu pagodas.

⑤ **The 11th-century Nathlaung Kyaung** was in its day the most important Hindu temple at Bagan. Its presiding deity, stolen in the 19th century, is now in a Berlin museum.

⑥ **Pahtothamya Temple** contains Mon-style paintings.

⑦ **The site museum** holds a poorly lit and labeled collection of stone Buddhas and inscriptions culled from Bagan's monuments.

Mimalaung Kyaung
This late-12th-century shrine became known as "the temple that does not catch fire" after it survived unscathed a devastating blaze in 1225.

Mataungta Gate

Tharabar Gate
The last surviving gateway in the old city walls, Tharabar is flanked by a pair of brick-walled shrines dedicated to the *nats*, or nature spirits, Min Mahagiri and Hnamadawgyi.

VISITORS' CHECKLIST

Practical Information
Road Map C3. 7 miles (11 km) west of airport. **Open** museum: 9am–4:30pm Tue–Sun; temples: dawn–dusk daily. 📷 covers all of Bagan; separate admission fee for museum. 📷 guides can be hired through most hotels; horse cart drivers also provide commentary.

Transport
✈ Mandalay Intl. ✈ Nyaung U Airport. 🚐 Pickups run between Nyaung U, Old Bagan, Myinkaba, & New Bagan. Bicycles, e-bikes, taxis, horse carts available for hire.

Shwegugyi Temple
This fine early-Bamar-style temple was erected by King Alaungsithu in 1131. Inscriptions inside record that it took just seven months to complete. Large windows and doors create a light, airy feel inside.

Kalay Gate

★ Thatbyinnyu Temple
Visible from all over Bagan, Thatbyinnyu, which means "omniscience," is the tallest structure on the site, rising to a majestic 210 ft (61 m). It was the first to adopt the double-story "hollow"" *(gu)* style.

Key

— Suggested route

0 meters 200
0 yards 200

❷ Ananda Temple

Surmounted by a classically proportioned corncob tower, the whitewashed Ananda Temple is among the most stylistically refined and impressive temples in Bagan. It is also the most revered by Burmese Buddhists. Its grand entranceways lead to four beautiful gilded Buddhas standing in huge recesses, interconnected by corridors that are adorned with wonderful stone sculpture and painting. The exterior surfaces are no less sumptuously embellished, featuring bands of green-glazed terra-cotta plaques showing scenes from the *Jatakas*, episodes from the Buddha's life. From afar, however, the golden spire is Ananda's most readily identifiable feature, as spectacular today as it was when Kyanzittha commissioned the building in 1105.

Door guardians, made of exquisitely carved and painted hardwood, flank the entrances on the east and west.

Outer wall and arched gateways
A high wall with arched gateways at the cardinal points encloses the whole complex. Inside the entrances, guardian deities in the seated *lalitasana* position, denoting spiritual ease, welcome worshippers.

KEY

① **The long north and south porticoes** are 19th-century Konbaung additions.

② **The gable-arched entrances** to the temple are decorated with exuberant stuccowork. Only those on the east and west sides are open.

③ **The upper terraces,** which are currently not open to the public, contain Ananda's finest paintings.

④ **The central roof** consists of six receding terraces.

⑤ **Corner stupas** adorn the roof.

⑥ **Over 1,000 stone sculptures** line the outer corridor, many of them set in niches.

⑦ **Carved stone reliefs** lining the inner ambulatory corridor recount the story of the Buddha's life.

Stone *chinthes*, or grinning leogryphs, stand guard at all the corners of the temple building.

★ **Central tower**
The splendid corncob tower, soaring 170 ft (52 m) above the sandy plains, underlines the fact the shrine was designed by Indian architects. It is crowned by a gleaming golden umbrella finial, or *hti*.

④

⑤

③

⑦

⑥

***Jataka* tiles**
Thousands of green-glazed terra-cotta tiles encrust the base, sides, and terrace of the temple, depicting scenes from the *Jatakas*.

★ **Four Buddhas**
One of the temple's most famous features are the four gilded wooden Buddhas standing in the main shrines. Only those in the north and south are original, the other two having been destroyed by fires.

South-facing Kassapa

North-facing Kakusandha

East-facing Konagamana

West-facing Gautama

❸ Ananda Oak Kyaung

Road Map C3. Old Bagan, W of Ananda Temple's northern entrance.

In ancient Pali-Sanskrit, "oak" means "brick," and this small *vihara* (chapel or sanctuary) is one of only a few brick monasteries surviving from the early Bagan period. The building is best known for the exceptionally well-preserved frescoes that cloak its interior walls and ceilings. Rendered in earthy reds, greens, blacks, and browns, these are particularly rich with scenes of everyday life in the 11th century: market shopping, Arab traders, soldiers marching, and people bathing, cooking, and playing musical instruments, including the *hsaing waing* (Burmese musical ensemble) and *saung gauk* (Burmese harp). There is also some erotica. Although Ananda Oak Kyaung is locked as a rule, the caretaker who has the key lives in a house next to the compound and will open it for visitors.

❹ Sin Myar Shin

Road Map C3. N of the Shwesandaw Pagoda.

One of a trio of shrines standing in a neat row just south of the main road, this double-story

Frescoes surrounding a statue of the Buddha in the tiny Upali Thein ordination hall

temple is capped by a richly gilded corncob spire. Two Buddha images preside over the main hall on the first floor, while four Buddhas facing the cardinal points sit in the upper chamber. Traces of original murals remain throughout, along with paintings from the Konbaung era of the 18th and 19th centuries.

However, the best reason to come to this shrine is for the chance to scramble up to its high terrace below the main tower for glorious views of the sunrise or sunset. Very few visitors to Bagan realize that the authorities still permit people to climb Sin Myar Shin, so the terrace rarely has more than a handful of people. This is a particularly good place to come to admire the Thatbyinnyu and Ananda temples, both located only a short distance north, and floodlit to spectacular effect in the evenings.

❺ Upali Thein

Road Map C3. 1 mile (1.5 km) NE of Ananda, Old Bagan–Nyaung U Rd. ✉

This diminutive ordination hall dating from the 13th century forms part of a larger monastic complex whose wooden portions have long since disappeared. It is noteworthy for the way its exterior mimics the design and decor of the now lost wood structures, and for the frescoes inside. Painted during the Konbaung era, they show scenes from the lives of past Buddhas as well as from the hall's consecration. The building was erected during the reign of King Kyazuco (r. 1234–50), known as the Philosopher King for his piety and knowledge of the Theravada canon. Kyazuco named the building after a famous monk, Mahasiha Upali, who was originally invited to Bagan by his father.

A Historical Theme Park?

The efforts of Myanmar's military government to restore the ancient ruins of Bagan after centuries of wear from weather and earthquakes were described by UNESCO as "[a] Disney-style fantasy version of one of the world's great religious and historical sites ... [using] the wrong materials to build wrongly shaped structures on top of magnificent ancient stupas." Since 1995, an estimated 1,299 stupas, monasteries, and temples have been speculatively rebuilt from piles of bricks scattered across the site of the medieval city, while another 668 have seen major renovations, funded largely by merit-making donations from wealthy Burmese. Archeologists, heritage architects, and UNESCO have been unanimous in their condemnation of the program, claiming that the results bear little relation to what the original structures would have looked like, and criticizing the use of cement and other modern materials. In reply, the Burmese authorities claim it is the government's "duty to preserve, strengthen, and

Ancient temples and pagodas scattered across Bagan

restore" Bagan's monuments, and have flown in the face of foreign disapproval by permitting the construction of an unsightly observation tower and gigantic museum complex that now dominate horizons where once only temple towers rose from the plains. The controversy, however, seems not to have deterred tourists, and, since 2010, foreign visitors have flocked to the archeological zone in record numbers to view the spectacular reconstructions.

The soaring lines of Htilominlo, one of the last great temples built in Bagan

❻ Htilominlo

Road Map C3. SE of Upali Thein, Old Bagan–Nyaung U Rd.

One of the greatest of all Bagan's temples, Htilominlo dominates the northern group of monuments and is the very antithesis of the nearby Upali Thein: a soaring, triumphant building whose tapering central spire reaches 150 ft (46 m) into the sky. King Nantaungmya (r. 1211–34), son of a concubine and therefore several notches down the line of succession, commissioned it to mark his ascent to the throne after a divination ritual involving a tilting white umbrella. Built in splendid late-Burmese style, with a main vestibule that is oriented to the rising sun, the temple is the last example of its kind erected in Bagan. Patches of ornate stone carving and stucco survive around the doorways, arches, and pediments outside. The interior houses four gilded Buddhas on each of its two floors, facing the cardinal points.

❼ Shwe Leik Too

Road Map C3. Outskirts of Wetkyin village, midway between Nyaung U and Old Bagan.

The 13th-century Shwe Leik Too is a midsized temple in late-Bamar style with four projecting porticos and a corncob tower, enclosed by a low perimeter wall. The temple is of interest primarily because it is among only a handful of monuments in Bagan which the government still allows visitors to climb. A low-roofed passageway leads from the vaulted inner chamber, which holds both standing and seated Buddhas, to the upper terrace from where fine panoramic views extend over the northern half of the archeological zone. To the southwest, Htilominlo looks resplendent in the dawn light, while the myriad temples and pagodas to the east form striking silhouettes as the sun rises behind them.

The 13th-century Bamar-style Shwe Leik Too Temple with its corncob tower

❽ Gubyauknge and Gubyaukgyi

Road Map C3. Wetkyin village.

East of Htilominlo, the 11th-century Gubyauknge, one of Bagan's oldest temples, retains some fine original stuccowork on its exterior. A pair of *nats*, or nature spirits, flank the doorway to the main shrine, reflecting the syncretic nature of Buddhism in the medieval city.

Gubyaukgyi, a stone's throw northeast, is a 13th-century building with a distinctive, pyramidal sanctuary tower surmounting its roof. Usually called the Wetkyin Gubyaukgyi to distinguish it from its namesake in Myinkaba, the temple retains some fine mural traces around the entrance ceiling.

Mural at the 13th-century Wetkyin Gubyaukgyi temple in Bagan

❾ Nyaung U

Road Map C3. 2.5 miles (4.5 km) NW of airport. ⟨⟩ 55,000. ✈ Mandalay International. ✈ Nyaung U Airport. 🚌 🚐 🚍 Pickups run a regular route between Nyaung U, Old Bagan, Myinkaba, and New Bagan. 🚢

Bagan's central market area lines the main street of Nyaung U village. Most visitors who travel up here do so to eat in one of the many restaurants flanking Thiripyitsaya 4 Street. Many also stop off at the quirky **Thanaka Museum**, which has displays showing how *thanaka*, the quintessentially Burmese face paste, is produced. The museum shop sells cosmetics made from this fragrant wood powder.

🏛 **Thanaka Museum**
Corner of Thiripyitsaya 4 St and Main Rd. **Open** 9am–9pm daily. 📷

⑩ Kyanzittha Umin

Road Map C3. Nyaung U. 🖼

A cave temple in a plot just southwest of the Shwezigon Pagoda, Kyanzittha Umin was originally part of a small monastery. The cave's exterior was encased in a brick facade, while inside it was excavated to create corridors whose walls and ceilings were decorated with murals, many of which survive intact. Although named after King Kyanzittha (1030–1112), the site was probably developed during the reign of his father, King Anawrahta (1015–78). A flashlight is recommended for a visit as the cave has no interior lighting.

⑪ Shwezigon Pagoda

Road Map C3. Western edge of Nyaung U. 🖼 Oct/Nov: Shwezigon pagoda festival.

The gilded Shwezigon Pagoda, on the outskirts of Nyaung U in the northeastern corner of the archeological zone, was Bagan's most important religious site during the reign of King Anawrahta, founder of the Bagan Empire (see pp50–51), and his son, King Kyanzittha, who completed work on this complex. Over the span of their two lifetimes, military conquests

and land reforms brought peace and prosperity to the kingdom, enabling an intense period of temple construction of which this, along with the Ananda Temple, is the shining example. It was Anawrahta's enthusiastic promotion of Theravada Buddhism, coupled with a tolerant attitude to *nat* worship, that also forged the distinctive religious culture of Burma in the 11th century – one that endures to this day. Evidence of this is to be found in the southeast corner of the pagoda's enclosure, where the Shrine of the 37 *Mahagiri Nats* is dominated by a stone statue of Thagyamin, the king of the *nats*.

Believed to enclose a bone and tooth relic of Gautama Buddha, as well as a gold image of Anawrahta and a Chinese emerald Buddha, the main *zedi* (stupa) measures 160 ft (49 m) high and 160 ft (49 m) across its base, with four smaller stupas at its corners and bands of 500 beautifully enameled *Jataka* plaques around its sides. Four other subsidiary shrines at the *zedi*'s cardinal points house beautiful cast-copper Buddhas dating from 1102. Also worth a close look, on the eastern façade of the pagoda near the great lion images, are the Edicts of King Kyanzittha, recounting the ruler's coronation and the foundation story of the site.

The unusual Sapada Pagoda, with a square relic chamber in the spire

⑫ Sapada Pagoda

Road Map C3. Junction of the main and airport roads, Nyaung U.

Standing incongruously at the intersection of the airport road and Nyaung U's main street, this late-Bagan-style pagoda owes its unusual shape to the career of the young monk after which it was named. Sapada was one of 20 novices dispatched to an illustrious monastery in Ceylon, where he spent 10 years. His teachings later had a great influence on Theravada philosophy in the Burmese capital. In honor of the monk's formative sojourn abroad, the stupa has a Sinhalese-style square *harmika*, or relic chamber, between its bell-shaped bottom and top spire.

The grand Shwezigon Pagoda, believed to contain relics of the Buddha

For hotels and restaurants in this region see pp203–4 and p212

⑱ The Southern Plain

Road Map C3. Minnanthu village.

The temples spread across the southeastern extremity of the archeological zone, around Minnanthu village, are the most remote on the site, but their superb murals, which include some of the oldest and best-preserved in Bagan, warrant the effort needed to reach them.

On the west side of the lane winding through Minnanthu is the whitewashed **Lemyethna Temple**. This single-storied edifice is built in late Bagan style on a square raised platform with four projecting porches and an upper section of receding terraces, surmounted by an Indian-style curvilinear spire and gilded pagoda. Dating from 1222, it is said to have been built in honor of a prime minister who, having been sentenced to execution by the king, wrote a famous poem expressing equanimity at the prospect of his death, described as merely part of the "ineluctable cycle of Karma." Lemyethna contains some well-preserved paintings, particularly around the arches framing the Buddha shrines, although many of these have been lost under a recent coat of limewash.

A short way north, on the opposite side of the lane, stands a trio of shrines conjoined by

Buddha images with hands positioned in the *dharmachakra* mudra, Payathonzu Temple

narrow vaulted passageways. **Payathonzu Temple** was never completed but is renowned for its wonderful 12th-century paintings dominated by floral motifs into which mythical animals, birds, and human figures are woven. Shown under the bodhi trees where they gained enlightenment, the 28 Buddhas of the Past also feature prominently. Several murals reveal a marked Tantric influence. Some scholars attribute this to Payathonzu's proximity to the last of Bagan's Ari monasteries. These were home to forest-dwelling monks who practiced Tantric rituals regarded as debauched by the Theravada order.

More wonderful paintings adorn the walls and arched ceilings of the **Nandamannya Temple**, a short walk north down a sandy track off the lane. Framed by decorative scrolls are a series of large panels showing scenes from the life of Gautama Buddha.

These include the Birth, with Prince Siddhartha coming forth from the right hip of his royal mother, and the Renunciation of the World, symbolized by the Buddha cutting off his hair. A small rectangular panel on the shrine's western side depicts the famous *Temptation of Mara*. Here the demon Mara, the personification of unwholesome influences and temptation, tries in vain to seduce the Buddha out of the meditation that led to his enlightenment by showing him visions of beautiful young women, who, in some legends, are said to be Mara's daughters.

A hot-air balloon floating past the exquisite temples of Bagan

Ballooning in Bagan

The sight of hot-air balloons drifting serenely over Bagan's otherworldly skyline has become almost as iconic of the archeological zone as the temples themselves. Operated by Balloons Over Bagan (balloonsoverbagan.com) and Oriental Ballooning (orientalballooning.com), these magical flights run every morning and evening through the winter season from October to March. The rides allow visitors an unrivaled perspective over the sprawl of Bagan, from the monuments and surrounding plain to the Ayeyarwady River and Rakhine-Yoma Hills. Ballooning trips typically last around an hour, ending with a gentle touch-down in the fields on the fringes of the site, where a champagne breakfast awaits, followed by a ride back to base. Tickets can be booked online, or at the Balloons Over Bagan and Oriental Ballooning sales desks located in Nyaung U.

The temples and pagodas of Old Bagan, with the great Thatbyinnyu Temple soaring up behind them ▶

⑭ New Bagan

Road Map C3. 5.5 miles (9 km) SW of Nyaung U Airport. ✈ Mandalay International. 🚌 Nyaung U Airport. Pickups run between Nyaung U, Old Bagan, Myinkaba, and New Bagan.

Bagan Myothit, or New Bagan, was created in the 1990s to house villagers relocated by the Tatmadaw (military government) from Old Bagan. Of the monuments around the village, the largest and most impressive is the **Dhammayazika Pagoda**. It was built in 1196 by King Narapatisithu (1138–1211), during whose peaceful reign Burmese culture first began to supersede that of the Mon and the ancient Pyu. The gilded stupa rests on three hexagonal terraces studded with five smaller gilded shrines that contain Konbaung-era Buddhas. Dhammayazika was one of many prominent sites in Bagan to receive a radical makeover by the government in the 1990s.

The **Anauk** (west) and **Ashe** (east) **Petleik pagodas**, in New Bagan's southern neighborhood of Thiripyitsaya, date from the 11th century. Neither would be of more than passing interest were it not for their superb collection of unglazed terracotta *Jataka* tiles discovered in vaulted corridors surrounding

Souvenir stalls lining the path to the gilded 12th-century Dhammayazika Pagoda

the stupas during excavation work carried out in 1905. The tiles are now protected by newly built brick walls and roofs.

At Bagan's southern edge, the **Lawkananda Pagoda** stands on a bluff above the river. Attributed to Anawrahta (1015–78), it dates from the 11th century and enshrines one of the four tooth relics of the Buddha that are said to have magically replicated themselves from the one set within the Shwezigon Pagoda *(see p128)*. The stupa, whose gold leaf and marble-tiled terrace are recent additions, stands on a platform that affords fine views over the river.

🏛 **Dhammayazika Pagoda**
Between New Bagan and Minnanthu village, north side of main road.

🏛 **Anauk and Ashe Petleik pagodas**
Southern edge of Thiripyitsaya, New Bagan.

🏛 **Lawkananda Pagoda**
Southwest of New Bagan.

⑮ Myinkaba

Road Map C3. Between Old Bagan and New Bagan. 🏙 800. ✈ Mandalay International. 🚌 Nyaung U Airport. Pickups run between Nyaung U, Old Bagan, Myinkaba, and New Bagan. 🎭 Sep: Manuha festival.

After the conquest of Thaton in 1057, King Anawrahta exiled the Mon King Manuha to the village of Myinkaba. The most stately and well preserved of the temples that sprang up around the displaced royal family is the **Nagayon Temple**. It was built by King Kyanzittha (1030–1112), allegedly at the spot where he took refuge from his brother and predecessor Sawlu (1050–84) during a feud in the 1080s. Kyanzittha had the temple built after he became king as an act of thanksgiving to a snake deity that protected him during his flight; a cobra hood above the head of the gilded standing Buddha in the main shrine underlines the connection. The ambulatory corridor retains some impressive 11th-century paintings, along with sculpted figures of previous Buddhas.

The 11th-century Lawkananda Pagoda overlooking the Ayeyarwady River

For hotels and restaurants in this region see pp203–4 and p212

The 11th-century Abeyadana Temple with a classical square base

The foundation myth of the nearby **Abeyadana Temple**, on the opposite side of the road, is linked to the same snake-related story, only in this version, the site was where the fugitive prince met Abeyadana, his Bengali lover, before fleeing Bagan. Some of the site's finest murals adorn the interior of the shrine, featuring images of Hindu deities and Mahayana Buddhist bodhisattvas, interpreted as reflecting the Bengali origins of the queen.

The **Nanpaya Temple**, a short way north on the edge of the village, is believed to have been the residence (some say prison) of King Manuha, accounting for the *hamsa* bird images on the outside of the building – the *hamsa* was the heraldic symbol of the Mon nation *(see p92)*.

Four pillars inside the pagoda are decorated with some of Bagan's most beautiful stone carvings, including one showing Brahma, a deity of the Hindu trinity, holding lotus flowers.

The **Manuha Temple**, still farther north, was built by the eponymous king in 1059 while he was in exile, using funds raised by the sale of his remaining crown jewels. A somewhat nondescript square block on the outside, the pagoda holds an extraordinary quartet of outsized Buddhas – three giant gilded sitting figures, and a huge reclining one – whose disproportionate scale and cramped confines are believed to have been intended to express the discomfort of the Mon king's incarceration and exile from his homeland.

Buddhist pilgrims pour through Manuha's compound during holiday periods, and the next stop on their itinerary is usually the **Gubyaukgyi Temple** beside the main road at the north end of Myinkaba. Built in 1113 by Prince Yaza Kumaya, it is famed for its murals, which were restored by UNESCO in the 1980s. The paintings lining the main hall illustrate scenes from 550 *Jataka* stories, including the 16 Dreams of Kosala. On the outside of the building, some exceptionally fine stucco decoration survives on the surrounds of the pierced-stone windows.

Adjacent to the temple stands a small structure enclosing a four-sided carved pillar. The oldest surviving text from medieval Bagan, the famous Myazedi Inscription is written in Pali, Pyu, Mon, and Burmese, and is one of a pair – the other is at the site museum at Old Bagan.

The Gubyaukgyi Temple, featuring some fine stuccowork around its windows

Artisan working on a laquerware pot, Bagan

Lacquerware

Myanmar has been a center for fine lacquerware since Bayinnaung's invasion of Siam in 1563, when skilled Laos-Shan artisans were brought back to his court. Bagan became the industry's main hub in the 20th century, and in the 1920s the British founded a lacquerware school in the ruined city to foster the craft. The largest concentration of workshops and showrooms is around Myinkaba and New Bagan. There visitors can watch the various stages of lacquerware production, from the weaving of bamboo and rattan frames, through the molding and drying of the lacquer putty, to the careful engraving and polishing required to finish the pieces. Prices are high, primarily because it can take a few months to complete even a small bowl; a large object with elaborate designs requires up to a year of work. The finer the detail, and the more colors and layers of lacquer that are applied – 15 coats is the norm for a quality article – the more the product will cost.

The graceful five-terraced Shwesandaw Pagoda, a popular sunset-viewing spot

ⓖ Mingalazedi Pagoda

Road Map C3. NE of Myinkaba village to the west of the road.

This giant pagoda between the main road and riverbank was the last major building project at Bagan before the Mongol invasion of 1287. Nothing about the structure, however, suggests an empire on the decline. The scale, complexity, and precision of the stonework is exceptional, and the number of expensive ceramic plaques adorning its three receding terraces unrivaled. It is a testament to the extravagance for which its sponsor, King Narathihapate (1238–87), was renowned – in a donatory inscription, the king boasts of commanding an army of 36 million men and eating "300 dishes of curry each day."

Yet beneath the bravado, the city's coffers were emptying fast and the king's grip on power slipping away. The black hole in the treasury's finances had grown during Narathihapate's reign. Even as his slaves toiled on the lavish Mingalazedi, Kublai Khan's Mongol army were attacking Bhamo, gateway to the Ayeyarwady and central Burma. Only a couple of years after work on the building was completed, the king fled in panic to Pyay (Prome), where he was arrested and forced to take poison, earning for himself the unflattering epithet Taok Pyay Min, "the king who ran from the Chinese."

Until 2012, it was possible to scale the steep flights of steps that lead to the cylindrical base of Mingalazedi's bell-shaped stupa, but access has since been forbidden.

ⓗ Shwesandaw Pagoda

Road Map C3. S of Anawrahta Rd/ Yangon–Mandalay Hwy.

One of the few monuments that the Bagan authorities allow visitors to climb is the Shwesandaw Pagoda, a 10-minute ride by horse cart to the northeast. Built by King Anawrahta in 1057, the enormous *zedi* was one of four that Bagan's founding father constructed outside the city walls to provide cosmic protection for the capital (Shwezigon was another).

The pagoda comprises five square terraces topped by a cylindrical stupa with a recently added *hti*, or finial. The old one toppled in an earthquake in 1975 and still lies where it landed, crumbling in the dusty compound below.

A hair relic of the Buddha that the king of Bago presented to Anawrahta for his help in repelling a Khmer invasion of the Mon kingdom is believed to be secreted inside the stupa. Flights of steep steps ascend the whitewashed monument on four sides, leading to a spacious terrace at the base of the stupa. The panoramic views from here over the archeological zone are magnificent, although at sunset, when a souvenir bazaar springs up in

Mingalazedi Pagoda, the last of the great stupas built at Bagan

For hotels and restaurants in this region see pp203–4 and p212

the enclosure below, the crowds and noise of camera shutters can be oppressive.

Environs

Housed in a long, rectangular, redbrick chamber on the west side of the Shwesandaw compound is a serene Buddha known as **Shinbinthalyaung**. Measuring 60 ft (18 m) from head to toe, the reclining figure was installed during roughly the same period as the nearby stupa. Broken traces of original frescoes adorn the plaster walls of the temple.

A two-minute walk north of the Shwesandaw Pagoda, the little-visited **Lawkahteikpan Temple** is a beautifully proportioned structure dating from the reign of Kyanzittha's successor, Alaungsithu (1089–1168). Inside, the walls and ceilings above the gilded, seated Buddha are decorated with well-preserved and intricate mid-12th-century frescoes. They require a flashlight to be viewed as there is no lighting in the building.

⑱ Dhammayangyi Temple

Road Map C3. SE of the Shwesandaw Pagoda.

Rising from the sand and scrub, Dhammayangyi, a massive walled temple a short walk southeast of the Shwesandaw Pagoda, is the largest and best preserved of all of Bagan's monuments. The temple was built in the late 1160s, during the short three-year reign of King Narathu (1118–71). The king was said to be a violent psychopath who ascended to the imperial throne after murdering his father, Alaungsithu, by smothering him with a pillow, and elder brother, Min Shin Saw, by poisoning him on his coronation day. The temple's colossal size is often interpreted as a gesture of atonement for the killings, though it seems to have done little to erase Narathu's nasty streak. He later strangled his Bengali queen, allegedly because he took objection to her Hindu rituals. Her father promptly dispatched an eight-strong suicide squad to exact revenge in 1171. Court chronicles record that the assassins were able to gain access to the palace by disguising themselves as Brahmin astrologers, hiding their swords beneath their robes. Having killed the king, they slit their own throats.

Similar in layout to Ananda, Dhammayangyi is thought to have the best masonry and brickwork in the archeological zone. King Narathu is said to have overseen construction work himself, threatening with summary execution any mason who left between the bricks a gap wide enough for a needle to be inserted.

The Sulamani Temple, one of the most beautiful structures of Bagan's late period

⑲ Sulamani Temple

Road Map C3. Central Bagan Plain.

The most refined of the temples of Bagan's late period, Sulamani forms a striking silhouette in the center of the archeological zone. Fusing the monumental verticality of structures such as Thatbyinnyu (see p121) with the horizontal planes of Dhammayangyi, it fully deserves its name, which translates as "Crowning Jewel." The temple was built on two major levels, with porches at the cardinal points, and seven tiers of ascending terraces whose corners are crowned by delicate tapering stupas. Surmounting the whole is a beautifully designed *sikhara* tower, comprising a pagoda placed on top of a curvilinear corncob base.

Only the first floor is open to the public. Encircling the inner shrine, where four Buddhas face the four directions, is an inner ambulatory with niches for Buddha statues on pedestals and murals depicting scenes from the life of the Buddha and a menagerie of mythological beasts, snakes, and sea creatures. Some of these are original, but most date from the Konbaung era of the 18th–19th centuries. Also of note are the exceptionally fine carved stucco moldings adorning the pediments over the exterior doorways and windows, and the glazed ceramic plaques lining the temple's base and terraces.

The colossal Dhammayangyi, the largest temple in Bagan

⑳ Popa Taung Kalat

The most popular day trip from Bagan is the drive to Popa Taung Kalat, or Mount Popa as the sheer-sided volcanic plug is more commonly known. Myanmar's most revered center of *nat* worship, it is visited in huge numbers by local people, who come to pray at the Mother Spirit shrine at the foot of the hill. Opposite the temple, a flight of covered steps winds up Taung Kalat to a small Buddhist monastery on the summit plateau. From here, stupendous views extend west across the plains of Bagan to the Ayeyarwady and the distant Rakhine-Yoma Hills, and east to the spectacular form of Mount Popa, an extinct volcano with a deep caldera and a cloak of dense forest. Visitors who spend a night at the nearby Popa Mountain Resort will be treated to the vision of the temple's golden spires illuminated by the first rays of daylight.

The small *hti*-topped golden rock stupa at the shrine of Popa Taung Kalat

Main entrance to Popa Taung Kalat
The entrance to the *zaungdan* (covered stairway) that winds up the hill is crowned with a seven-tiered ceremonial *pyatthat* roof tower and flanked by a pair of large white elephants.

37 *Mahagiri Nats*
The elaborately decorated Mother Spirit shrine at the base of the hill holds life-sized statues of the 37 *Mahagiri Nats*, or Great Spirit Heroes. Dressed in golden crowns and vibrant silk, the deities are joined by various ogresses, wizards, and necromancers.

KEY

① **The Shrine of the Mother Spirit of Popa Nat**, opposite the main entrance, is visited by all pilgrims to Popa Taung Kalat. The shrine's doorway is flanked by a pair of tigers.

② **The bazaar** at the base of the hill contains souvenir stalls, shops selling flowers and religious paraphernalia, and teashops offering Burmese snacks and drinks.

③ **Taung Kalat (Pedestal Hill)** rises 2,400 ft (730 m) above sea level.

④ **The 777-step *zaungdan*** offers a 20-minute hike to the summit.

⑤ **Mount Popa** (4,981 ft/1,518 m) to the east is a national park. Trails wind up its forested slopes to the rim of the huge caldera at the summit.

Nat Worship in Myanmar

One of the most intriguing aspects of Burmese religious life is the worship of *nats*, nature spirits who represent human flaws, weaknesses, or vices, and who died unnatural and often violent deaths. Propitiated daily with flowers, fruit, and incense, *nats* may reside in trees, rocks, caves, or summits such as Popa Taung Kalat, the high altar of *nat* worship in Myanmar. *Nat* veneration in the country is known to predate Buddhism, which arrived in the 3rd century BC. King Anawrahta of Bagan wisely incorporated *nats* into Theravada ritual, which is why Burmese temples today nearly always also contain *nat* shrines. In addition, he fixed the official number of *nats* at 36, adding a 37th, Thagyamin, king of the *nats*, derived from the ancient Hindu deity Indra. In this way, he established the *nat* pantheon as subordinate to the Buddha, a position they retain to this day.

Tiger statue at the entrance to the Shrine of the Mother Spirit of Popa Nat

For hotels and restaurants in this region see pp203–4 and p212

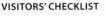

★ **Taung Kalat Buddhist Monastery**
The whitewashed and gilded monastery crowning the summit of Popa Taung Kalat is an important place of pilgrimage for Buddhist monks and nuns, as well as laypeople from across the country.

VISITORS' CHECKLIST

Practical Information
Road Map C3. 32 miles (52 km) SE of Bagan (90-minute drive). **Open** 7am–10pm daily. 🛈 guides can be hired in Bagan and Popa Taung Kalat. 🛈 donation. 🛈 🛈 May/Jun & Nov/Dec: *nat pwe*.

Transport
✈ Mandalay International. ✈ Nyaung U Airport. Taxis (individual and shared) & pickup trucks are available from Bagan; truck passengers may have to change at Kyaukpadaung.

Hti-topped golden rock stupa

Macaques
Troops of pilfering macaques patrol the *zaungdan* up to the shrine and have become a well-known presence on Taung Kalat.

MANDALAY REGION

Scattered among the sand flats and low hills in and around the city of Mandalay are the remnants of four royal capitals spanning more than 500 years of Burmese history. They encompass some of the country's most iconic sights, from Mandalay's exquisite teak Shwenandaw Monastery and Amarapura's much-photographed U Bein's Bridge to Inwa's stucco monastery and the glittering, pagoda-encrusted ridges of Sagaing. Just upriver from Mandalay, the massive unfinished stupa at Mingun is another of the region's unmissable sights.

The first of the great centers built in the region was at Sagaing, on the west bank of the Ayeyarwady, where a huge concentration of religious monuments are a legacy of a kingdom that ruled over much of central Burma in the early 14th century. On the opposite bank, Inwa (Ava) was founded in 1364 on a man-made island protected by formidable walls. Today, its scant remains rise forlorn from an expanse of rice fields, best explored by horse cart via a tangle of sandy tracks.

Amarapura, spread around a lake on the southern fringes of Mandalay, became the next Konbaung capital in 1783 and retains some imposing monuments, among them the majestic Pahtodawgyi Pagoda and U Bein Bridge. Much of the city was ruined by the massive earthquake of 1839, and it was finally deserted in the mid-1850s in favor of a site at the foot of Mandalay Hill.

Called Yadanabon – a Burmese corruption of the site's ancient Pali name, Ratanapura ("City of Gems") – Mandalay city was founded in 1857 as the Konbaung capital, a role it retained until the Third Anglo-Burmese War in 1885. Although shortlived, Yadanabon's golden era left in its wake an array of superb religious buildings, as well as the colossal royal palace – a forbidden city hidden behind walls and a wide moat.

Modern Mandalay has grown into a vast metropolis, whose heat and chaotic traffic are well worth braving for its wealth of historic sites, which include the Mahamuni Temple, Myanmar's second most venerated shrine, and the Shwenandaw Monastery, a remnant of the old palace. While most of the royal enclave was destroyed in World War II, many of the city's gilded and carved structures still survive, hinting at the splendor that must once have held sway here.

Statue of King Mindon outside the Kuthodaw Pagoda at the base of Mandalay Hill

◄ Yedanasini Pagoda, an atmospheric complex of crumbling brick stupas and stone Buddhas at Inwa (Ava), near Mandalay

Exploring Mandalay Region

Mandalay is the only practicable base from which to explore the sights in the city and its sandy environs. Foremost among these are the rebuilt royal palace and the finely carved teak Shwenandaw Monastery. Mandalay Hill and the bustling Mahamuni Temple warrant a detour, as does U Bein's teak bridge at Amarapura. Other essential stops in the area include the vestiges of the giant unfinished stupa at Mingun, reached by a memorable boat trip upriver; the elegant brick and stucco ruins of medieval Inwa (Ava); and the pagoda-covered hill at Sagaing. With two or three more days to spare, excursions can be made to a trio of lesser-visited sights around Monywa to the west, and to the colonial hill station of Pyin U Lwin to the east, which offers a leafy escape from the heat of the central plain.

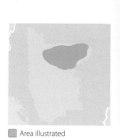

☐ Area illustrated

Key

════ Highway

──── Main road

──── Other road

─ ─ ─ Railroad

──── Regional border

Sights at a Glance

❶ Mandalay City pp142–9
❷ Amarapura
❸ The Ayeyarwady Bridges
❹ Sagaing
❺ Inwa (Ava) pp154–5
❻ Mingun pp156–7
❼ Monywa

❽ Thanboddhay Pagoda
❾ Bodhi Tataung
❿ Pho Win Taung Caves
⓫ A Myint
⓬ Pyin U Lwin (Maymyo)
⓭ Gokteik Bridge
⓮ Meiktila

The colorful exterior of the distinctive Thanboddhay Pagoda near Monywa

For hotels and restaurants in this region see p204 and pp212–14

Getting Around

Mandalay's palace and hill can be covered on foot, but a taxi will be needed to get to the Mahamuni Temple and Amarapura on the city's southern edge, and for day trips to Inwa (Ava) and Sagaing. Mingun can be accessed by boat. Monywa is reachable by bus, and the sights around it are accessible using the Chindwin ferry and motorcycle taxis. There is a train service from Mandalay city to Pyin U Lwin and the Gokteik Bridge. Meiktila is on the Mandalay–Yangon bus route, and Thazi train station, east of the town, is on the Yangon, Mandalay, and Taunggyi lines.

The colonial-era Sacred Heart Catholic Church in Pyin U Lwin (Maymyo)

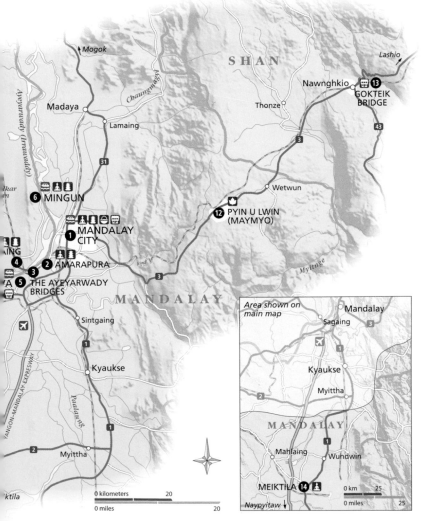

For additional map symbols *see back flap*

❶ Mandalay City

Spurred by massive Chinese investment in recent years, modern Mandalay is one of Southeast Asia's boom cities, and a far cry from the low-rise, slow-paced, bicycled-powered backwater it was after the great fires of the 1980s. Today, glass-sided malls and tower blocks loom over its main arteries, while the roads below are jammed with imported cars and motorcycles. Navigating the mayhem is easy, though, thanks to its regular grid plan. Streets running east–west are numbered 1–49, beginning in the far north, and those running north–south are numbered 50 onward, starting in the far east. Therefore the address 81st St (28/29) means on 81st Street between 28th and 29th streets.

Cast-bronze seated Buddha statue in the Setkyathiha Pagoda in Mandalay

Worshipper touching one of the Angkor statues in the hope of curing an ailment

🏛 Mahamuni Temple
82nd St, S of 45th St (Boba Htu Rd). **Open** 4am–11pm daily. 📷

The Mahamuni Temple is the country's second most revered shrine after the Shwedagon Pagoda in Yangon. Its stately bronze Buddha is said to be one of only five likenesses of the historical Buddha cast in his lifetime, although it was probably made 500 years later. More certain is that it came here in 1784 as plunder from Bodawpaya's raid on Arakan *(see p115)*. While women are not allowed to enter the inner sanctum, men are permitted to press gold leaf on to the figure – so much has been added over the years that large lumps of solid gold have formed. Only the face, polished daily, remains shiny and smooth.

In a hall off the main temple are six fine Hindu-Buddhist figures originally plundered from Angkor Wat, but subsequently looted from Arakan by Bodawpaya's army. Worshippers traditionally rub various body parts of the images in the hope of curing medical afflictions.

🏛 Jade Market
87th St (39/40). **Open** 8–11am & 2–4pm daily. 🏛 entrance charge.

Myanmar is the source of the world's finest jade and nearly all of it passes through the huge jade market on 87th Street. It is a fascinating place, although only confirmed experts are advised to part with any cash – jade is notoriously difficult to price. All morning, buyers and traders meet to haggle around long Formica tables, shining lights through pieces of jade to assess their quality. Elsewhere, cutters and polishers can be seen transforming stones into finely worked pieces for export.

🏛 Shwe In Bin Kyaung
89th St (37/38). **Open** 7am–10pm daily.

Commissioned in the 1890s by two wealthy Chinese jade merchants, this elegant teak monastery was created in classic Konbaung style, with a slender central tower of seven receding tiers capped by a golden finial. The cornices and eaves retain splendid, intricately carved ox-horn embellishments, similar to those of Shwenandaw Monastery, although unlike its more famous cousin across town, Shwe In Bin receives only a trickle of visitors. An oasis of calm, it offers one of the most atmospheric retreats in the city.

🏛 Setkyathiha Pagoda
85th St (30/31). **Open** 7am–10pm daily.

This inconspicuous temple, seven blocks north of the Shwe In Bin Kyaung, houses a 16-ft (5-m) seated Buddha cast in bronze by King Bagyidaw in 1823, just before the outbreak of the First Anglo-Burmese War. Also housed in the complex is a sacred golden boulder and bodhi tree planted by the first prime minister of independent Burma, U Nu.

Gold Leaf

Mandalay is one of the few places in Myanmar where gold leaf, prized by the Burmese as a temple offering, is still made in the traditional way. At workshops concentrated around the intersection of 36th and 77th streets, teams of pounders thump at booklets of bamboo pages between which tiny morsels of gold have been placed. The resulting foil is cut, replaced, and thumped again for hours until it is only a few molecules thick. Packets of these leaves make great souvenirs.

Teams of craftsmen pounding at gold morsels to make gold leaf

⬛ Eindawya Pagoda

Eindawya St (88/89). **Open** 8am–9pm daily.

Three blocks northwest of Setkyathiha stands the gilded Eindawya Pagoda. Resting on four square, receding terraces, the beautifully proportioned bell-shaped *zedi* (stupa) was built by Pagan Min (1811–80), ninth ruler of the Konbaung Dynasty, on the site of a royal palace where he lived while still a prince. In the popular imagination the pagoda is closely associated with rebellion: Pagan Min was the king whose noncompliance sparked the Second Anglo-Burmese War of 1852, and in 1919 a party of Europeans was expelled from the complex for not taking off their shoes (the monks responsible were subsequently sentenced to life imprisonment). One of Burma's best-loved singers of the 1930s, Myoma Nyein, later immortalized the shrine in his hit song, *Eindawya Paya Zay*, composed in support of Zegyo Market shopkeepers who occupied the temple precincts to protest against the British-imposed penal code.

The beautifully proportioned stupa of the golden Eindawya Pagoda, Mandalay

⬛ Zegyo Market

84th St (26/27). **Open** 9am–7pm daily.
Mandalay's main shopping area, Zegyo Market is centered on a couple of Chinese-style multistory malls and has a vast number of stalls where it is possible to buy everything from pickled tea to traditional felt slippers. The surrounding streets, where fresh produce is sold from vibrant stalls, also offer plenty of local flavor. The best time to visit is in the early morning before the crowds and heat build, and when local monks file through collecting alms. Between 5pm and 10pm in the evenings, a night market springs up in this area with barbecue stalls.

⬛ Mandalay Palace

See pp144–5.

⬛ Mandalay Hill

See pp146–9.

Sights at a Glance

① Mahamuni Temple
② Jade Market
③ Shwe In Bin Kyaung
④ Setkyathiha Pagoda
⑤ Eindawya Pagoda
⑥ Zegyo Market
⑦ Mandalay Palace
⑧ Mandalay Hill

VISITORS' CHECKLIST

Practical Information
Road Map C3. ⬚ 1,100,000.
ℹ️ Myanmar Travels and Tours, 68th St at 27th, (02) 60356. ⬚ all major sights are covered by the Archeology Department's combination ticket, valid for one week.
⬚ ⬚ Feb/Mar: Mahamuni temple festival; Jul/Aug: Waso *chinlone* festival at the Mahamuni Temple.

Transport
✈ Mandalay International.
⬚ Mandalay Central. ⬚ ⬚

Map labels:

Mandalay Hill 1 mile (1.5 km) ⑧
12TH STREET
North Gate
Mandalay Palace ⑦
East (Main) Gate
West Gate
South Gate
STREET
86TH STREET
19TH STREET
82ND STREET
81ST STREET
80TH STREET
22ND STREET
Thiri Mandalar
23RD STREET
24TH STREET
25TH ST
Zegyo Market
26TH STREET
26TH STREET
27TH STREET
Eindawya Pagoda ⑤
Mann Myanmar Plaza
28TH STREET
29TH STREET
30TH STREET
Mandalay Central
Setkyathiha Pagoda ④
31ST STREET
32ND STREET
79TH STREET
78TH STREET
ADIPADILI STREET
Diamond Plaza
33RD STREET
85TH STREET
84TH STREET
34TH STREET
83RD STREET
82ND STREET
81ST STREET
77TH STREET
76TH STREET
75TH STREET
74TH STREET
72ND STREET
ADIPADILI ROAD
89TH STREET
35TH STREET
35TH STREET
36TH STREET
36TH STREET
Shwe In Bin Kyaung ③
37TH ST
78 Mall
37TH STREET
86TH STREET
38TH STREET
89TH ST
Jade Market ②
39TH STREET
40TH STREET
Mandalay University
41ST STREET
41ST ST
42ND STREET
80TH STREET
81ST STREET
78TH STREET
84TH STREET
ADIPADILI ROAD
Mahamuni Temple ①
Mandalay International Airport 25 miles (35 km)

0 meters 800
0 yards 800

Mandalay Palace

The seat of the last rulers of independent Burma, Mandalay Palace was built in the mid-19th century by King Mindon, but is most closely associated with his son, Thibaw, who was expelled from it by General Prendergast in 1885. The complex was commandeered by the British army for use as a barracks, before being destroyed by Allied bombs in 1945 while it was occupied by the Japanese during World War II. The present structures, built by the Tatmadaw in the 1990s, bear little more than a passing resemblance to the richly carved and gilded teak originals. To gain a sense of the architectural splendor of Mindon's time, visit the Shwenandaw Monastery nearby, a transplanted fragment of the original Glass Palace, and the only piece of the former palace to have survived.

★ **Nan Myin Watchtower**
This is one of the few original fort buildings to survive the Allied bombings of World War II.

Glass Palace
Decorated with mosaic and gilt iron trellis work, this sumptuous building contained the king's living chambers as well the Bee Throne Room.

KEY

① **Lion Throne (Sihasana) Room**

② **The Zetawunzaung**, containing the Goose Throne (Hamsasana), was where ambassadors were received. The Byedaik hall to its north held the Elephant Throne (Gajasana), which vanished after the British invasion.

③ **The Baungdawzaung** (Royal Crown Room), holding the Conch Throne (Sankhasana), was used for audiences with palace officials.

④ **The Lapetyezaung** (Tea Room) held the king's personal armory.

⑤ **The Bee Throne (Bhamarasana) Room** was where the Queen's nomination and nuptials took place.

⑥ **The Peacock Throne (Mayurasana) Room** was used to review troops and watch races.

⑦ **Deer Throne (Mrigasana) Room**

⑧ **Chief Queen's Apartments**

⑨ **Central Queen's Apartments**

⑩ **The Queen's Audience Hall** held the Lotus Throne (Padmasana) and is now the palace museum.

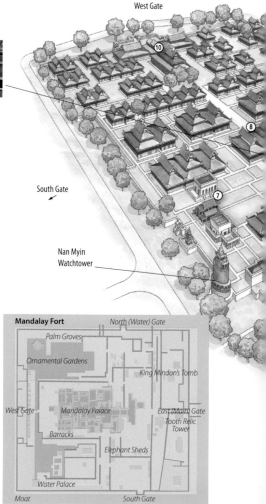

West Gate

South Gate

Nan Myin Watchtower

Mandalay Fort

Palm Groves
North (Water) Gate
Ornamental Gardens
King Mindon's Tomb
West Gate
Mandalay Palace
East (Main) Gate
Tooth Relic Tower
Barracks
Elephant Sheds
Water Palace
Moat
South Gate

Moat, walls, and bastions
Mindon's palace was encased by 1.2-mile- (2-km-)
long walls on each side and a 210-ft- (64-m-) wide
moat. Each of the walls had several bastions, and three
gateways topped by tall, gold-tipped *pyatthat* roofs –
12 in total, corresponding to the signs of the zodiac.

VISITORS' CHECKLIST

Practical Information
Half a mile (1 km) N of the train
station, east (main) entrance
another 2 miles (3 km) NE; foreigners can enter only via this
gate. **Open** 7:30am–4:30pm daily.
🚲 all major sights in Mandalay,
Inwa, and Amarapura covered by
Archeology Department's combination ticket, valid for one week.
🛏 hotels can arrange guides.

Transport
Taxis and motorcycle taxis easily
available. Trishaws wait at the east
gate for the 0.5 mile (1 km) ride to
the palace complex.

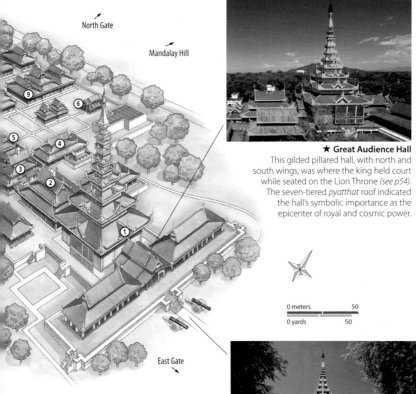

North Gate

Mandalay Hill

⑨

⑥

⑤

④

③

②

①

★ **Great Audience Hall**
This gilded pillared hall, with north and
south wings, was where the king held court
while seated on the Lion Throne *(see p54)*.
The seven-tiered *pyatthat* roof indicated
the hall's symbolic importance as the
epicenter of royal and cosmic power.

| 0 meters | 50 |
| 0 yards | 50 |

East Gate

Entrance to the palace complex
Most of the area within Mandalay Fort is an army
base, and the palace complex is a 15-minute walk
in from the east gate. The entrance to the complex
is flanked by a pair of 9.5-ft (3-m) British cannon,
originally cast for the Royal Navy and stamped
with the cipher of King George II (1727–60).

Mandalay Hill

According to Theravada lore, the Buddha visited Mandalay Hill, prophesizing that on the 2,400th anniversary of his death a great city would be founded at its foot. The vision was realized in 1857, when King Mindon moved his capital from Amarapura to carve out the foreseen "Golden City." Visitors continue to make the auspicious ascent in large numbers, both to pay their respects at the shrines punctuating the stepped pathway to the summit, and for the views of the distant Shan Hills. A perfect preamble to the climb is a tour of the structures at the base of the hill. Dating from Mindon's era, they include one of the last surviving fragments of the great teak palace of the Konbaungs.

Shweyattaw Buddha
The country's only pointing Buddha marks the convergence of the two main walkways up Mandalay Hill.

Main entrance with *chinthes*
The start of the main walkway up the hill is flanked by two huge *chinthes*, the grinning, luck-bringing leogryphs who gave their name to Orde Wingate's Chindits during World War II *(see p57)*.

Atumashi Monastery
This handsome structure opposite the Shwenandaw is a copy of the one built by King Mindon in 1857. The original burned down in 1890, when its huge lacquered Buddha was lost.

Mandalay Palace

KEY

① **Sandamuni Pagoda**, companion to the nearby Kuthodaw Pagoda, houses a huge collection of stone slabs inscribed with Buddhist scriptures, plus a particularly splendid brass statue of the Buddha that dates from 1802.

② **Kyauktawgyi Temple**, built between 1853 and 1878 during Mindon's reign, stands near the start of the walkway and is worth a visit for its monolithic marble Buddha.

③ **Pedestrian walkway** up the hill.

Shwenandaw Monastery
Arguably the most beautiful Konbaung teak building to have survived, this masterpiece of classical Burmese architecture is famed above all for its carvings.

Mwegyi Hnakaung (Two Great Snakes)
Just over the summit are the statues of two great cobras and of the *nats* they transformed into after their death. The snakes were believed to visit the hill to worship the Buddha.

VISITORS' CHECKLIST

Practical Information
Immediately NE of the Mandalay Palace complex. 🚩 all major sights in Mandalay, Amarapura, and Inwa are covered by the Archeology Department's combination ticket, which is valid for one week. 🎫 guides can be hired through most hotels.

Transport
Taxis and motorcycle taxis can be hailed on the streets and will go up to the summit.

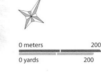

Sataungpyei Temple
At the summit, this gilded, brightly decorated shrine affords spellbinding views over the city and its surroundings. The site witnessed fierce fighting during World War II.

Kuthodaw Pagoda
Centered on a magnificent golden stupa, this complex was built in 1857 by King Mindon to house a vast assembly of stone tablets carved with the entire text of the sacred *Tipitaka* scripture.

Exploring Mandalay Hill

The fact that nearly all of Mandalay Palace was destroyed in 1943 lends great significance to the Konbaung-era monuments grouped northeast of the palace complex. The pick of the bunch is the transplanted Shwenandaw Monastery, the only part of Mindon's inner palace to have survived the Allied bombs. Nearby, a string of whitewashed and gilded temples holding tablets bearing the entire *Tipitaka* canon set the scene for the ascent of Mandalay Hill itself, best undertaken barefoot on the long, stepped *zaungdan* (walkway).

The entrance of the teak Shwenandaw Monastery, Mandalay

🔹 Shwenandaw Monastery
Golden Palace Monastery, off 62nd St near the NW corner of the moat. **Open** 8am–5pm daily. 🎫 combination ticket.

The sole remnant of the Konbaung Dynasty's magnificent Golden Palace is the Shwenandaw Monastery. Formerly part of the personal apartments of King Mindon, the building only survived the Allied bombing raids of World War II because in 1880, Mindon's son Thibaw had it dismantled and moved to its current site outside the palace walls. His father had passed away inside the hall in 1878 and Thibaw is said to have found the space too distressing to be in.

The rich exterior carving of the monastery and the gilded pillars and ceilings inside give visitors a vivid impression of how sumptuous the complex of which it formed a part must have looked in its prime.

🔹 Atumashi Monastery
63rd St. **Open** 8am–5pm daily. 🎫 combination ticket.

West of the Shwenandaw Monastery stands a modern reconstruction of a grand edifice originally built by Mindon

in 1857. Surmounted by five rectangular terraces, rather than the more usual Konbaung-style receding tiers, it formerly held a 30-ft (9-m) Buddha made from the king's own lacquered silk clothes. The enormous diamond that was once embedded in its forehead was looted during the British invasion of 1885, and five years later the Buddha itself was lost in a fire, along with the rest of the building. Although ornately decorated, the present structure, built by the Tatmadaw using convict labor in 1996, does not approach the refinement of its predecessor.

🔹 Kuthodaw Pagoda
62nd St. **Open** daily.
🎫 combination ticket.

King Mindon commissioned the sumptuously gilded Maha Lawka Marazein stupa, at the foot of Mandalay Hill, as the centerpiece of the walled Kuthodaw Pagoda in 1857. The 100-ft (30-m) *zedi*, or stupa, stands in a complex dominated by 729 slender, whitewashed ancillary pagodas, each containing carved alabaster slabs inscribed with a page of the *Tipitaka*, the Theravada Pali canon. The inscriptions were created to mark the Fifth Buddhist Synod of 1871 and, when they were completed, took 2,400 monks six months to recite. Local guides love to describe the collection as the "World's Largest Book." In common with most of the Konbaung capital's sacred sites, this one fared badly at the hands of the British in 1885, losing precious stones off the stupa's *hti* or crowning finial, gold leaf from the *zedi* itself, and 6,370 bells from the miniature pagodas, which were melted down and used to cast ammunition. The original *Tipitaka* slabs were also looted for use by the British army in road construction.

🔹 Sandamuni Pagoda
Off East Moat. **Open** 6am–9pm daily.
🎫 combination ticket.

Adjacent to the Kuthodaw stands the lookalike Sandamuni Pagoda, where 1,774 more inscribed marble slabs are

The gilded iron Buddha commissioned by Bodawpaya, now in the Sandamuni Pagoda

For hotels and restaurants in this region see p204 and pp212–14

housed in rows of neatly whitewashed shrines. Often dubbed "Volume II of the World's Largest Book," the inscriptions are commentaries on the *Tipitaka*. Before this pagoda was built, the site was where King Mindon and his family lived while waiting for work on their new palace to be completed. It is synonymous with the bloody coup of 1866 in which two of the king's sons mounted a bid for the throne, killing the incumbent crown prince and two others ahead of them in the line of succession. The victims were buried where they died, along with other members of the royal family who perished in the rebellion. A mausoleum in the complex is their final resting place. Pride of place in the Sandamuni Pagoda, however, goes to the large iron Buddha cast by the despotic, expansionist King Bodawpaya in 1802, which is now heavily encrusted in gold leaf.

Painting of King Mindon at Mandalay's Kyauktawgyi Temple

🏛 Kyauktawgyi Temple

10th St. **Open** 7:30am–8pm daily. 🎫 combination ticket.

An even larger Buddha occupies the main shrine hall of the late-19th-century Kyauktawgyi Temple, diagonally opposite the southern entrance to the hill. It reportedly took between 10,000 and 12,000 men 13 days to drag the single piece of solid, pale-green marble 15 miles (25 km) from the quarry at Sangyin to Mandalay city. Several smaller statues of the *arahants*, or Great Disciples, attend the Buddha.

The unusual Shweyattaw Buddha, the only pointing Buddha statue in Myanmar

🏛 Mandalay Hill

Open 7am–10pm daily. ♿ through the elevator to the Sataungpyei Pagoda, reached via a surfaced road around the north side of the hill.

Four different *zaungdans*, or stepped, covered paths, wind up Mandalay Hill, each taking around 45 minutes to climb. A motorable road also zigzags up the north side to the summit.

The start of the southern stepway, the most popular, is flanked by a pair of huge leogryphs, or *chinthes*. First of the numerous landmarks along this route is the **U Khanti Tazaung**, a hall built as a memorial to the hermit-monk U Khanti who lived on the spot during the colonial era. The holy man was instrumental in the creation of Mandalay Hill as a pilgrimage site, raising funds to build numerous shrines and pagodas. The *tazaung* is also noteworthy for being the place where the Peshawar Relics were enshrined until World War II, when they were removed for safekeeping. Unearthed in 1905 inside the remains of a massive stupa on the outskirts of Peshawar, Pakistan, the three fragments of clavicles encased in crystal were brought to Burma by the British in 1924 as a gift. However, anticolonial sentiment was rife at the time and the Burmese never really accepted the relics as genuine. They are now in a pagoda near the base of the hill.

A short way farther up the steps, the unusual pose of the gilded **Shweyattaw Buddha**, sited where two paths meet, refers to Mandalay's foundation legend. The Buddha was said to have prophesized that a city would spring up at the foot of the hill 2,400 years after his death – hence the statue's outstretched arm and finger, which point directly to the palace where King Mindon fulfilled this prediction in 1857.

The penultimate shrine on the route centers on a statue of **Sanda Mukhi**, an ogress to whom the Buddha is said to have made the famous prophecy. On first meeting the great teacher, she entered a devotional frenzy of such force that she purportedly cut off her breasts and placed them at his feet as an offering. So impressed was the Buddha that he told her she would be reincarnated 2,400 years after his death as the king of the great city whose foundation he had foreseen.

The terrace encircling the **Sataungpyei Temple** at the summit offers stupendous views over Mandalay city. Surmounted by a forest of gilded spires and a central pyramidal pagoda covered in gold, the building is set amid colorful flame trees and magnolia bushes. Although a peaceful spot now, the slopes witnessed ferocious hand-to-hand fighting during World War II, when Japanese forces dug into machine-gun posts mounted a desperate defense against battalions of Gurkha and British troops.

2 Amarapura

Road Map C3. 8 miles (12 km) SW of Mandalay city center. 🚶 56,000. ✈ Mandalay International. 🚌
Note: all major sights covered by Archeology Department's combination ticket, valid for one week.

On the southwestern fringes of Mandalay, Amarapura (literally "City of Immortality") succeeded Inwa (Ava) as the Burmese capital in 1783. The move is said to have been recommended by the court astrologers of the megalomaniac King Bodawpaya to expiate the bad karma the ruler had accrued by drowning his grandnephew, King Maung Maung (1763–82), in order to seize the Konbaung throne.

The strip of lush, leafy land between the east bank of the Ayeyarwady and the shores of Taungmyo Lake (also called Taungthaman) provided the perfect setting for the old Inwa palace, which Bodawpaya dismantled and rebuilt near the waterside, with four pagodas protecting its corners. Of the latter, the most impressive is the soaring **Pahtodawgyi**, which the king built in 1820. With a spectacular bell-shaped *zedi* raised on five terraces decorated with beautifully carved *Jataka* friezes showing episodes from the Buddha's life, the stupa still dominates the town's skyline. Male visitors are

Stone carving of a mythical animal at the early-19th-century Pahtodawgyi Pagoda

allowed up the steep steps to its uppermost terrace, from where a fine view extends over the adjacent pagodas to the lake.

A low-rise town of sandy, tree-lined lanes and wooden houses, Amarapura has a very different feel from the nearby metropolis. Most of its residents earn their living in workshops that specialize in fine-quality wedding *longyis* and *htameins*; the distinctive sound of looms at full tilt is a constant backdrop.

Amarapura's back roads all seem to converge on the town's most iconic sight, **U Bein Bridge**, built by Bodawpaya's

eponymous mayor using timber from Inwa, the old capital. Spanning a neck in the lake 0.7 miles (1.1 km) wide, this impressive teak walkway – the world's longest – rests on wooden piles which stand at least 20 ft (6 m) proud of the waterline in the dry season, but are almost completely submerged during the monsoons. Tourists descend in droves to photograph the bridge in the morning and evening light as villagers, market gardeners in traditional *kaukyoe* straw hats, and red-robed monks stride across it. Boatmen offer trips over the water to the eastern shore, where the **Kyauktawgyi Pagoda** is the largest of a scattering of mid-19th-century monuments. Built by King Pagan Min in 1847, the five-tiered temple, gilded in high Konbaung style, houses a giant seated Buddha of jade-colored Sangyin marble. Its entrance porches contain wonderful frescoes of traditional Burmese monuments and scenes, including one (in the northeast entranceway) showing the pagoda as it looked in its prime.

🏯 **Pahtodawgyi Pagoda**
Off Kanthitan St.
Open 7am–11pm daily. ♿

🏯 **Kyauktawgyi Pagoda**
East bank, Taungmyo Lake.
Open daily.

U Bein's Bridge, supported by over 1,000 piles, spanning Amarapura's Taungmyo Lake

❸ The Ayeyarwady Bridges

Road Map C3. 11 miles (17 km) SW of Mandalay, via the expressway. 🚌

Connecting Amarapura with Sagaing, the **Old Inwa Bridge**, with 16 spans and two decks (one for road and another for rail traffic), used to be the only route across the Ayeyarwady from Mandalay when it was built by the British in 1934. They sabotaged it in 1942 by destroying two of the spans to forestall the Japanese advance. The bridge was repaired 14 years later and served as the main link between the two banks until 2008, when the three-span **Ayeyarwady Bridge**, carrying a four-lane highway, was built next to the old bridge.

Buddha statues lining the crescent-shaped colonnade of Umin Thounzeh, Sagaing

The Old Inwa Bridge, one of the two bridges connecting Amarapura and Sagaing

❹ Sagaing

Road Map C3. 13 miles (21 km) SW of Mandalay. 🚹 70,000. ✈ Mandalay International. 🚌 **Note:** major sights covered by Archeology Department's Sagaing-Mingun joint ticket.

One of the great spectacles of Upper Burma is that of Sagaing Hill rising from the bleached west bank of the Ayeyarwady, its denuded ridges encrusted with whitewashed domes and shimmering golden spires. Thousands of Buddhist pagodas and monasteries cluster in and around this riverside market town southwest of Mandalay. They are the legacy of a brief period in the early 14th century when, as the country plunged into turmoil following the demise of the Bagan Empire, it served as the capital of a powerful regional dynasty led by the young King Sawyun (1300–27). After only 50 years, however, one of Sawyun's descendants, Thadominbya (1345–67), decided to move the royal palace across the river to a new, more easily defensible site at Inwa (Ava). Sagaing has since devoted itself largely to spiritual rather than political matters. Today around 6,000 monks reside in the numerous *kyaungs* (monasteries) dotted around the town, and buses loaded with pilgrims are very much part of the local scene.

Crowning the southern extremity of a long ridge rippling north all the way to Mingun, the gilded **Soon U Ponya Shin** is the most prominent of the many temples scattered across Sagaing Hill. It can be reached on foot, by following one of several covered walkways leading to the summit via a constellation of ancillary shrines, or on a bumpy metaled road that ends at the temple gates. Either way, visitors first pass through a hall lined with dazzling turquoise glass mosaic where a huge, golden-robed Buddha smiles down beneficently. Beyond, the east terrace affords a spellbinding view over the Ayeyarwady and the myriad temples that overlook it.

Just below the Soon U Ponya Shin, a northern spur of the main Sagaing Hill approach road winds up to the **Umin Thounzeh**, a cave temple housing 45 Buddha images arrayed in a grand semicircular shrine. Decorated with a backdrop of sparkling glasswork, the richly gilded statues offer one of Sagaing Hill's most distinctive photo opportunities.

From the terrace of Umin Thounzeh another great view extends west over a patchwork of millet and sesame fields toward Monywa, a landscape dominated by the huge golden dome of the **Kaunghmudaw Pagoda**, on the outskirts of Sagaing. Rising to a height of 150 ft (46 m), the gigantic *zedi* dates from 1636 and was built to celebrate the foundation of Inwa (Ava) as the royal capital. Local legend claims its unusual shape was inspired by that of the breast of Thadominbya's queen, although the Abhayagiri Dagoba in Anuradhapura, Sri Lanka, was more probably the model. Interred inside the stupa is the fake tooth relic with which the Ceylonese famously hoodwinked King Bayinnaung of Bago (Pegu) *(see p95)*, and which was brought here as plunder by the Taungoo ruler Anaukpetlun in 1599.

🏯 **Soon U Ponya Shin**
Sagaing Hill. **Open** 7am–10pm daily.

🏯 **Umin Thounzeh**
Sagaing Hill. **Open** 7am–10pm daily.

🏛 **Kaunghmudaw Pagoda**
5 miles (8 km) NW of Sagaing city center. **Open** 7am–11pm daily.

❺ Inwa (Ava)

Called Ava by the British, Inwa served as the Burmese capital for longer than any other city – over six centuries in all – and retains evocative temples, stupas, and monasteries, the finest of them being Konbaung structures of the early 1800s. The crumbling edifices occupy a spit of land protected by fortified walls, moats, and earthworks in the south and west, by the Myitnge River in the east, and by the Ayeyarwady in the north – this gave rise to the site's name, which means "Mouth of the Lake." A massive earthquake in 1839 left the city and its structures in ruins, after which King Tharrawaddy shifted the court to Amarapura. While it is possible to travel to Inwa by road, most visitors arrive by ferry, transferring to a horse cart for a tour of the monuments.

Horse carts driving down a tree-lined road on a tour of the ruins of Inwa

Yedanasini Pagoda
Just off the route to the Bagaya Kyaung is this complex of brick stupas, roofless pillars, and meditating stone Buddhas surrounded by palmyra palms and flame trees.

KEY

① **Ferry point**

② **Horse cart waiting area**

③ **Htilangshin Pagoda**, next to the Maha Aungmye Bonzan Kyaung, consists of a group of gilded stupas with elegantly tapering spires. They date from the Bagan era, but were substantially renovated during the Konbaung period.

④ **Ticket point**

⑤ **Shwedigon Pagoda**, Inwa's largest stupa, presides over the southwest corner of the site, overlooking the old moat.

⑥ **Nogatataphu Pagoda**, whose golden spire towers high above the surrounding rice fields, is the largest stupa at Inwa after the Shwedigon Pagoda.

↖ Sagaing

Ayeyarwady River

Key

— Suggested route

| 0 meters | 500 |
| 0 yards | 500 |

★ **Maha Aungmye Bonzan Kyaung**
Designed in the style of a teak monastery, this brick and stucco structure is among the few survivors from the Ava era. It dates from the reign of King Bagyidaw (r. 1819–37), who moved the capital back here from Amarapura in 1824.

Mandalay City ↑

Nan Myin Tower
Inwa's own "leaning tower," damaged during the 1839 earth-quake, was part of Bagyidaw's now vanished palace complex.

★ **Bagaya Kyaung**
One of Myanmar's finest surviving teak monasteries, the Bagaya Kyaung retains some superb carving. Particularly noteworthy are its ornate door surrounds. Young novices attend school here in the mornings.

❻ Mingun

Bodawpaya (1745–1819) was one of the most expansionist and militarily daring rulers in Burmese history, and the mighty stupa he raised on the banks of the Ayeyarwady at Mingun was intended to match in scale his prowess as an empire builder. Commissioned in 1790 to house a tooth of the Buddha, Pahtodawgyi (also called the Mingun Pagoda) was constructed by slaves, whom the king supervised personally while living on an island nearby. However, the upheavals of the early 19th century caused a shortage of funds and labor, and the project was never completed. Had it been, the stupa would have risen even higher than the Great Pyramid of Giza in Egypt. A massive earthquake in 1839 reduced its upper portions to rubble, and left huge cracks in the façades. Even so, King Bodawpaya's folly remains an imposing sight, particularly when first glimpsed from the Ayeyarwady River.

The eastern entrance
Facing the river and rising sun, the eastern doorway leads to a shrine containing a Buddha image that is much venerated by the Burmese.

Settawya Pagoda
This whitewashed shrine was built in 1811 to house a footprint of the Buddha. Although somewhat extravagant in its design, the temple provides a splendid backdrop for passengers alighting at the nearby boat jetty.

KEY

① **Settawya's five-level terrace**, with rows of statues of *nats*, leads down to the river.

② **The south and north façades**, badly damaged in the 1839 earthquake, receive the least interest from visitors, although both have beautifully ornamented Konbaung-style door arches and surrounds.

③ **The proportions of the stupa** are impressive, even in its unfinished state. Each of its sides is about 230 ft (70 m) in length, and its walls rise 164-ft- (50-m-) high, only one third of their intended height. To see what it was meant to look like when complete, visitors can stop off at its scale model, Pondaw Pagoda, sited 600 ft (182 m) to the south.

④ **The eastern entrance**

★ **Hsinbyume Pagoda**
To the north stands this extraordinary pagoda, built in 1816 by Bagyidaw, Bodawpaya's grandson. It depicts the mythical Mount Meru, the wavy concentric terraces below the stupa representing the seven ranges that encircle the sacred peak.

Magnificent views

Pahtodawgyi was designed to make an impact when viewed from the river, and to provide sweeping vistas of it. Since further earthquake damage in 2012, climbing to the upper levels is discouraged. Nonetheless many still do so, often led by local guides. Take great care if climbing.

VISITORS' CHECKLIST

Practical Information
Road Map C3. 14 miles (24 km) N of Sagaing; 29 miles (47 km) from Mandalay Hill by road, one hr upriver from Mandalay.
Open daily. 🎫 covered by the Archeology Department's Sagaing-Mingun joint ticket. 🛈 guides available at the bell. 🎉 Feb/Mar: brother and sister teak tree *nat* festival, 5–10th waxing moon days of Tabaung.

Transport
✈ Mandalay International.
🚌 9am, west end of 26th St; private boats at 8am, Gawain Jetty, 35th St, Mandalay.

The western entrance
The more peaceful western entry is the place to sidestep the crowds, especially in the evening when its cracked façade looks dramatic in the warm light.

Giant ruined *chinthes*
Only the ruined haunches remain of the pair of colossal stone *chinthes* (leogryphs) that originally flanked the stupa's landing stage and main approach.

★ The great bell of Mingun
Cast on a vast scale and weighing 200,000 lb (90,700 kg), the stupa's bell had to be floated into position via a specially built canal.

The multicolored spires of the unique Thanboddhay Pagoda

❼ Monywa

Road Map C3. 84 miles (136 km) W of Mandalay. 190,000. Mandalay International. direct from Mandalay & Bagan; also from Pakokku on the Ayeyarwady River, where some cruisers may pause on the Bagan–Mandalay trip.

Monywa is the main port on the Chindwin, Myanmar's second most important river, whose headwaters rise just across the Patkai Range in Assam. The town has long been a hub for trade with northeast India, although with little traffic now crossing the northern border, its principal modern role is as a clearing house for produce grown in the fertile Sagaing plains. While the town's two pagodas are worth a look, the few foreigners who travel here tend to do so en route to or from Bodhi Tataung, the Thanboddhay Pagoda, and the Pho Win Taung Caves, which are more comfortably explored using Monywa as a base than as day trips from Mandalay.

Novice monks shopping at one of Monywa's open-air produce markets

❽ Thanboddhay Pagoda

Road Map C3. 6 miles (10 km) SE of Monywa via Highway 71. Open 6am–5pm daily.

The riotously colorful Thanboddhay Pagoda is a temple unlike any other in Myanmar. The brainchild of a local abbott named Moe-hnyin Sayadaw, it was built in the 1930s as a monument to the 512,028 souls who are believed to have achieved Buddhahood in the era of Gautama – a concept artistically expressed in a multitude of Buddha figures, both large and small. Every inch of the building's exterior is festooned with statues, along with the pillars, niches, walls, and ceilings inside, which are smothered in vibrantly painted and gilded stucco. The pagoda's distinctive roof is layered with rows of small gilded stupas, and the temple itself is flanked by 30-ft- (9-m-) high obelisks covered in tiny Buddha statues.

The somewhat kitsch theme-park effect is further enhanced by the pastel-colored monks' cells, the large masonry fruits seen around the complex, the pair of large white concrete elephants standing guard at the main entrance, and the Arlin Nga Sint, a lofty watchtower built in the form of a snake. Men (but not women) may climb this tower via a spiral staircase for a bird's-eye view over the complex.

❾ Bodhi Tataung

Road Map C3. 5.5 miles (8 km) E of Thanboddhay. Open 7am–9pm daily.

An astonishing apparition rises from a hilltop to the east of Thanboddhay at Bodhi Tataung, where two colossal gilded Buddhas – one standing, one reclining – gaze serenely across the Chindwin Valley. The giant figures form part of a modern complex founded by a globe-trotting Burmese monk named Sayadaw Bhaddanta Narada, who traveled the Buddhist world to raise funds for the project, but died before seeing it completed.

Bodhi Tataung's spectacular centerpiece, on the summit of the hill, is the **Laykyun Setkyar**, a 424-ft (116-m) standing Buddha depicted with arms held stiffly at his side. A staircase winds halfway up the hollow interior, via a series of galleries featuring gaudy moral murals, to a viewing platform that is not for the fainthearted.

Immediately below the standing figure, his neighbor measures 312 ft (95 m) from head to toe and is the second largest reclining Buddha in Myanmar after the one at Win Sein Taw Ya near Mawlamyine *(see p193)*. Finally, on level ground at the foot of the hill stands a gleaming golden pagoda, the 430-ft (131-m) **Aung Setkyar**, which, like the Laykyun Setkyar, can be scaled via an inner passageway. The stupa is set in a park featuring thousands of parasol-wielding Buddhas placed in perfect rows.

The massive reclining and standing Buddhas of Bodhi Tataung

The Pho Win Taung cave complex, with hundreds of caves containing wood and stucco Buddha statues

⑩ Pho Win Taung Caves

Road Map C3. Pho Win Taung village, 4 miles (6 km) S of the Yinmarbin Rd; 15 miles (25 km) SW of Monywa via the Chindwin ferry, or 26 miles (43 km) SW via the Chindwin Bridge. ✈ Mandalay International. 🚌 🚢 **Open** 8am–6pm daily. 🎫 🚻

Buried deep in the rural hinterland west of the Chindwin River is one of Upper Burma's less-visited gems, a complex of Buddhist cave temples hollowed from a oddly shaped outcrop of sandstone near the village of Pho Win Taung (also known as Hpo Win Daung). The name translates as "Mountain of Solitary Meditation" and the site, which holds more than 520 rock-cut chambers, has about it an aura of great sanctity, despite being in generally poor condition, with no visitor facilities beyond a ticket office and a handful of basic local food stalls.

Carved between the 14th and 18th centuries, the first group of caves, close to the village, contain numerous wood and stucco Buddhas, and a few retain some vibrant murals of geometric patterns and episodes from the *Jatakas*. Local guides are on hand to show visitors around – worth employing to help fend off the aggressive macaques who patrol the stone steps connecting the various sites. A smaller, more recent complex of 46 rock-cut monuments lies about half a mile (1 km) beyond the village at **Shwebataung**, where the

entrances to the cave chambers are approached via a series of steep stone staircases hewn from an impressive limestone cliff face.

⑪ A Myint

Road Map C3. 15 miles (25 km) S of Monywa on the Chindwin River. By road, reachable via Chaung U village on Highway 71. 🏔 1,500. ✈ Mandalay International. 🚌 🚢

On the banks of the Chindwin River amid the flat riverine countryside south of Monywa is the unspoiled backwater village of A Myint, where luxury cruisers occasionally pause for passengers to explore a complex of **ancient stupas**. Smothered in weeds and mildew, the crumbling *zedis* are scattered around a plot of slender palm trees on the edge of the village. Some retain

superb murals on their walls and ceilings. Near the stupas, a picturesque **teak monastery** sports a traditional seven-tiered tower, beneath which a cavernous interior holds antique Buddhas and some fine wood-carving. The young novices of the *kyaung* (monastery) obligingly pose for photographs beneath the building's delicately carved window surrounds.

The only other structure of note in A Myint is the home of the former village headman. The grand double-storied mansion, built in Neo-Classical style and painted terra-cotta and ocher, dates from the British colonial era. The family who own the house, like the building itself, have seemingly fallen on hard times and retain only one vestige of their ancestral prosperity: an old windup gramophone that is still in perfect working order.

Crumbling *zedis* in the ancient stupa complex of A Myint

⑫ Pyin U Lwin (Maymyo)

Road Map D3. 43 miles (73 km) E of Mandalay. 👥 66,000. ✈ Mandalay International. 🚌 🚐

Located on the western edge of the Shan Plateau, Pyin U Lwin (formerly known as Maymyo or Maytown after its first governor, Colonel May) was founded in the 1890s by the British as a military post. When the rail line to Lashio was completed, the town became the official summer capital of the colonial administration. At an elevation of 3,510 ft (1,070 m), the town enjoys a much cooler climate than that of Mandalay on the central plains, which appealed to the homesick British. Mock-Tudor and Scottish Baronial mansions with turrets and ample verandas duly sprang up under the pine trees, along with a whites-only club, a golf course, and botanical gardens. After Burma gained its independence, the sizable Anglo-Burmese community gradually dwindled, but the Sikh and Nepali minorities whose forebears were brought here to work on the railroads are still very much in evidence. Although Pyin U Lwin is often described as a hill station, the term is a misnomer, as the town is set on a plateau rather than a mountain. Its role as a hot-season retreat from the plains, however, has seen a new lease of life in recent years with the rise of an affluent Burmese middle class. Several of the old hotels have been renovated, and dozens of new establishments have also opened since the NLD-led tourist boycott was relaxed in 2010. Most visitors pass time in the town by shopping for soft fruit and flowers grown in the local nurseries, and taking sightseeing rides around the pleasant tree-lined roads in horse-drawn carriages (locally called "wagons"), along with an obligatory visit to the **National Kandawgyi Botanical Gardens**. The gardens were created in 1915 and modeled on London's Kew Gardens. Today the 150-acre (60-ha) site holds nearly 600 species of trees, over 500 of them endemics, and 480 kinds of flowers, including 25 types of roses, all displayed around rolling lawns and ornamental lakes spanned by pretty wooden bridges. The rock gardens, fountains, playgrounds, and a small zoo are popular with local children. There is also a delightful Orchid Garden featuring more than 300 species of indigenous blooms, and a well-stocked Butterfly Museum, with beetles and butterflies displayed in cases.

Tower made of flowers at Pyin U Lwin's botanical gardens

🔷 National Kandawgyi Botanical Gardens

Nandan Rd (on the southern edge of town). **Open** 8am–5:30pm daily. 🚾 ♿ 🖥

⑬ Gokteik Bridge

Road Map D3. 47 miles (76 km) NE of Pyin U Lwin. 🚌

The linchpin of the railroad line connecting Mandalay and Lashio is the dizzying Gokteik Bridge, a gravity-defying construction that the travel writer Paul Theroux aptly described as "a monster of silver geometry in all the ragged rock and jungle." Commissioned at the end of the 19th century, it spans a precipitous gorge between two sheer limestone bluffs, above a carpet of dense forest. The challenge of spanning this wild terrain fell to the Pennsylvania and Maryland Bridge Company,

National Kandawgyi Botanical Gardens

The gilded *karaweik*-shaped Phaung Daw U Pagoda at Meiktila

which shipped all of the steel used in the construction from New York, transporting it to the site on a specially constructed trackway. Measuring 2,260 ft (689 m) across and 335 ft (102 m) in height, the bridge is supported by 15 latticework trestles and was the largest structure of its kind in the world when it was completed. Catching a first glimpse of the giant, with its silvery steel girders soaring above the trees and red-tinged cliffs, is an experience few passengers on the rattling ride to Lashio forget.

⑭ Meiktila

Road Map C3. 106 miles (171 km) S of Mandalay. 🏙 280,000. ✈ Mandalay International. 🚉 🚌

Travelers following the inland route between Bagan and Mandalay, rather than the slower journey by river, generally pass through the lakeside town of Meiktila, at the head of the Sittaung Valley. Its strategic position as the gateway to Upper Burma made it the scene of an epic battle in 1944, when the Allies took it from the Japanese, and were then promptly surrounded by the enemy. Two months of bitter fighting ensued before the siege could be broken. A legacy of the conflict is the large air base on the city's outskirts, which ensures a high-profile military presence. Tatmadaw

troops have taken to the streets several times in recent years to quell outbreaks of communal violence, including in March 2013, when dozens of people were killed and around 12,000 displaced in mob attacks by Buddhists on Muslims.

The city itself holds no sights worthy of a special detour. With time to kill, however, the path around the lake makes for a pleasant cycle ride, passing the picturesque **Phaung Daw U Pagoda**, a floating shrine made in the shape of a gilded *karaweik* bird. Among the old British-era mansions on its western shore is the one where NLD leader Aung San Suu Kyi and her husband Michael Aris spent their honeymoon.

🏛 **Phaung Daw U Pagoda**
Meiktila Lake, near Main Bridge.
Open 6am–9pm daily. ♿

The Abode of Kings

Rare are the first-time visitors to Myanmar who can correctly name the country's capital, and rarer still those who actually travel there. But since 2005, the seat of the government has been Naypyitaw (literally "Abode of Kings"), 200 miles (320 km) north of Yangon. Why the military junta saw fit to lavish an estimated US$4 billion on constructing a brand-new city in the middle of nowhere remains a subject of much speculation.

Ministers' villas and workers' apartments in the capital, Naypyitaw

Rumors circulated at the time that it was in response to astrological predictions that a foreign power was about to invade – located in the center of the country, the site is more easily defensible than its predecessor Yangon. Whatever the reason, Naypyitaw now serves as the permanent home of the Myanmar parliament, as well as the army and civil service. Around a million soldiers and bureaucrats had to be relocated to the new site, leaving their families behind until schools, hospitals, and other essential facilities could be built. While the low-ranking office workers live in color-coded blocks, the ruling elite inhabit luxury villas in the surrounding hills. Sprawling over the dusty plains of the upper Sittaung Valley, the new capital is a city of vast proportions, a concrete metropolis of empty multilane highways and huge civic structures, mostly unused and expensive to maintain. As such, it holds little of interest to foreign travelers, but does reveal a great deal about the priorities of Myanmar's former military rulers.

EASTERN MYANMAR

Much of Eastern Myanmar falls within Shan State, a vast upland of remote valleys divided by bare ridges and tracts of scrub forest, with the mighty Thanlwin River slicing through its heart. Although now largely denuded of their original forest cover, the grand river valleys and rippling mountains of the Shan Plateau include some of the country's signature landscapes, foremost among them Inle Lake, with its backdrop of misty hills and soaring ridgetops. The east also boasts an exceptional cultural diversity and is home to several ethnic groups.

Arriving in Shan from other parts of the country, the differences between this hill region and lowland Myanmar are immediately apparent. The climate is noticeably cooler, and the stupas are more slender and tapered than in the rest of the country. The population is mostly ethnic Shan – Thai-speaking descendants of the tribes who accompanied Kublai Khan on his 13th-century invasion of the Bagan Empire. However, there are several other ethnic minority groups from the hills – including the Pa-O, Padaung, and Danu – who, with their distinctive head-gear, clothes, and jewelry, are also among the defining features of the region.

On the western edge of the plateau, beautiful Inle Lake is the area's undisputed highlight. Every year, thousands of visitors come to experience the unique way of life of the Intha people, symbolized by the distinctive leg rowers standing on the back of their long-tailed canoes. Boat trips to Shan stupa sites, monasteries, and stilt villages provide the focus for lakeside stays, while in the surrounding hills a network of trails offers outstanding treks.

For more adventurous travelers, Hsipaw in the north and Kengtung in the far east are springboards for long-distance treks to still more remote hill-tribe villages. In the past few decades, the Golden Triangle – where the borders of Thailand, Laos, and Myanmar meet – was a no-go zone for foreign tourists. The drug cartels who control the opium trade for which this area has long been notorious had been waging war against the state. With the signing of various accords in recent years, however, the region is slowly moving toward peace, allowing visitors to again travel to most parts of the region.

Long-tailed Intha boat moored in one of the quieter reaches of Inle Lake, surrounded by the distant hills of the Shan Plateau

◀ Young novice monks standing at the distinctive wooden oval windows of Shwe Yaunghwe Kyaung monastery, Nyaungshwe, Inle Lake

Exploring Eastern Myanmar

Most of this region lies within Shan State, the largest administrative division in Myanmar, extending from China's Yunnan province in the northeast to the borders of Thailand and Laos in the southeast. Inle Lake is easily accessible to visitors, and the busy market town of Nyaungshwe on its northern fringes makes an ideal base for boat trips. To the west, the former colonial hill station of Kalaw is the recommended departure point for treks through the surrounding minority villages. Farther north, Hsipaw is another trekking hub, with trails leading through a variety of different terrains and ethnic zones, as is Kengtung in the east, from where day trips can be made on foot to Golden Triangle villages. Local markets across the region provide opportunities to meet minority people, who travel down from the hills dressed in their traditional finery on market days.

Detail of woodcarving, Hsin Khaung Taung Kyaung, Pindaya

A patchwork of fields in the countryside around Kalaw

Getting Around

As most of the roads in the region are in a dismal state, flying is the best way to reach the principal hubs – take the journey from Mandalay to Inle Lake: a grueling nine hours by bus; only 40 minutes by air. For overland travel to Kengtung from other parts of Myanmar a permit is required, and foreign visitors are only allowed to travel in a private vehicle. No permit is required to fly into Kengtung. Those entering from Mae Sai, Thailand, may cross at Tachileik and continue as far as Kengtung by public transport. Bicycles are usually available for rent in the major towns for getting around. On Inle Lake, a fleet of long-tailed boats is on hand to transport visitors to otherwise inaccessible sites.

For hotels and restaurants in this region see p205 and pp214–15

A long-tailed boat on Inle Lake moving past the floating gardens of the Intha

Sights at a Glance

1. *Inle Lake pp166–8*
2. Nyaungshwe
3. Kalaw
4. Green Hill Valley Elephant Camp
5. Taunggyi
6. Kakku
7. Wineries around Inle Lake
8. *Pindaya Caves pp174–5*
9. Hsipaw
10. Lashio
11. Kengtung

Detail of a carving at the remote Buddhist site of Kakku

A monk teaching young children at a village school in the Inle Lake area

Key

— Main road
= Other road
⋯ Railroad
▬ International border
▬ Regional border

0 kilometers   60
0 miles   60

For additional map symbols *see back flap*

❶ Inle Lake

Enfolded by the rippling Shan Hills, Inle Lake forms a world apart from the rest of Myanmar. The Intha people *(see p168)* who live in stilt villages along its fringes have evolved a unique way of life, beautifully adapted to the seasonal ebb and flow of the shoreline, where slender-topped stupas overlook a mosaic of rice paddies and floating vegetable gardens. Each morning, a fleet of long-tailed motorboats skim across Inle's glassy surface, ferrying visitors to monasteries and temples, and workshops where silk is handwoven from lotus fiber. The idyll is only slightly marred by the hordes who descend on the lake in the tourist season. Plenty of quiet corners remain, however, where it is possible to experience the essential tranquillity of wood-and-thatch villages far removed from the road network.

Ywama, a key tourist hub with a rotating market and silver jewelry workshops

Floating gardens of the Intha
The Intha of Inle Lake are famous for their amazingly productive vegetable beds, made by piling weeds and compost on long poles fixed to the lake floor.

Paramount Resort

Nga Hpe Kyaung

Phaung Daw U Pagoda
Inle Lake's main shrine holds five Buddhas that are now unrecognizable under innumerable layers of lumpy gold leaf.

Ywama

④ ⑤ ⑥ ⑦ ③

Nga Phe Kyaung
Long famed as the "Jumping Cat Monastery." The monks no longer prompt resident felines to jump through hoops, but the beautiful wooden meditation hall is worth exploring.

0 kilometers 2
0 miles 2

For hotels and restaurants in this region see p205 and pp214–15

Nyaungshwe

Inle Lake View

①

Inle Princess

Inle Resort

Myanmar Treasure Resort

Aureum Resort and Spa

Maing Thauk

②

Inle   Lake

Villa Inle

VISITORS' CHECKLIST

Practical Information

Road Map D4. 170 miles (275 km) SE of Mandalay. 🛏 hotels can arrange guides. 🛒 five-day markets in Ywama, Phaung Daw U, Inthein, Nampan, Nyaungshwe. 🎭 Sep/Oct: Golden Bird Festival, Phaung Daw U Pagoda (waxing moon of Thadingyut month).

Transport

✈ Mandalay International.
✈ Heho Airport (23 miles/38 km N of Inle). Nyaungshwe & resorts have long-tailed boats for excursions. Bicycles for rent at hotels.

Maing Thauk An atmospheric village of two halves, linked by a wooden bridge and partly built on stilts above the water.

KEY

① **Khaung Daing** is the site of famous hot springs where trekkers ease their aching limbs. It also has some of Inle's oldest resort hotels.

② **Inle Bo Teh**, marooned in the middle of the lake, is a British-era government guesthouse, now deserted and derelict.

③ **Nampan** is the largest village actually on the lake, with whole streets of stilt houses. Cheroots are handmade here by rolling a mixture of tobacco and aromatic herbs into Indian cherry leaves.

④ **Alodaw Pauk Pagoda**

⑤ **Inpawkhon** is a major silk weaving center where fine textiles are woven with fiber drawn from lotus stems.

⑥ **Inthein** is one of the largest settlements around Inle, and the venue of one of the region's busiest five-day rotating markets.

⑦ **Nyaung Ohak** is a small, weed-choked collection of Shan stupas at the base of the hill on which stands the Shwe Inthein stupa complex.

Resorts on Inle Lake
Around the lake are a host of luxury resorts *(see p205)*, most of them featuring stilt chalets with teak decks from which to admire the sublime effect of the changing light on the water.

★ **Shwe Inthein stupa complex**
A total of 1,054 slender-spired Shan *zedis* (stupas) are packed into this enclosure above Inthein. Most date from the 17th and 18th centuries. The site is reached via a long *zaungdan* (covered stairway).

The Intha of Inle Lake

Handmade cheroots produced by the Intha

The glassy waters of Inle Lake support a population of between 70,000 and 100,000 people, most of whom are members of an ethnic minority group called the Intha. Originally from Dawei (Tenasserim), in the far southeast of Myanmar, the Intha settled in the region in the 18th century, fleeing invasions by their Thai neighbors across the border. It is said that the local Shan chief refused to grant them rights to land around Inle, which is allegedly why the Intha built their stilt houses on the fluctuating waterline of the lake itself. Brilliantly adapted to the climate and ecosystem, the way of life they have since evolved – from their distinctive one-legged rowing style to their impressively fertile floating gardens – is unique in Southeast Asia.

Traditional Intha stilt houses on Inle Lake

The unusual floating gardens in which the Intha grow their fruit and vegetables are anchored to the lake bed by bamboo poles.

Leg-rowing position, used only by men

Traditional Intha conical net

Inle Lake fisherman standing on a long-tailed boat in the distinctive leg-rowing stance used by the Intha people

Leg-rowing races are part of the Phaung Daw U Pagoda's Golden Bird Festival, Inle's biggest religious celebration.

Fried red tree ants and crickets are among the local delicacies available at markets around the lake.

Exquisitely fine silk spun from lotus stalks is woven in local workshops into vibrant *longyis* and *htameins*.

The unique octagonal stepped stupa of the Yadana Mon Aung Pagoda

❷ Nyaungshwe

Road Map D4. 296 miles (477 km) SW of Mandalay, to the north of Inle Lake. ⚑ 12,000. ✈ Mandalay International. ✈ Heho Airport, 19 miles (31 km) west. 🚉 Shwenyaung, 7 miles (12 km) north. 🚌 🚕 five-day market. **Note:** a fee must be paid on entering the town and lake area.

Nyaungshwe is the principal hub for Inle Lake, to whose northern shore it is joined by a 3.5-mile (5.5-km) feeder canal. Fleets of motorized long-tailed boats leave on sightseeing trips throughout the day from the jetties lining the waterway's banks, and the sound of their engines churning through the green-blue water has become characteristic of the town.

Set on an orderly grid plan, Nyaungshwe is bisected by Yone Gyi Road, a broad main street running east–west, lined by open-fronted hardware shops, restaurants, and cafés. Northeast of the point where it crosses Main Road, the principal

north–south axis, is **Mingalar Market**, the town's main source of fresh produce, sold by Pa-O and other ethnic minority villagers from the surrounding hills. Every five days, their ranks swell when the covered bazaar plays host to the area's rotating market, worth catching in the early morning, when the air is filled with the aroma of cooking as stallholders prepare Shan-noodle breakfasts for shoppers.

The sandy streets south of Yone Gyi Road are dotted with numerous stupa complexes and Buddhist monasteries, best explored by bicycle. The largest is the **Yadana Mon Aung Pagoda** on Phaung Daw Seiq Road, whose centerpiece is a gilded stupa of unusual octagonal stepped design, set in a white-walled compound. A couple of blocks east, along the banks of the Mong Li Canal, the adjacent **Hlaing Gu** and **Shwe Gu** monasteries are home to the 200 or so novices and monks who file through the town with their alms bowls each morning at dawn.

Prettiest of all the monasteries in the area, though, is the **Shwe Yaunghwe Kyaung**, about 1.5 miles (2.5 km) north of town. Retaining its splendid carved teak eaves and whitewashed staircases, the traditional *thein*, or ordination hall, is lined with unique oval windows, creating frames in which the young novices happily pose for photographs when foreign tourists visit the monastery.

View of the hill town of Kalaw, located on the edge of the Shan Plateau

❸ Kalaw

Road Map D4. 37 miles (61 km) W of Nyaungshwe. ⚑ 11,000. ✈ Mandalay International. ✈ Heho Airport, 20 miles (33 km) east. 🚌 🚕 five-day market.

Situated in the green hills on the western edge of the Shan Plateau, Kalaw was originally developed by the British as a summer retreat. Swathed in pine forest, groves of orange trees, and stands of bamboo, it remains a pleasant, if somewhat disheveled, hill town. Its Raj-era roots are underlined by a scattering of colonial houses and its cosmopolitan population of Tamils, Sikhs, and other Indians descended from workers brought here in the 19th century. The main reason to visit Kalaw, however, is for the chance to trek in the hills separating it from Inle Lake (see pp222–3). Wrapped in terraced fields and forest, picturesque wooden villages nestle on the slopes, most of them hours away from the nearest road, and inhabited by ethnic minorities such as the Pa-O and Danu.

Young monks walking through Nyaungshwe to collect alms

Slender, graceful Shan stupas in the Buddhist shrine at Ywama near Inle Lake ▶

The resident elephants of the Green Hill Valley Elephant Camp

❹ Green Hill Valley Elephant Camp

Road Map D4. 14 miles (24 km) out of Kalaw; 17 (5A) Kyaung St, Ahlone, Yangon (bookings). **Tel** (0) 973107278. 🛫 Mandalay Intl. 🛫 Heho Airport. 🚉 Kalaw. **Open** 8am–7pm daily. 🅿 ♿ partial. 🍴 🏪 🌐 ghvelephant.com

Myanmar may hold the world's largest population of domesticated elephants, but visitors rarely catch sight of one unless they travel to remote timber camps *(see p96)*. A more easily accessible alternative is the Green Hill Valley Elephant Camp, a sustainable tourism initiative set up to care for retired pachyderms by a vet who used to work for the government timber company in the hills around Kalaw. Among them are a few young, fit animals who take visitors on short rides through the orchid, bamboo, and teak jungle. As well as providing a humane home for its charges, the camp promotes education in local villages and oversees a forest recovery program – visitors are encouraged to help by planting a tree in the camp.

❺ Taunggyi

Road Map D3. 175 miles (283 km) SE of Mandalay. 👥 210,000. 🛫 Mandalay International. 🛫 Heho Airport, 22 miles (37 km) west. 🚉 🚌 ℹ Pa-O National Organization (PNO) office, West Circular Rd, four blocks W of Myoma Market (10am–4pm Mon–Sat). 🍴 🎭 May: Pa-O Rocket Festival; Nov: Balloon Festival.

The capital of Shan, Taunggyi sits on a plateau surrounded by sheer cliffs, crags, and high ridges. It was founded by the British in 1894 when the former administrative offices at Fort Stedman, on Inle Lake's eastern shore, were moved to this more elevated spot 4,712 ft (1,436 m) above sea level to take advantage of its cooler climate, widely regarded as the most pleasant in Myanmar. Taunggyi is today the fifth largest urban area in the country and has the feel of a big city. Pa-O and Intha people account for the majority of its inhabitants, although there has been a deluge of illegal immigrants from southwest China in recent years, many of them importing cheap manufactured goods overland from Yunnan. This merchandise can be seen at **Myoma Market**, in the center of town, which is Shan State's largest bazaar and a great place to experience local life.

Although few visitors choose to stay in the city, a couple of monuments warrant detours. Crowning a ridge to the east, the **Shwe Phone Pwint Pagoda** affords a fine panoramic view of Taunggyi. Just off National Highway 4 on the city's southeast edge, the **Sulamani Pagoda** is a huge white structure surmounted by a gilded corncob stupa inspired by the design of the stately Ananda Temple in Bagan; the Sulamani Pagoda was built in 1994 to commemorate the centenary of Taunggyi's founding.

❻ Kakku

Road Map D4. 28 miles (45 km) SE of Taunggyi. 🛫 Mandalay International. 🛫 Heho Airport. 🚌 ℹ PNO office, West Circular Rd, four blocks west of Myoma Market, Taunggyi (10am–4pm Mon–Sat). **Open** 7am–7pm daily. 🏛 fee per person plus separate fee per group for a guide; pay at Taunggyi's PNO office. 🍴 🚻 🏪 🏪 🎭 Mar: Kakku annual pagoda festival.

A recommended day trip from Taunggyi or Inle is the drive south to Kakku, a remote Buddhist site near the village of Mway Taw where thousands of medieval stupas stand in a walled compound above a bend in the river. There are said

---

Taunggyi Balloon Festival

The most famous, colorful, and potentially lethal celebration in Shan State is Taunggyi's Balloon Festival, held annually over the full moon of Tazaungmon (November). Legend says the festival originated 1,000 years ago, although the balloons are probably a more recent addition. Seen as offerings to the Sulamani *cetiya* (memorial) in one of the heavens of Buddhist cosmology, extravagantly decorated giant hot-air balloons made of rice paper are lit and released over a period of three nights, watched by crowds of 10,000 or more. The loudest cheers are reserved for the massive explosions that occur when the fireworks in the balloons ignite, sending rockets spiraling and showering cascades of sparks and fire onto onlookers below.

Launching lit paper lanterns into the night sky, Taunggyi Balloon Festival

---

The elongated, slender stupas of the Shan people at the sacred Buddhist site of Kakku

to be 2,548 monuments in total. Most of the pagodas date from the Bagan period (11th–13th centuries), but the largest, in slender Shan style, is believed to have been built by Ashoka, the Mauryan emperor of India, in the 3rd century BC. A permit to visit Kakku has to be obtained in advance from the PNO office in Taunggyi. The cost covers the services of a guide, in traditional Pa-O dress, who will explain the cultural significance of the site.

The vineyards of the Red Mountain Estate near the town of Nyaungshwe

❼ Wineries around Inle Lake

Road Map D4. ✈ Mandalay Intl. ✈ Heho Airport. Taxi from Inle/Taunggyi.

While Myanmar may not be internationally renowned for its viticulture, a couple of wineries around Inle Lake do a brisk trade supplying the country's top hotels and tourist resorts. Both lie an easy day trip away from Inle and offer tours and tastings. On the outskirts of Nyaungshwe, **Red Mountain** was set up in 2003 and comprises two separate estates where a team led by a French winemaker produces New

World-style vintages, from Shiraz-Tempranillo and Pinot Noir to Sauvignon Blanc and Chardonnay. The estate has a delightful restaurant where visitors can enjoy fine local cuisine after a tasting tour.

Closer to Taunggyi, **Aythaya** was set up in 1999 by a German entrepreneur. The site, at an altitude of 4,000 ft (1,200 m), was chosen for its climate and soil, which provide perfect growing conditions for Shiraz and Cabernet Sauvignon, as well as Sauvignon Blanc and Chenin Blanc. Visitors can tour

the site, dine in a pretty garden restaurant, and stay overnight in teak lodges that offer views over the estate and Aythaya Valley.

🏨 **Red Mountain Estate**
Mya Thein Tan, Taung Chay village, 3 miles (5 km) south of Nyaungshwe. **Tel** (81) 209366. **Open** 9am–6pm daily. 🍴 🚗 📷 🅦 redmountain-estate.com

🏨 **Aythaya Vineyard**
Off NH 4, Aythaya, west of Taunggyi. **Tel** (81) 208653. **Open** tours: 8:30am–6pm daily; restaurant: 8:30am–11pm daily. 🍷 🍴 🚗 📷 🍴
🅦 myanmar-vineyard.com

Trekking in the Inle Region

The hill tracts between Kalaw *(see p169)* and Inle Lake *(see pp166–8)* are interlaced with footpaths connecting the area's many villages, which are home to several ethnic minorities, including the Pa-O, Danu, Padaung, and Intha. Local travel agents and hotels arrange trekking trips through the region, offering foreign visitors the chance to witness life in these remote subsistence farming communities, most of which have changed little in decades. Winding across forest, orchards, terraced hillsides, and field borders, the trails pass through varied, and often bucolic landscapes, although it is the local scene rather than scenery that tends to be the main incentive to visit here. Routes range from three- to five-hour walks to ridgetop settlements around Kalaw to multistage, multiday treks (including a well-liked three-day route from Inle Lake to Kalaw), where walkers stay overnight in village houses and share meals with local families.

Trekkers walking on the popular route between Inle Lake and Kalaw

❽ Pindaya Caves

A popular day trip from Inle, Pindaya is a complex of three caverns honeycombing the flanks of a steep hillside. The largest of them, extending 490 ft (150 m) into the rock, has become a major Buddhist pilgrimage site due to the 8,000 gilded Konbaung-era Buddhas inside. Dating to the late 1700s, they come in a variety of sizes and styles, but it is the ensemble that makes the real impact. After a stiff walk up the 200-step pathway, or via the road and elevator, the sight of the golden statues vividly illuminated against the stalactite-encrusted ceiling and rock walls is one few visitors forget. After a tour of the caves, the restaurants along the breezy shores of nearby Pone Ta Lote Lake offer a welcome break.

Elevator to the cave entrance
Pilgrims' donations paid for an elevator that bypasses 130 of the steepest steps of the *zaungdan*.

Diorama showing Prince Kummabhaya shooting the spider

The Archer and the Spider

The diorama at the head of the path to the caves recalls the legend of the giant spider that captured seven princesses who were bathing in Pone Ta Lote Lake and imprisoned them in the Shwe Umin cave. Prince Kummabhaya of Inle Lake bravely battled the outsized arachnid, shooting it with a single deadly arrow. The name of the site, derived from *pinguya*, literally "taken the spider," was inspired by this event.

Main road up to the caves

Shwe Umin cave

KEY

① **Hsin Khaung Taung Kyaung**, at the foot of Pindaya Hill, is an elegant 200-year-old teak monastery built in traditional Shan style. Inside are bronze and bamboo Buddhas.

② **Archer and spider diorama**

③ **Zaungdan to the lake**

④ **Pone Ta Lote Lake**, lined with banyan trees, *zedis* (stupas), and temples, separates the cave complex from the main part of Pindaya village and the market area.

⑤ **Pindaya village**, spread around the lake, is a typical Shan market hub where locally made Shan paper parasols, pottery, and conical bamboo hats can be found.

Zaungdan to the caves
Chinthes, or leogryphs, flank the entrance to the main *zaungdan* (covered, stepped path) up to the Shwe Umin cave, a steep 30-minute ascent punctuated by small pavilions with traditional, multi-tiered *pyatthat* roofs.

★ Shwe Umin Cave
About 8,000 gilded Buddha images fill the interior of Shwe Umin (literally "Golden Cave"), the oldest of them dating from 1773. The cave's entrance has a spectacular wall of seated Buddhas, and the main cavern beyond is a labyrinth of statues and stupas.

Giant seated Buddha
Ih the cave north of Shwe Umin is a seated Buddha depicted in *bhumisparsha* mudra with a halo of flashing lights.

Nget Pyaw Taw Pagoda
This large complex of gleaming white and gold Shan stupas close to the start of the main eastern walkway to the caves is an impressive sight. *Nat* statues and monumental *taguntaing* towers crowned by gilded *hamsa* birds complete the ensemble.

The gilded bamboo Buddha of the Maha Nanda Kantha, Hsipaw

❾ Hsipaw

Road Map D3. 124 miles (200 km) NE of Mandalay. 🏔 22,000. 🚍 🚐

Set on the banks of the Dokhtawady River in the hills of northern Shan State, Hsipaw is a bustling little market town. It is the obvious place to break the long journey between Pyin U Lwin and Lashio, and it is the base for some excellent trekking. But Hsipaw is an attractive place in its own right, and increasing numbers of visitors are stopping here to absorb the local atmosphere in the lively markets and peaceful surrounding countryside. The town is the setting for *Twilight Over Burma*, the best-selling autobiography

of Austrian-born Inge Sargent, who in 1953 married Sao Kya Seng, the hereditary Shan prince or *saopha* (literally "sky lord"). Sao Kya Seng disappeared during the military coup in 1962, but his nephew, Mr. Donald still lives in the old **Shan Palace (East Haw)**. He and his wife, Mrs. Fern, show visitors around, talking about the history of the family and the building.

The hills around Hsipaw, home to numerous ethnic minorities, offer first-class trekking. Single and multiday trekking circuits are offered by local guesthouses and hotels, and are much less frequented than routes around Kalaw and Inle Lake. An ideal way to prepare for hiking in the

high country is to climb Five Buddha Hill, an ascent rewarded with a spectacular view over the town and valley. The **Thein Daung Pagoda** on the hill is popular for evening walks. In the old quarter of Myauk Myo, on Hsipaw's northern fringes, it is worth visiting the **Madahya Kyaung** monastery and the **Maha Nanda Kantha** opposite, whose bamboo Buddha is covered in gold leaf.

🏛 **Shan Palace (East Haw)**
Open 9am–noon, 3–6pm daily.
🎫 donation.

🛕 **Thein Daung Pagoda**
Open 7am–10pm daily.

🛕 **Madahya Kyaung and Maha Nanda Kantha**
Open daily.

Environs
Hsipaw's most important Buddhist shrine is the **Bawgyo Pagoda**. Thousands of Palaung minority people come for its annual festival, when the temple's four Buddhas are processed around the complex in decorated palanquins. A lively fair and market are held at the same time, where local handicrafts can be purchased.

🛕 **Bawgyo Pagoda**
5 miles (8 km) W of town. **Open** 7am–9pm daily. 🎊 Mar: annual festival over the full-moon period.

Women tend the irrigated rice paddies in the countryside around Hsipaw

⑩ Lashio

Road Map D3. 45 miles (73 km) NE of Hsipaw. 123,000. Lashio Airport.

The extent of the recent surge in Chinese migration to eastern Myanmar can most keenly be felt in Lashio, terminus of the railroad line from Mandalay. Only 66 miles (100 km) southwest of the Ruili–Muse border crossing point into Yunnan, the large market town now has a significant Chinese majority. During World War II, it played a crucial role in the engagement against the Japanese by forming a waystage on the famous Burma Road, by means of which the Allies were able to resupply Chiang Kai-Shek's Kuomintang nationalist forces. Today, contraband electronic goods, rather than the Chinese tea, walnuts, silk, and Yunnanese camphor of former times, pack the convoys of trucks lumbering to and from the frontier.

Little remains of the former Shan princely capital that stood here in the British era. The old, mainly wooden town burned to the ground in a massive fire in 1988. However, on a forested hill overlooking the southern flank of Lashio, stands a photogenic modern Chinese temple, the **Quin Yin Shang**, complete with upswept eaves and corpulent Buddha.

Quin Yin Shang
Open 7:30am–9pm daily.

Buddhist monk outside the painted exterior of the Wat Jong Kham stupa in Kengtung

⑪ Kengtung

Road Map E3. 262 miles (422 km) E of Taunggyi. 23,000. Kengtung Airport. May: Wat Jong Kham festival; Aug: Swing Festival (Women's New Year); Dec: New Year.

Off-limits for decades due to the long-running conflict between the Burmese Tatmadaw, Shan insurgents, and local opium barons, Kengtung (also spelled Kyaingtong; pronounced cheng-*dong*) is the capital of the Golden Triangle region and a springboard for exploring one of the most fascinating regions in Southeast Asia. Tai minorities (mostly Tai Lü, Tai Nuea, and Tai Khün) dominate the town itself, while surrounding hill villages are divided between Ann, Akha, Wa, and Palaung, all of whom retain their traditional ways of life. The best introduction to the various groups, who are distinguished by their elaborate costumes, is the daily **Gard Luang Central Market**, for which shoppers from the hill tracts don their finest clothes and jewelry. Local agencies arrange guided treks that take in a cross section of the area's minorities. Permits may be required, and overnight stays are not allowed, although this may change.

Kengtung itself makes a pleasant base for day trips. The road around Naung Tung Lake, in the center of town, affords great views of the somewhat ramshackle skyline, dominated by the graceful profile of the **Wat Jong Kham** (Zom Kham), a gilded stupa crowned by a golden *hti* (finial). The wat is said to date from a 13th-century migration from Chiang Mai's Lanna kingdom. At an intersection nearby stands the **Maha Myat Muni** (Wat Mahamuni), whose interior is richly decorated with traditional gold-leaf Tai murals on burgundy backgrounds. The Buddha here is a replica of Mandalay's shiny-faced Mahamuni. Near the lake's southwest corner, the **Yet Taw Mu**, an impressive 60-ft (18-m) standing Buddha swathed in gold leaf, is among the town's more distinctive landmarks.

Myanmar's Golden Triangle

After Afghanistan, Myanmar is the second largest producer of opium in the world, and the center of this lucrative trade is in the hill tracts of eastern Shan, the notorious Golden Triangle region where the borders of Myanmar, Laos, and Thailand intersect. Remnants of the defeated Kuomintang army ran the drugs trade in the 1950s and 1960s, but local warlords later took control in order to finance insurgencies against the state, often with the collusion of Myanmar government officials. Despite the concerted US-led crackdown of the 1990s and 2000s, opium is again flowing freely from these hills. Peasants earn five times as much by growing poppies rather than tea, rubber, or fruit. A 50 per cent rise in the price of raw opium in recent years has seen a surge in the land given over to its cultivation. Illicit opium money, laundered via Yangon banks and state-owned oil and gas companies, is said to percolate through almost every part of Myanmar's economy, including the tourism industry.

Opium poppies, grown widely in the hills of eastern Shan

NORTHERN MYANMAR

From the sun-scorched plains of the Ayeyarwady Valley to the eternal snows of the eastern Himalayas, Northern Myanmar encompasses a spectacular gamut of landscapes. Red pandas and tigers roam the dense jungles along the border with India, while endangered freshwater dolphins arc through the wakes of the ferries that remain this remote region's main form of long-distance transport. Over the past decade, however, few foreign travelers have experienced these natural wonders at close quarters due to the long-running armed conflict between Kachin insurgents and the Myanmar army.

Myanmar's far north has long been the prime source of the country's legendary teak, and although much of the forest cover disappeared during the 20th century, huge tracts survive. Carpeting the hills that hug the main river valleys of the Chindwin and Ayeyarwady, these jungles remain some of the most inhospitable, unexplored territory in the world, particularly the regions lining the border with India, which form the traditional homeland of the Naga tribes. Although for the most part converted by Christian missionaries, the Nagas have retained many aspects of their traditional way of life. Prior to the closure of the region to visitors, a handful of river cruise operators ran luxury steamer trips up the Chindwin River and included visits to the Naga New Year festivities in their itineraries.

Farther north, the Hukawng Valley forms the heart of a vast wildlife sanctuary that may, in time, become a major visitor attraction, along with the pristine valleys of the Hkakabo Razi National Park, site of Myanmar's highest mountains.

However, due to sporadic outbreaks of fighting between the army and Kachin insurgents, overland and river travel is often restricted. Until recently, foreigners were only permitted to reach Myitkyina and Putao by air, but backpackers are once again starting to take Ayeyarwady ferries between Mandalay and Myitkyina. However, with the peace accord between the Myanmar government and the Kachin Independence Army (KIA) still relatively untested, it remains to be seen whether travel along Myanmar's great northern artery will remain open to all.

The Ayeyarwady flowing past the red-roofed Nondo Zedi stupa on its banks at Kyaukmyaung

◀ A Tangkhul Naga in ceremonial finery celebrating the Naga New Year festival at Leshi village in the Naga Hills

Exploring Northern Myanmar

The great travel experience of the north is without doubt the journey along the Ayeyarwady from Myitkyina to Mandalay. Passing remote settlements, supply jetties, and gold-panners' encampments, the trip can take upward of a week on the old two- and three-story ferries of the Inland Water Transport (IWT) company. This route is rarely attempted by foreigners, which makes it a uniquely intense way of experiencing local life at close quarters. Ferries and privately owned motorboats also depart regularly from Bhamo. Kachin State's other main attractions, at least potentially, are two protected areas in the far north – the Hukawng Valley Tiger Reserve and Hkakabo Razi, Southeast Asia's highest peak. With the former off-limits due to the ongoing insurgency, only the latter is currently accessible.

Area illustrated

Iconic green-and-white IWT ferry at Kyaukmyaung on its way north to Bhamo

Getting Around

Uncertainty still surrounds the travel restrictions in Kachin State. The Mandalay–Myitkyna train line – via Katha and Indawgyi Lake – is usually open to foreigners. The river journey between Mandalay and Myitkyina is also technically open, but some travelers have not been allowed farther north along the Ayeyarwady than Kyaukmyaung. Road travel remains subject to controls; the only way to reach Putao in the far north is by air from Myitkyina. Daily flights connect Myitkyina with Mandalay and Yangon. Hkakabo Razi is accessible via expensive tours and trekking trips organized through hotels in Putao; access to the Naga Hills above the Chindwin River is granted via Burmese tour operators who set up bespoke transport and accommodations *(see p229)*.

Key

— Main road

= Other road

⋯ Railroad

▬ International border

▬ Regional border

△ Peak

For hotels and restaurants in this region see p205 and p215

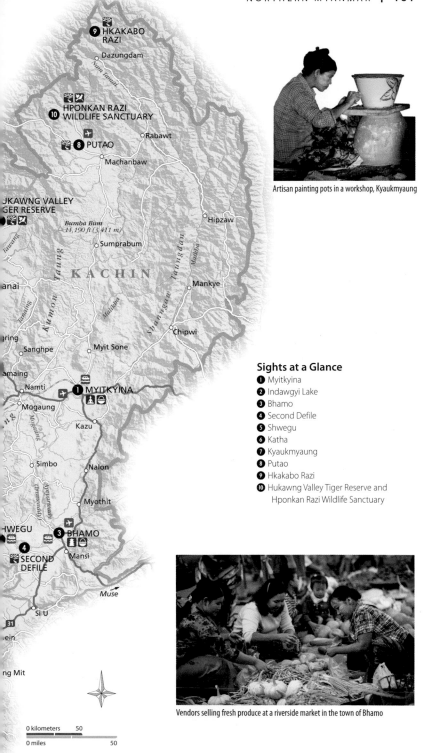

9 HKAKABO RAZI

Dazungdam

10 HPONKAN RAZI WILDLIFE SANCTUARY

8 PUTAO

Rabawt

Machanbaw

JKAWNG VALLEY GER RESERVE

Bumha Bum
11,190 ft (3,411 m)

Sumprabum

Hipzaw

K A C H I N

Kumon Taung

Shangaw Taungdan

Mankye

Chipwi

Myit Sone

Sanghpe

anai

jring

amaing

Namti

1 MYITKYINA

Mogaung

Kazu

Simbo

Nalon

Myothit

HWEGU

3 BHAMO

Mansi

4 SECOND DEFILE

Muse

Si U

31

ein

ng Mit

Artisan painting pots in a workshop, Kyaukmyaung

Sights at a Glance

1 Myitkyina
2 Indawgyi Lake
3 Bhamo
4 Second Defile
5 Shwegu
6 Katha
7 Kyaukmyaung
8 Putao
9 Hkakabo Razi
10 Hukawng Valley Tiger Reserve and
   Hponkan Razi Wildlife Sanctuary

Vendors selling fresh produce at a riverside market in the town of Bhamo

0 kilometers   50
0 miles   50

For additional map symbols *see back flap*

The delicate gilded spires of the Hsu Taung Pyi Pagoda in Myitkyina

❶ Myitkyina

Road Map D2. 345 miles (555 km) N of Mandalay. 🏛 63,000. ✈ Mandalay International. ➤ Myitkyina Airport, 5 miles (8 km) W of the center. 🚂 🚌 🛥 📷 Jan: Manau festival.

Capital of Kachin State and the main market town in the north of the country, Myitkyina has, since ancient times, been a center for trade between China and Myanmar. Lying on the west bank of the Ayeyarwady, it became the terminus of the British-built railroad line in the 1890s, and stands at the nexus of several major routes across the Himalayas to the north, including the Ledo Road to Assam *(see p185)*, constructed during World War II. This strategic importance explains why the town was the scene of a fierce battle in 1944 between a combined force of Chinese and Allied troops and Lieutenant General Honda's 33rd Imperial Japanese Army, during which it was virtually destroyed.

As a consequence, modern Myitkyina holds no sights of great note beyond the small but beautifully gilded **Hsu Taung Pyi Pagoda** overlooking the river, which has been restored by Japanese veterans.

A two-minute walk north of the stupa, the Sheduna Stadium is the venue for the nationally significant, annual **Manau Festival** *(see p43)*, held in mid-January, when teams of elaborately costumed dancers

from all of Kachin's seven tribal subgroups perform around tall totem poles, or *manautaing*. Although almost all of the Kachin population are Christian these days, the minority's animist roots are clearly discernible in styles of dress and dance. The Manau Festival is derived from a pre-Christian *nat* (nature spirit) worship ritual traditionally performed before the annual harvest, or for other important occasions such as weddings.

🏯 Hsu Taung Pyi Pagoda
Hsu Taung Pyi Pagoda Rd, two-minute walk S of Sheduna Stadium. **Open** 7am–10pm daily.

❷ Indawgyi Lake

Road Map C2. 105 miles (170 km) southwest of Myitkyina. ✈ Mandalay International. ➤ Myitkyina Airport. 🚌 🚂 Myitkyina to Hopin, then pick-up truck. Can hire cars in Myitkyina.

One of the few standout attractions in Kachin State

accessible to foreign visitors is beautiful Indawgyi Lake, a long day's journey by rail and road west of Myitkyina. Despite being marginally larger than Inle, the lake sees hardly any tourists and supports only a scattering of poor Kachin and Shan villages along its shores – a consequence of an old superstition stating that the waters were the home of a demon. Not until a Buddhist pagoda was built on an islet in the middle of the lake during the Konbaung era did people start to settle in the area. Connected to land by a narrow causeway that is only accessible during the dry season, the gilded **Shwe Myintzu Pagoda** has become a revered pilgrimage destination. Worshippers from all over the country travel here during Tabaung for the 10-day pagoda festival.

🏯 Shwe Myintzu Pagoda
1 mile (2 km) SE of Nampade village. **Open** daily. 📷 📷 Feb/Mar: annual pagoda festival.

Fisherman drawing in his nets on Indawgyi Lake

The Four Faces Pagoda, one of the modern Buddhist shrines in Bhamo

❸ Bhamo

Road Map D2. 119 miles (193 km), south of Myitkyina. 🏔 32,000. 🛫 Mandalay International. ✈ Bhamo Airport, 2 miles (3.5 km) to the east. 🚌 ⛴

The largest town on the Ayeyarwady between Myitkyina and Mandalay, Bhamo is also the one closest to the Chinese border, 40 miles (60 km) east. Traders, merchants, emissaries, and holy men have for hundreds of years traveled here along the Daying Jiang Valley to reach the mighty river. Among the visitors in medieval times was Marco Polo, who penned an account of the route in the 13th century. Then, as now, jade mined in the surrounding hills dominated the region's trade.

Evidence of the site's ancient commercial importance lies 3 miles (5 km) north at **Old Bhamo** (Bhamo Myo Haung), where the ruins of a lost city are scattered around two gold-tipped stupas, the Eikkhawtaw and Shwekyaynei pagodas, believed to date from the Pyu era (1st century BC–9th century AD). Modern Bhamo was gutted by fire in the 1990s and holds little to detain visitors, although its daily market, attended by ethnic minority people from the nearby hills, is worth a browse early in the morning. On the riverfront, a large open-air pottery bazaar provides the town's best photo opportunity.

❹ Second Defile

Road Map D2. 37 miles (61 km) SW of Bhamo. 🛫 Mandalay International. ✈ Bhamo Airport. 🚌

One of the most beautiful stretches on the Ayeyarwady River lies a couple of hours downstream from Bhamo, where the river narrows to just 330 ft (100 m) as it flows through a belt of thickly wooded mountains. Water levels along this scenic 7.5-mile (13.5-km) segment, known as the Second Defile (the First Defile lies north of Bhamo), can reach nearly 200 ft (60 m) in the rainy season, when boat-men have to keep a close eye on the famous green and red Parrot's Beak warning marker painted on a rock – if the bird is not visible, the flood is dangerously high and vessels are obliged to turn back.

Equally emblematic of the Second Defile is the impressive 985-ft- (300-m-) high **Nat Myet Hna Taung** or Welatha Cliff, a soaring limestone escarpment reminiscent of those that line parts of the Mekong River in neighboring Laos.

❺ Shwegu

Road Map D2. 63 miles (102 km) W of Bhamo. 🏔 16,500. 🛫 Mandalay International. ✈ Bhamo Airport. 🚌 ⛴

Just west of the Second Defile, Shwegu is a remote agricultural town on the Ayeyarwady's south bank where IWT ferries make an obligatory stop. Much of the fruit and rice sold in the local market is grown on the sandy soil of the two islands visible in the river opposite. The smaller, **Kyundaw**, holds the remnants of between 6,000 and 7,000 old stupas from the Bagan era of the 11th–13th centuries. While some have recently been renovated and sport coats of whitewash, most remain in a state of charismatic dereliction.

Stacks of decorated pottery for sale in the open-air market in Shwegu

Irrawaddy Dolphins

The Upper Ayeyarwady is among the last places in the world to support a breeding population of Irrawaddy dolphins (*Orcaella brevirostris*). Only 60 to 70 of these rare cetaceans survive along this stretch of the river, where they have evolved a unique bond with local fishermen. When summoned by a knocking of an oar on the side of the boat, the dolphins drive shoals of fish into the waiting nets, a service for which the animals receive a share of the spoils. Sightings are most common along a 46-mile (74-km) stretch of the Ayeyarwady between Kyaukmyaung and Mingun, officially designated as a sanctuary for this group, which has been listed as Critically Endangered on the IUCN Red List of Threatened Species.

Irrawaddy dolphin swimming alongside a fishing boat

A view of Katha, once home to George Orwell, from the Ayeyarwady River

➏ Katha

Road Map C2. 196 miles (317 km) southwest of Bhamo. 🚹 29,000. ✈ Mandalay Intl. ✈ Bhamo Airport. 🚌 Mandalay to Naba, then bus. 🚤

One of the more appealing stops on the Upper Ayeyarwady river journey, Katha surveys the river from its high bank, over-shadowed by the densely wooded hills of the Gangaw Taung to the west. This quiet, tree-lined administrative town is perhaps best known for being the place to which the British writer George Orwell was posted in 1926–7 as a District Superintendent in the Imperial Indian Police. His short sojourn here inspired his 1934 autobiographical novel, *Burmese Days*. A few buildings mentioned in the book still stand, including the half-timbered British Club, the double-storied police commissioner's house, and the Anglican church.

Stonework logo of the British Club, Katha

➐ Kyaukmyaung

Road Map C3. 28 miles (46 km) N of Mandalay. 🚹 11,000. ✈ Mandalay International. 🚉 Shwebo. 🚌 🚤 🚣

About an hour's drive north of Mandalay, Kyaukmyaung is a small river port renowned for its ceramics, especially the huge, kiln-fired pots which were used to transport oil, fish paste, and other foodstuffs for export. Known as Martaban jars, these distinctive containers are characterized by their glossy brown glaze and sweeping floral designs. Hundreds of newly turned specimens lie drying on the riverbank and outside the potteries in the Ngwe Nyein area, where visitors are welcome to watch the manufacturing process. It is thought that these giant receptacles were first made here in the 18th century, after King Alaungpaya brought families of potters back from his conquest of Bago (Pegu).

Large Martaban jars drying on the banks of the Ayeyarwady in Kyaukmyaung

➑ Putao

Road Map D1. 520 miles (837 km) N of Mandalay. 🚹 10,000. ✈ Mandalay International. ✈ Putao Airport. ℹ Putao Trekking House, No. 424/425 Htwe San Lane, Kaung Kahtaung, Putao, (0) 98400138. 🌐 **putaotrekkinghouse.com**

In the far north of Kachin State, 220 miles (345 km) beyond Myitkyina, Putao is a distant outpost reached by very few foreign travelers. Thanks to its proximity to the snow-clad mountains of the Myanmar–China border, the town holds great potential as a hub for trekking trips.

In British times, Putao was known as Fort Hertz, after William Axel Hertz, the intrepid District Commissioner who first mapped the area in 1888. Not much has changed here since then, beyond the addition of an airstrip – famous in the annals of World War II for being the only one in Burma not taken by the Japanese, and playing a role in the legendary Allied airlift over the "Hump" of the eastern Himalayas to resupply Kuomintang forces.

Weather permitting, flights from Mandalay land here twice a week – the only sanctioned route into the region for foreign nationals. Trekking must be pre-arranged through a Yangon-based agency or one of the few hotels in the town *(see pp222–3)*; fees generally include permits, excursions, and food. The hotels also organize trips to waterfalls, local beauty spots, minority villages, and timber camps.

The icy summit of Hkakabo Razi, thought to be the highest mountain in Southeast Asia

⑨ Hkakabo Razi

Road Map D1. Hkakabo Razi base camp is about 200 miles (320 km) N of Putao. 🛈 Putao Trekking House, Htwe San Lane, Kaung Kahtaung, Putao. 🕸 **putaotrekkinghouse.com**

Putao's northern horizon is dominated by the convoluted, ice-encrusted summit of Hkakabo Razi, Myanmar's highest mountain at 19,294 ft (5,881m). The first ascent of the peak was made by a Japanese expedition as recently as 1996. In the same year, American conservationist Alan Rabinowitz surveyed the area's wildlife and discovered herds of

Leaf deer found in Northern Myanmar

Himalayan blue sheep, takin, red panda, stone martens, and an endemic species of leaf deer *(Muntiacus putaoensis)* hitherto unknown to science. His findings led to the creation of a national park, which now nominally protects a 1,500-sq-mile (2,424-sq-km) tract of rain forest and Alpine valleys around the mountain.

A 10-day round trip is required to reach Hkakabo Razi's base camp, and access to the park is permitted only to those foreign travelers who are on prearranged tours, either via government-approved agents or through the two hotels currently operating in Putao.

⑩ Hukawng Valley Tiger Reserve and Hponkan Razi Wildlife Sanctuary

Road Map D1. 124 miles (200 km) NW of Myitkyina.

Dubbed the "Indiana Jones of Wildlife Protection" by *Time* magazine, Alan Rabinowitz was also the driving force behind the Hukawng Valley Tiger Reserve and Hponkan Razi Wildlife Sanctuary, a vast, contiguous 8,452-sq-mile (13,602-sq-km) tract of swampy rain forest and jungle-covered mountains that forms the world's largest tiger reserve. When it was set up by the Myanmar government in 1999, it was estimated that around 100 tigers inhabited the area. However, since then, a combination of poaching and habitat erosion through logging and mining has resulted in a sharp fall in numbers. Some Myanmar experts have even suggested that the creation of the sanctuary was merely a ruse by the Tatmadaw military regime to wrest control of the area – and its lucrative uranium, oil, and teak reserves – from the Kachin Independence Army (KIA).

Visits to the Hukawng Valley are currently not allowed, although following the recent reduction in hostilities between the KIA and the Myanmar government, restrictions may well be relaxed in the future.

The Ledo Road

The great wilderness of jungle, roadless valleys, and peaks in the far north of Myanmar was a region notorious among US airmen during World War II as the "Hump." In 1942, dozens of cargo planes vanished while flying missions across it to resupply troops in northern Burma and China. The Allies, under the command of General "Vinegar Joe" Stilwell, were keen to replace the airlift with an all-weather overland route from India. A new road through the 3,727-ft (1,136-m) Pangsau "Hell" Pass over the Patkai Range dividing Assam and the Hukawng Valley was key to the project's success. In December 1942 work began on the Ledo Road, named after the Assamese town where it began. Conditions in the jungle were appalling. By the time the first bulldozers reached Shwingbyiang in Burma a year later, 1,100 US servicemen and many more local laborers had died from malaria and Japanese sniper bullets. Eventually, the Ledo Road reached Myitkyina to link with the old Burma Road from Bhamo to Kunming in China, a total distance of 1,079 miles (1,736 km), which the first convoy completed in 1945. As a result of the insurgencies on both sides of the Myanmar–India border, the route has been closed for decades.

A 1945 US military booklet by S/Sgt C. M. Buchanan and Sgt J. R. McDowell

SOUTHEASTERN MYANMAR

Extending from the mouth of the Sittaung River to the Isthmus of Kra, Southeastern Myanmar encompasses three states. Mon State is home to the sublime Kyaiktiyo Pagoda, the region's main pilgrimage spot. Kayin offers visitors the otherworldly sight of karst outcrops rising from lush paddy, while Tanintharyi's magnificent landscape includes the myriad coral-fringed islands and islets of the unspoiled Myeik Archipelago.

Facing Yangon across the Gulf of Mottama (Martaban) is the heartland of the Mon, who until the rise of Bagan had been Burma's most powerful ethnic group, but were thereafter confined to an ever-shrinking enclave around Thaton port. Today, Mawlamyine, known as Moulmein in colonial times, is the Mon capital, while the state itself occupies a mere sliver of lowland tapering down the Andaman coast. During World War II, the hills lining the Thai border inland became notorious as the site of the "Death Railway," built by the Japanese in the 1940s using a slave labor force of Allied PoWs. Overgrown for most of its length, the rail route sees far fewer visitors today than the one leading to the top of Kyaiktiyo Hill north of Mawlamyine, where a golden boulder perched precariously above a cliff is the region's principal pilgrimage destination.

Buttressed between Mon State and the Dawna Hills along the Thai frontier, Kayin is the stronghold of the Karen, who, since Independence, have been engaged in a war with the Myanmar army that has forced thousands of them into refugee camps. While a 2012 ceasefire promises a long-awaited opening up of this beautiful region, currently Kayin's only officially accessible area is the karst landscape around Hpa-an, an area of extraordinary limestone rock formations and caves spreading from the banks of the Thanlwin.

Farther south, Tanintharyi extends to Thailand, its pristine coastline of sand and coral tracked by forested hills. Offshore, the Myeik (Mergui) Archipelago, where Moken sea gypsies still lead a nomadic lifestyle, is regarded by many as the area of Myanmar most likely to be transformed by tourism over the coming years.

The spectacular Myeik Archipelago, offering opportunities for diving, snorkeling, and kayaking

◀ The delicately balanced golden rock on Kyaiktiyo Hill, one of Myanmar's most revered sites

Exploring Southeastern Myanmar

The undisputed highlight of Southeastern Myanmar is Kyaiktiyo, site of the fabled Golden Rock Pagoda, a shrine at its most ethereal at dawn or dusk. A half-day drive away is Mawlamyine (Moulmein), a coastal city with great Burmese character and a string of hilltop pagodas with spectacular views over the mouth of the Thanlwin River. A short detour inland leads over the Kayin State border to Hpa-an, springboard for forays into spellbinding karst country to the southeast. The unspoiled Myeik Archipelago is currently off-limits to all but keen divers on cruises and tours for which special permits issued in Yangon are required. Most of these trips are run out of Ranong or Phuket, Thailand, but anyone traveling from other parts of Myanmar can usually join the boats in Kawthaung.

Area illustrated

Bago

KYAIKTIYO GOLDEN ROCK PAGODA

Sittaung

8

Ki

Kyaikto

Taunkz

Zokth

Gulf of Mottama (Martaban)

Getting Around

Foreigners may travel freely in Mon State, and from Mawlamyine to Hpa-an (in Kayin State) on local buses and ferries. Travelers to Kyaiktiyo can choose between regular buses and a dedicated air-conditioned express train that leaves Yangon on Saturday and returns on Sunday. Tickets are cheap but must be bought in advance at Yangon's Myanmar Railways booking office *(see p239)*. In Tanintharyi foreigners are only allowed to visit the towns on National Highway 8, and can take a bus or train from Mawlamyine to Dawei, then a bus to Myeik (Mergui), and then a boat to Kawthaung. However, the easiest way is to take one of the daily flights from Yangon. The Myeik Archipelago can only be explored on prearranged cruises or expensive live-aboard diving tours *(see p223)*.

Sights at a Glance

1. Kyaiktiyo Golden Rock Pagoda *pp190–91*
2. Mawlamyine (Moulmein)
3. Thanbyuzayat
4. Hpa-an
5. Mount Zwegabin
6. Saddar Cave
7. Kyauk Kalap Pagoda
8. Dawei
9. Myeik (Mergui)
10. Kawthaung

Buddhist shrine located in the Saddar Cave, a vast limestone cavern near the town of Hpa-an

For hotels and restaurants in this region see p205 and p215

Buddha statues at the start of the trail up Mount Zwegabin

Andaman
Sea

THAILAND

DAWEI **8**

TANINTHARYI

MYEIK
(MERGUI) **9**

KAWTHAUNG **10**

Pyintha

Chaungnakwa

Shwegwun

lin

8

eik

KAYIN

nggala

Thaton

85

HPA-AN

4

Yinnyein

KYAUK KALAP
PAGODA **7** **5** MOUNT
ZWEGABIN

MON **6** SADDAR CAVE

Nwa-la-bon
Taung Pagoda

Paung

Mutkyi

Kawpamagon

Myawaddy

Zatabyin

Gyaing

Khindan

Kalwi

2 MAWLAMYINE
(MOULMEIN)

Chaungzon

8

Atran

Kadonsit

Kyauktalon
Kyaung

Win Sein Taw Ya

Hintha
Island

Mudon

Kada

Andaman
Sea

Kamawet

Kyaikkami

Nipado

Kwanhlar

3 THANBYUZAYAT

Setse

Karoppi

8

↓ *Dawei*

0 kilometers   20

0 miles   20

The gilded rocks of Nwa-la-bon Taung Pagoda

Key

━━ Highway

━━ Main road

━━ Other road

━━ Railroad

━━ International border

━━ Regional border

For additional map symbols *see back flap*

❶ Kyaiktiyo Golden Rock Pagoda

One of the most iconic sights Southeast Asia has to offer is that of the gravity-defying Golden Rock Pagoda, perched on its ledge above a jungle-cloaked valley, seemingly about to plunge into the void. From the roadhead at Kinpun, an arduous six- to seven-hour hike takes visitors up the Paung Laung ridge to the rock; less devout pilgrims are carried up on litters or take one of the pickup trucks that grind up a bumpy, potholed track for an hour to the mountaintop. Visitors who spend the night in or near the pagoda will be well placed to see the ethereal sight of the setting or rising sun illuminating the richly gilded boulder, which is the third most revered site in Myanmar after the Shwedagon Pagoda in Yangon and the Mahamuni Temple in Mandalay.

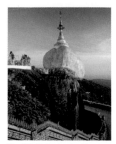

The gilded balancing boulder, revered by Burmese Buddhists

Lower terrace
A paved walkway has been built around the base rock from which female visitors, prohibited from touching the boulder, may admire the pagoda at close quarters, as well as the amazing views of the forested valley below.

KEY

① **Pilgrims' bazaars**, both in the main approach and adjacent village, are crammed with restaurants and shops selling fruit, flower, and incense offerings to pilgrims.

② **The Mountain Top Hotel** is the most comfortable place to spend the night within easy reach of the boulder; foreigners are not allowed to join the Burmese pilgrims who sleep on the main terrace.

③ **Viewing pavilion** on the upper terrace.

④ **Polished bells** strung with red ribbons are a popular pilgrim offering, and are tied to spikes on the railings of the upper terrace.

⑤ **A narrow causeway** flanked by low railings leads to the boulder. Only men are permitted to cross it.

⑥ **The famous golden boulder**, measuring 50 ft (15 m) around, is balanced on a rock decorated with a lotus pattern.

⑦ **The 24-ft- (7-m-) tall pagoda on top of the boulder** enshrines a hair of the Buddha and is, contrary to appearances, the main object of veneration rather than the boulder.

The route
Devout pilgrims walk all the way to the top from Kinpun, a few hire sedan chairs to carry them up, and the majority squeeze into trucks with slat benches that run through the day to bus stops just below and at the summit.

★ The gilded boulder

The culmination of any visit to Kyaiktiyo for men is the chance to apply gold leaf to the rock. Large protuberances of solid gold have, as a result, built up around the base of the boulder.

The *taguntaing*
With images of Thagyamin, king of the *nats*, around its base, and a *hamsa* bird crowning its tip, this monumental column reaffirms the subordination of animist *nat* spirits to Theravada Buddhism.

★ Festival of 9,000 Lamps

The number of pilgrims visiting Kyaiktiyo soars during the annual pagoda festival (held over the full moon of Tabaung in March), when the upper terrace is illuminated by 9,000 candles.

The Legend of Kyaiktiyo

The hair of the Buddha now secreted inside the Golden Rock Pagoda is said to have been given as a gift to King Tissa in the 11th century by a hermit, who had kept it for 100 years in his topknot. The holy man asked the king to find a boulder in the shape of a head upon which the hair could be enshrined. Tissa, who was blessed with magical powers, dived to the bottom of the ocean where he found a suitable rock and magically transported it to its present position. The weight of the sacred hair is believed to prevent the boulder from toppling into the ravine below.

❷ Mawlamyine (Moulmein)

Road Map D5. 195 miles (314 km)
E of Yangon on National Highway 8.
🏙 326,000. ✈ Yangon Mingaladon;
Mawlamyine Airport, SE edge of town.
🚉 🚌

Known as Moulmein in colonial times, Mawlamyine became the capital of British Lower Burma when it was ceded by the Konbaungs as part of the Treaty of Yandabo, following the First Anglo-Burmese War of 1824–6. Strategically sited at the mouth of the Thanlwin (Salween) River, the town provided a convenient harbor for steamers traveling between the cities of Calcutta (India) and Singapore, and on to the Straits Settlements and the Pacific. Among the legions of linen-suited passengers to have admired its gilded hilltop pagodas en route to more distant corners of the empire was Rudyard Kipling, who immortalized it in his popular 1892 poem "Mandalay." George Orwell was also briefly a resident of the town in 1926, while he was serving as a police officer in Burma. It is believed that he drew on an experience he had here for his famous 1936 essay "Shooting an Elephant."

The great bridge spanning the estuary at Mawlamyine, carrying road and rail traffic

Since Independence, the town has become the capital of Mon State, and is one of the largest cities of Myanmar. The sizable Anglo-Burmese community for which Mawlamyine was once known dispersed long ago, but the old quarter overlooking the riverfront retains plenty of faded charm. Dominating its low-rise, tin-roofed skyline from atop Pagoda Hill inland is the huge **Kyaikthanlan Pagoda**, a classic Mon-style stupa founded in the 9th century, but enlarged several times since. A fancily decorated elevator leads to its terrace, a popular spot for a sunset stroll from where the views across the Thanlwin are glorious.

Farther north along the hill stands the equally grand **Mahamuni Temple**, whose glittering central shrine houses a much-revered replica of Mandalay's Mahamuni, donated by Mibayagyi, one of Mindon's queens. During the British annexation of Upper Burma, after Thibaw was deposed and the court exiled in 1885, she is said to have pined for her beloved Mahamuni statue, and commissioned this replica image in 1904.

🔆 Kyaikthanlan Pagoda
Pagoda Hill, just off NH 8.
Open 7am–10pm daily. ♿ via the elevator. 📷 🏛

🏛 Mahamuni Temple
Pagoda Hill, just off NH 8.
Open 7am–10pm daily. 📷 🏛

Environs
Flowing 1,749 miles (2,825 km) from the Tibetan Plateau to its mouth in the Gulf of Mottama (Martaban), the **Thanlwin (Salween)** is one of the world's longest free-flowing rivers – as

Dramatic limestone outcrop housing the Kyauktalon Kyaung pagoda, offering superb views of the surrounding countryside

For hotels and restaurants in this region see p205 and p215

yet, not a single dam blocks its route to the sea. Appropriately enough, the great bridge spanning the estuary at Mawlamyine, where the river meets the Andaman Sea, is the longest in Myanmar and carries both the highway and main rail line north.

Overlooking the coastal transport artery from a hilltop inland is the **Nwa-la-bon Taung Pagoda**, a golden boulder temple much less well known than the one at Kyaiktiyo. It consists of three gilded rocks balanced on top of each other. A fleet of 4WD trucks, with wooden slats in the rear for passengers, waits to shuttle pilgrims to the summit, which offers fabulous views of the coastal plain and river-mouth.

On a scrub-covered hillside south of Mawlamyine, just off the main highway at Yadana Taung, reclines a huge, red-robed Buddha, **Win Sein Taw Ya**, depicted at the moment of *parinirvana*, or attaining freedom from the cycle of rebirth. Measuring 600 ft (180 m) in length, it is the largest statue of its kind anywhere in the world and, like the one at Bodhi Tataung near the town of Monywa *(see p158)*, is hollow. Pilgrims may venture inside to see dioramas depicting scenes from moral tales and the life of the Buddha.

Rising sheer from the rice paddies across the National Highway from Win Sein Taw Ya, a dramatic outcrop of limestone is the site of a small but

Old locomotive marking the starting point of the "Death Railway" at Thanbyuzayat

spectacularly located pagoda called the **Kyauktalon Kyaung**. A flight of whitewashed steps leads to the summit of the rock, from where the views across the surrounding fields to the river are superb.

🧍 Nwa-la-bon Taung Pagoda
17 miles (28 km) NW of Mawlamyine, via a cement road branching off National Highway 8 (NH 8) between Kawpamagon and Mutkyi.
Open 7:30am–9:30pm daily.
Closed during the monsoons. 📷

🧍 Win Sein Taw Ya
Yadana Taung, 12 miles (20 km) S of Mawlamyine on NH 8.
Open 7am–9pm daily. 📷 📷

🧍 Kyauktalon Kyaung
12 miles (20 km) S of Mawlamyine on NH 8. **Open** 7am–10pm daily.

❹ Thanbyuzayat

Road Map D5. 40 miles (65 km) S of Mawlamyine on NH 8. 🚌 **Open** cemetery: 7am–5pm daily. ♿

The infamous "Death Railway" connected with the Burmese rail network at Thanbyuzayat. The large **War Cemetery** on the northwest side of town is the final resting place of 3,617 of the estimated 16,000 Allied PoWs who died working on the line. Memorials on the site also feature dog tags taken from some of those who were buried where they fell beside the tracks. Maintained by the Commonwealth War Graves Commission, the immaculate headstones are set amid lawns around a single white cross.

Burma's "Death Railway"

One of the most notorious human rights atrocities committed during World War II was the use of slave labor by the Japanese to carve a rail link between Bangkok and Rangoon in 1942–3. The line was later called the "Death Railway" because so many lives were lost during its construction.

Allied submarines off Malaysia made it difficult for the Japanese to resupply troops in Burma, so it was decided that Allied PoWs and Asian workers would be used to cut a rail track through 258 miles (415 km) of jungle and mountains. Begun in late 1942, the work was carried out at great speed in appalling conditions. The men worked 24-hour shifts, used shovels and pickaxes instead of

Gravestones and memorials at the Thanbyuzayat War Cemetery

mechanical equipment, and were fed meager rations of rotten meat and rice. Disease, exhaustion, starvation, and torture killed 16,000 PoWs and around 90,000 Malaysian and Burmese laborers over the 15 months it took to finish the job. The most severe loss of life occurred when 69 men were beaten to death and hundreds more died from disease during the construction of a cutting called the "Hell Fire Pass" through the watershed ridge of the Tenasserim Hills. Shortly after it was finished, the Allies bombed the line and it is no longer in use.

Giant reclining Buddha statue at Win Sein Taw Ya, the largest of its kind in the world

The Thanlwin flowing through Hpa-an, with Mount Zwegabin in the background, the tallest of the hills around the town

❹ Hpa-an

Road Map D5. 186 miles (300 km) SE of Yangon. 🏠 52,000. ✈ Yangon Mingaladon; Mawlamyine. 🚌 🚢

A peaceful, predominantly Karen market town on the banks of the Thanlwin (Salween) River, Hpa-an features on the southeastern tourist circuit due to its proximity to the spectacular karst terrain of the surrounding countryside. Apart from the unremarkable Shweyinhmyaw Pagoda, whose terrace juts out over the river, sights are thin on the ground. The most enticing option for a late-afternoon stroll is the trip across the river to **Hpa-pu Mountain**, a prominent peak on the far side of the Thanlwin whose summit may be reached via a stepped path in a little under half an hour. The reward for the effort is sweeping, magnificent views, over the river and beyond to Mount Zwegabin.

❺ Mount Zwegabin

Road Map D5. The trailhead begins 5 miles (9.5 km) south of Hpa-an at Zwegabin Junction. **Note:** carry sufficient food and water for the climb.

The definitive landform among the many outlandish limestone outcrops and massifs blistering the otherwise flat terrain beyond Hpa-an is Mount Zwegabin (2,373 ft/732 m), whose forested flanks surge upward from the vivid green rice fields. Legend has it that the hill is the home of local spirits and souls.

Reached via a steep flight of stone and cement steps, Zwegabin's summit holds a small, lonely monastery, staffed by a couple of young monks who welcome visits from the odd party of pilgrims willing to brave the heat and the voracious troops of macaques that patrol the approach path. After a stiff hike of around two hours, the effort is repaid with an astounding view that is at its most sublime around sunrise. To reach the top in time, however, visitors will have to set out in the middle of the night, as foreigners are no longer permitted to spend the night in the monastery.

❻ Saddar Cave

Road Map D5. 17 miles (27 km) SE of Hpa-an via Naung Lon village. **Open** daily.

Southwest of Hpa-an, just off the main road to Eindu, is the Saddar Cave, the largest grotto in the area. A pair of monumental white elephants flank the entrance to the cavern, a reference to the local legend that an elephant king once took shelter inside it. Narrow, winding staircases lead from there through a series of immense chambers encrusted with Buddha statues and impressive rock formations and populated by bats, until the passage emerges on the far side of the mountain at a small lake – a magical experience.

The passage through the Saddar Cave emerging at the lake on the far side of the mountain

Kyauk Kalap Pagoda perched on an outcrop of limestone outside Hpa-an

Boats leave from Myeik's harbor for Kadan, a twin-peaked barrier island opposite the mouth of the river. The port is also the main embarkation point for the 800 or more islands of the stunning **Myeik Archipelago**, one of the last pristine marine wilderness zones in Southeast Asia. The region, homeland of the Moken sea gypsies, is strictly off-limits to land-based tourists; some cruises and diving tours travel there from Ranong and Phuket, Thailand (see p223).

⑦ Kyauk Kalap Pagoda

Road Map D5. 7 miles (12 km) south of Hpa-an. **Open** 8am–noon and 1–5pm daily.

Rising from the glassy waters of an artificial lake, the golden Kyauk Kalap Pagoda caps a thin, knobbly finger of limestone draped in vegetation, a spectacle all the more amazing for its backdrop of beautiful karst outcrops. Visitors are permitted to visit the small monastery at its base and climb to the top for views of Mount Zwegabin. The resident monks are vegetarians and animal lovers, which explains the colony of rabbits hopping around the grounds.

⑧ Dawei

Road Map D6. 383 miles (617 km) SE of Yangon. 🚇 140,000. ✈ Yangon Mingaladon; Mawlamyine. 🚄 Dawei Airport. 🚌 🚢 from Myiek, Kawthaung.

The provincial town of Dawei was a port for the Siamese Sukhothai and Ayutthaya kingdoms from the 13th to 16th centuries, and later came under the control of the British, who knew it as Tavoy. Today it is a sleepy, low-rise settlement with colonial-era shophouses. North of the center stands the huge gilded **Shwe Taung Zar Pagoda**.

Around 7 miles (12 km) west of Dawei is **Maungmagan beach**, where simple shacks serve seafood. Further south are numerous deserted beaches.

⑨ Myeik (Mergui)

Road Map D7. 569 miles (916 km) SE of Yangon. 🚇 210,000. ✈ Yangon Mingaladon; Mawlamyine. 🚄 Myeik Airport. 🚌 🚢 from Kawthaung.

Myeik (formerly Mergui) juts into the mouth of the Tanintharyi River – a strategic location from which it dominated the area's maritime trade for centuries. To avoid the pirates and tropical storms that plagued the Malacca Straits, the kings of Siam used Myeik as the main port for Ayutthaya, transferring goods by road through the peninsular jungles.

Today the **Theindawgyi Pagoda**, a slender, gilded stupa on a low rise above the covered riverfront market, is the only noteworthy sight in Myeik.

⑩ Kawthaung

Road Map D7. 500 miles (804 km) by air from Yangon. 🚇 56,000. ✈ Yangon Mingaladon; Mawlamyine. 🚄 Kawthaung Airport. 🚌 🚢 from Myeik and Ranong (Thailand).

Kawthaung is the main border crossing point between Myanmar and Thailand, with a population fluent in both languages. The tourists milling around are nearly all on visa runs from Ranong, Thailand, on the opposite side of the Kra Buri River. For those who stop off for a couple of days, it is worth visiting the **Pyi Taw Aye Pagoda**. Standing on a low rise west of the harbor, this Mon-style stupa is set in a compound with gleaming ceramic floors. The interior features dazzling glass mosaics.

The Moken Sea Gypsies

Moken sea gypsies diving in the Myeik Archipelago

In the far southeast of Myanmar, the beautiful Myeik (Mergui) Archipelago is the last bastion of an indigenous minority whose nomadic lifestyle has earned them the nickname "sea gypsies." Somewhere between 2,000 and 3,000 Moken, as they refer to themselves, live amid the turquoise waters and coral reefs of the islands, traveling between fishing sites and sheltered mooring places in long-tailed houseboats. Their ability to free-dive to astonishing depths and hold their breath underwater while spear fishing is the stuff of legend. Many Moken children do not set foot on dry land for years, unless accompanying their parents to trade seafood for rice in markets on the mainland. Widespread resettlement programs initiated by the Myanmar government in recent years have led to the creation of dedicated Moken villages on the archipelago, an attempt to clear the sea gypsies from areas rich in oil and gas. Despite this, many continue to roam as they have for centuries.

TRAVELERS' NEEDS

WHERE TO STAY

Accommodation options in Myanmar cover the full spectrum, from boutique luxury to run-down guesthouses. While the big city hotels tend to be characterless, international-style blocks, the more appealing places are those with a Burmese atmosphere, where local handicrafts, art, and building materials enliven the interiors. Hotels of all grades are expensive by Southeast Asian standards. Reluctance on the part of the government to grant new trading licenses, coupled with the sudden spike in demand when the tourism boycott ended in 2010, has ensured a chronic shortage of rooms across the country, particularly in the more popular visitor destinations such as Bagan and Inle Lake. Numerous new hotels are being built, and licenses for extensions to existing guesthouses fast-tracked by the government, but there remains a dearth of accommodations in all categories.

Hotel Grading

Accommodation licenses in Myanmar are issued by the Ministry of Tourism, which grades hotels in the country according to a star-rating system of one to five stars. Every establishment is obliged to display its grade plaque in reception. Only a handful of ultra-luxurious places in Yangon make the five-star category, whereas, at the other end of the scale, there are numerous one-star hotels.

The ministry does not publish its grading criteria, but the stars give a fair reflection of a hotel's standard. Not all hotels and guesthouses achieve star status, however. And just because an establishment does not display a plaque, it does not mean that it is not licensed.

Luxury and Business Hotels

The recent rise in foreign investment in Myanmar, in particular from Singaporean chains, means that the coming years are likely to see a sharp rise in the number of luxury hotels in the country. For the time being, however, capacity barely keeps pace with demand, and falls well below it at the height of the tourist season between November and March, when rates soar.

Myanmar's top five-star hotels are nearly all in Yangon. Places such as the Strand and the Chatrium (*see p202*) are on a par with other Asian counterparts, with international-grade facilities, standards of service,

The gracious lobby of the luxury Chatrium Hotel Royal Lake in midtown Yangon

and comfort. Popular with both visiting business clients and foreign tourists, the five-star hotels all occupy landmark properties downtown. Rooms are spacious, richly furnished, and centrally air-conditioned. Flat-screen TVs and in-room Wi-Fi are the norm, and the complexes include state-of-the-art leisure facilities such as large outdoor pools, gym, and spa, as well as a choice of restaurants, cafés, bars, and, in a few cases, glamorous clubs attracting the rich and famous of Yangon.

Only slightly less luxurious are business hotels, which are to all intents and purposes five-stars, but with fewer frills and lower tariffs. Some business hotels lack a pool, but the rooms are always very comfortable.

If you are making your own reservation (rather than staying as part of a package tour) it is worth knowing that the best rates for high-end hotels are always posted online; booking in person or over the phone invariably means being offered the far higher "rack rate." As with high-end hotels in other countries, extras such as mini-bar purchases and in-room phone calls can add significantly to the final bill.

Note that payments made by card will incur an additional charge of 5 per cent or more, so it is better to settle in cash (usually in US dollars).

Yangon's Kandawgyi Palace Hotel, with the Karaweik Palace in the background

◀ Visitors floating over the ancient temples and pagodas of Bagan in a hot-air balloon

Belmond Governor's Residence in Yangon, a boutique hotel housed in an exquisite teak mansion from the 1920s

Boutique Hotels

In recent years, a handful of small-scale luxury hotels have started to appear in Myanmar, where the emphasis is as much on bespoke designer style as comfort. As well as being more compact, boutique places tend to favor Burmese aesthetics, fusing traditional woodcarving, stone sculpture, art, and crafts with contemporary chic. The effect can be memorable, but so can the prices: places such as Bagan's Hotel @ Tharabar Gate *(see p204)*, Mandalay's Hotel by the Red Canal *(see p204)*, and Yangon's Governor's Residence *(see p202)* are in particularly high demand in peak season from November through February and their tariffs reflect this.

Resort Hotels

Large self-contained hotels that are a destination in themseves are few and far between in Myanmar, although this is bound to change over the coming decade as areas such as the Myeik (Mergui) Archipelago *(see p195)* are developed for tourism. Boasting pools, stylish accommodations, smart restaurants, and sports and games facilities, Myanmar's few bona fide resort hotels tend to be situated on the shores of Inle Lake. Places such as the Aureum Resort and Spa and Inle Lake View *(see p205)* make the most of their spectacular situation, with chalets on stilts or facing

the waterfront. Ngapali beach, in the northwest state of Rakhine, is the other place where resort hotels tend to dominate. Set in the shade of mature palms, the likes of Amazing Ngapali, Sandoway, and Bayview *(see p203)* offer beautiful swimming pools and sea views from their luxurious designer chalets, only a few steps away from the surf of the Andaman Sea.

The dividing line between a boutique hotel and a resort is often a fine one, depending on the amount of effort that has been put into the decor, and many places categorize themselves as "boutique resorts." This is the preferred option among foreign tour operators, which is why these places tend to be full of tour groups. Bookings are usually made through agents, or via email or telephone, rather than online reservation systems. Payment is in cash (US dollars).

Conventional Hotels

The "conventional" category used in the listings *(see pp202–5)* refers to a class of upper- and mid-range hotels that are lacking the kind of glitz that may appeal to foreign tourists. Sometimes dubbed "Chinese-style," they are often intentionally bland to appeal in the main to visiting Chinese business-people, with rooms in simple, motel-style chalets or multi-storied blocks. The furniture and

fixtures are usually worn and smell of cigarette smoke, but the tariffs are more affordable.

Guesthouses, B&Bs, and Budget Hotels

Small, family-run hotels, guesthouses, and what might be classed as B&Bs or homestays (allowed in a few places where no other accommodations are available, such as in the hill tracts and ethnic minority villages of the north, *see p200*) are in short supply across the country. While standards of cleanliness tend to be high and the welcome warm, prices are, as a consequence, prone to inflation. When booking a room on spec, always check the quality of the plumbing, the thickness of the mattresses, and the airconditioning, which can vary greatly. Many mid-range hotels also offer different categories of rooms and it is always worth comparing these if vacancies are available.

Budget hotels generally offer the poorest value for money, especially those popular with foreign backpackers. Often with small or no windows, old-style air-coolers ratherthan modern air-conditioning, and blighted by unpleasant odors from their tiny bathrooms (if they have them), the rooms may be stuffy and cramped. When traveling on a tight budget, always ask to see the rooms before parting with any money.

Villas arranged like an Intha stilt village at the Myanmar Treasure Resort, Inle Lake

Homestays

It is against the law in Myanmar for foreign visitors to stay in the homes of local people. Exceptions, however, are made in some parts of the country such as Shan State – notably between Kalaw and Inle Lake, and around Hsipaw – where trekking is a popular activity, but where no other accommodations are available. Trekkers wishing to undertake two- or three-stage routes are allowed to stay overnight in the villages of ethnic minority people along the way *(see p173)*. All the necessary arrangements will be made by your guesthouse or by the travel agent hired to organize the trek.

Staying in Monasteries

Many monasteries accept guests for a night or two in exchange for a small donation. In the rural hinterland of Inle Lake, this enables tourists to undertake multistage hikes, an arrangement formally ratified by the Ministry of Tourism in March 2013 to ease pressure on beds in the area. Elsewhere, monasteries may serve as a last resort when the only other lodgings in the region are occupied. Monastery visitors should not expect much in the way of creature comforts beyond shared bathrooms and a thin cotton mattress or straw mat to sleep on.

Booking

Given the shortage of rooms, it is essential to book as far ahead as possible – at least a month, or more, in advance. Reservations may be made verbally by telephone (although the English spoken may not always be fluent, and the cost of calls extremely high), or directly by email or through the hotel's website. Either way, it is wise to ask for confirmation via email, and to reconfirm the reservation a couple of days before the intended date of arrival. Always check the rate in advance. Most upscale hotels expect full payment at the time of booking. Some of the less expensive places require payment at check-in, while others waive payment until check-out.

Travel agents in Myanmar *(see p229)* will be happy to make all the necessary arrangements on behalf of travelers. Charges for this service vary: larger agents

Staff at the reception desk of one of Mandalay's mid-range hotels

have access to discounted rates that they may hand on in part to clients, which can work out cheaper even after their mark-up. In addition, many hotels in Myanmar accept bookings via the website agoda.com, and some smaller guesthouses even insist that guests make reservations this way.

Prices

Tariffs are high compared with other countries in Southeast Asia as a result of the shortage of accommodations. A very basic budget room in downtown Yangon can cost upward of US$25–30 per night, and a threadbare mid-range one more than double that. At the high end, rates are even more inflated: a room in one of the landmark five-star hotels in the November–February peak season can cost US$500–900, excluding government taxes.

Bargaining

It was once easy in Myanmar to haggle down the cost of accommodations – vacancies were plentiful and alternatives close to hand. Far from being able to negotiate a reduction, visitors are now more likely to find the rate has increased since the time of booking. If demand is high, many hotels, particularly those in tourist areas, will adjust their tariffs accordingly.

Taxes

Service charges of between 5 and 10 per cent are routinely collected on rooms in luxury hotels and resorts, in addition to the flat-rate 10 per cent government tax. These amounts tend not to be included in the price quoted at the time of booking. These taxes do not, however, apply to cheaper places.

Tipping

Although tipping didn't use to be customary, the practice has gradually become more widespread over the past few years. If a staff member has been particularly helpful, a gratuity of a few US dollars will be welcomed. Bear in mind that upscale hotels already levy a service charge of 10 per cent on top of the bill.

Checking In

When checking in, foreign visitors are required to fill in government forms listing their passport and visa details, date of arrival in Myanmar, and onward itinerary. Some places also insist that you hand over your passport for the duration of your stay, although they can usually be dissuaded from doing this if you are firm enough. Ask to have a look at the room you have been allocated before any money is handed over, as it will be easier to change at this stage than later. Some hotels require payment in full and in cash at check-in; the balance for any extras will need to be paid when checking out.

The stylish Arakan-style villas of the Amazing Ngapali resort complex

Facilities for Disabled Travelers

Visitors with mobility problems will find high-end hotels more straightforward than budget ones. Luxury places tend to have wheelchair-friendly luggage runways to their lobbies, spacious elevators, and help for any heavy lifting. Beyond that, however, disabled travelers can expect no dedicated facilities. Staying in cheaper hotels can mean endless stairs, cramped lifts, and small bathrooms with only squat toilets and no tubs.

Facilities for Children

Very few hotels in Myanmar offer dedicated facilities for kids; those that do tend to be the most expensive five-stars, where "kid's clubs" are sometimes featured on weekends. Nearly all hotels, however, allow under-12s to share a bed with their parents for free, or charge a small amount for an extra bed or cot. Babysitter services are available in some hotels. Upscale places are likely to have extensive grounds and gardens with areas where youngsters can let off steam, as well as swimming pools with special shallow sections for children.

Recommended Hotels

The hotels in this guide have been selected across a wide price range and represent the most commendable options in their location and category. Value for money, quality of furnishings, facilities, the overall setting and atmosphere, and the warmth of the welcome have been taken into consideration. The best of these are highlighted as DK Choice. The prices listed are those charged by the hotel during the high season from November to February for a double room, inclusive of all taxes. Hotels are listed by region (further divided into towns) and by price range.

The swimming pool at The Hotel @ Tharabar Gate, a luxury boutique hotel in Old Bagan

Where to Stay

Yangon

Wai Wai's Place $
B&B
30, Pearl St, Kamayut Tsp
Tel *(0) 9421150524*
W waiwaisplace.com
Quiet, friendly B&B near Inya Lake offering unusually restrained rates and genuine hospitality.

Bike World $$
B&B
10F, Khabaung Rd, 6 Miles Pyay Rd
Tel *(01) 527636*
W myanmarpanorama.com
Quirky, cycling-themed B&B run by an Australian-Burmese couple. Immaculate, comfortable rooms, a relaxing terrace, sound travel advice, and guided cycle tours.

Central Hotel $$
Conventional **City Map** D4
335–357, Bogyoke Aung San Rd
Tel *(01) 241001*
W centralhotelyangon.com
A bit frayed around the edges, but in a great location. Ask for a top-floor room as traffic noise can be loud on the lower floors.

Classique Inn $$
B&B **City Map** C1
53B, Shwe Taung Gyar St (Golden Valley Rd), Bahan Township
Tel *(01) 525557*
W classique-inn.com
Smart, professionally run guesthouse. Staff are friendly, and there is a relaxing pebble-and-brick terrace to lounge on.

Clover City Center $$
Conventional **City Map** D4
217, 32nd St (Upper Block)
Tel *(01) 377720*
W cloverhotelsgroup.com
Service is average and small rooms for the price, but it is well maintained and its location is hard to beat.

Garden Home $$
B&B **City Map** E2
10, Bogyoke Museum Lane, Bahan Township
Tel *(01) 541917*
W gardenhomebnb.asia
One of the cozier, more welcoming B&Bs in the city, with a relaxing garden and terrace. Walking distance from the Shwedagon Pagoda.

Hotel Alamanda $$
Boutique **City Map** C1
60B, Shwe Taung Gyar St (Golden Valley Rd), Bahan Township

The Chatrium's huge, palm-lined pool, one of the hotel's main selling points

Tel *(01) 534513*
W hotel-alamanda.com
This French-run boutique B&B offers stylish rooms in an old house that has plenty of character, with varnished wood floors, wicker chairs, and deep verandas.

Hotel 51 $$
Conventional **City Map** F4
154/156, 51st St, Pazuntaung Township
Tel *(01) 293022*
W hotel51myanmar.com
This mid-range newcomer in the east of the colonial quarter has small but comfortable rooms with modern bathrooms at decent rates. Staff are helpful.

DK Choice

**Belmond Governor's
Residence** $$$
Boutique **City Map** B3
35, Taw Win Rd, Dagon
Tel *(01) 229860*
W belmond.com
Now part of the international Belmond Group, this historic hotel occupies a beautifully renovated 1920s mansion. The paddle fans, split-cane blinds, and liveried staff re-create the colonial-era ambience to perfection. Lotus ponds in the grounds add to the charm.

Chatrium Hotel Royal Lake Yangon $$$
Conventional **City Map** E2
40, Nat Mauk St
Tel *(01) 544500*
W chatrium.com
Extensive grounds, a huge pool, an excellent location next to the

historic royal Kandawgyi Lake, and spectacular views of the Shwedagon Pagoda are this five-star hotel's greatest assets.

Inya Lake Hotel $$$
Business
37, Kaba Aye Pagoda Rd
Tel *(01) 9662866*
W inyalakehotel.com
Set amid wonderful lakeside gardens, this Soviet-built five-star hotel has a faded 1960s feel, but comfortable furnishings. It is owned by the government.

Kandawgyi Palace Hotel $$$
Business **City Map** E3
Kan Yeik Tha Rd, Mingalar Taung Nyunt Township
Tel *(01) 382919*
W kandawgyipalace-hotel.com
Occupying a great lakeside spot, this government-owned, five-star hotel is run to high standards. Well placed for sightseeing.

The Savoy $$$
Boutique **City Map** C1
129, Dhammazedi Rd
Tel *(01) 526289*
W savoy-myanmar.com
Gorgeous boutique hotel in a colonial mansion, with in-period fixtures, furniture, and decor, down to the claw-foot bathtubs. Walking distance from the Shwedagon Pagoda.

The Strand $$$
Boutique **City Map** E5
92, Strand Rd
Tel *(01) 243377*
W hotelthestrand.com
The grandfather of Yangon's colonial-era hotels, the Strand dates from 1903 and is still replete with old-world elegance. The delectable high tea service here is a must.

Sule Shangri-La $$$
Business **City Map** D4
223, Sule Pagoda Rd
Tel *(01) 242828*
W shangri-la.com/yangon/suleshangrila
Myanmar's top business hotel, and a landmark to rival the nearby Sule Pagoda, of which its best rooms have superb views.

Bago Region

BAGO: Bago Star $
Conventional   **Road Map** D5
11–21, Kyaik Pun Pagoda Rd, Oatha Myothit
Tel *(052) 23766*
Few people stay in Bago, due to the lack of decent accommodations. While overpriced, this place is the best of the bunch, with wooden chalets in a garden plot.

PYAY: Lucky Dragon $$
Resort   **Road Map** C4
772, Strand Rd, Sandaw Quarter
Tel *(053) 24222*
W luckydragonhotel.com
Well-maintained, comfortable, modern bungalows set around leafy gardens in the heart of town. Jacuzzi and pool. Good value.

DK Choice

TAUNGOO: Royal Kaytumadi $$
Resort   **Road Map** D4
Taw Win Kaytumadi Rd
Tel *(054) 24761*
W royalkaytumadi.kmahotels.com
This beautiful lakeside five-star hotel offers generous-sized air-conditioned rooms and an outdoor pool looking across the lake to the Shwesandaw Pagoda. As befits the location, the architecture, decor, and fixtures are in regal Burmese style.

Western Myanmar

CHAUNGTHA: Belle Resort $$
Boutique   **Road Map** C5
Chaungtha
Tel *(042) 42112*
W belleresorts.com
Chalets and bungalows with Thai gabled roofs sit right behind the beach. The suites are huge.

MRAUK U: Shwe Thazin $$
Boutique   **Road Map** B3
Sun Sha Seik Quarter
Tel *(043) 24200*
W shwethazinhotel.com
An attractive two-star hotel close to the ruins. Air-conditioned bungalows sport local art.

MRAUK U: Mrauk Oo Princess $$$
Boutique   **Road Map** B3
Aungdat Creek
Tel *(043) 50232*
Luxurious Arakan-style villas scattered around leafy tropical gardens. They have their own boat for transfers from Sittwe.

DK Choice

NGAPALI: Amazing Ngapali Resort $$$
Resort   **Road Map** C4
27, Inya Myaing Rd, Zee Phyu Gone village
Tel *(043) 42011*
W amazingngapaliresort.com
Set well away from the bustle of the main beach area, this complex of Arakan-style villas is flawlessly stylish. The rooms are huge and most face the ocean.

NGAPALI: Bayview $$$
Resort   **Road Map** C4
205, Hnget Pyaw Khaung Kwin
Tel *(01) 504471*
W bayview-myanmar.com
A small-scale resort hotel with a perfect location. Large, cool, wood-floored rooms, lovely pool and pretty restaurant.

NGAPALI: Sandoway $$$
Resort   **Road Map** C4
Mya Pyin village
Tel *(043) 42244*
W sandowayresort.com
Glamorous, Italian-owned boutique resort. Palm trees frame the poolside and cottages; the villas have beach views.

NGWE SAUNG: Bay of Bengal $$$
Resort   **Road Map** C5
North side, Ngwe Saung
W bayofbengalresort.com
Ultra-stylish resort hotel arranged around a central pool, with gorgeous teak-and-stone chalets facing the beach.

PATHEIN: La Pyae Wun $
Conventional   **Road Map** C5
30, Mingyi St
Tel *(042) 25151*
The most comfortable option in town and well situated for the market area and riverfront. The rooms – all twin – have tiled floors and are generous-sized and air-conditioned.

Bagan Archeological Zone

NEW BAGAN: Kumudara $$
Resort   **Road Map** C3
Corner of 5th St and Daw Na St, Pyu Saw Htee Quarter
Tel *(061) 65142*
W kumudara-bagan.com
One of the few budget hotels where you can admire the ruins while lounging in a pool. Tired but acceptable for the price.

NEW BAGAN: Ruby True $$
Conventional   **Road Map** C3
Myat Lay Rd
Tel *(061) 65043*
W rubytruehotel.com
Clean and comfortable chalets in a peaceful spot on the edge of the village. The hotel's remote location explains the low tariffs.

DK Choice

NEW BAGAN: Bluebird $$$
Boutique   **Road Map** C3
Myatlay St, Bagan Myothit (East), Naratheinkha 10
Tel *(061) 65440*
W bluebirdbagan.com
This boutique hotel has been exquisitely designed by its French owner, who has used local arts and crafts to create a romantic, stylish hideaway near the ruins. The rooms are minimalist and cool, and there is a small, gorgeous pool in a walled spice garden to lounge beside.

OLD BAGAN: Bagan Thande Hotel $$
Conventional   **Road Map** C3
Near Gawdawpalin Temple
Tel *(061) 60025*
W baganthandehotel.net
Bagan's oldest hotel was built in 1922 for a visit by the Prince of Wales. On a raised plot overlooking the river. The refurbished, spacious, teak-paneled rooms offer good value.

The cottages of the glamorous Sandoway Resort, located on the beachfront

For more information on types of hotels *see pages 198–201*

**OLD BAGAN: Aye Yar
River View Resort** $$$
Resort Road Map C3
Near Bupaya Pagoda
Tel *(061) 60352*
W ayeyarriverviewresort.com
Set in vast river-facing gardens,
this resort has had an expensive
makeover and offers smartly fur-
nished rooms with great views.

**OLD BAGAN: The Hotel @
Tharabar Gate** $$$
Boutique Road Map C3
Tharabar Gate
Tel *(061) 60037*
W tharabargate.com
Five-star, boutique luxury on a
small scale, set in an oasis of
dense greenery. In a prime loca-
tion near the river and ruins.

**OLD BAGAN: Thiripitsaya
Sanctuary** $$$
Resort Road Map C3
Old Bagan
Tel *(061) 60048*
W thiripyitsaya-resort.com
Large riverside resort boasting
spectacular sunset views and
a good-sized swimming pool.
Popular with tour groups.

**POPA TAUNG KALAT: Popa
Mountain Resort** $$$
Resort Road Map C3
Mount Popa
W myanmartreasureresorts.com
Dreamy views from the poolside
terrace of this boutique resort
extend over the spectacular Popa
Taung Kalat monastery – one of
the country's most exotic sights.

Mandalay Region

**MANDALAY CITY: Peacock
Lodge** $
B&B Road Map C3
60th St (25/26)
Tel *(02) 042059*
W peacocklodge.com
Peaceful, clean, and cool, with
quality Myanmar meals served
on a sociable garden terrace.
This is by far the best budget
option in Mandalay, but book
well ahead.

**MANDALAY CITY: Hotel
Yadanarbon** $$
Conventional Road Map C3
125, 31st St (76/77)
Tel *(02) 71999*
W hotelyadanarbon.com
The Yadanarbon is a large,
modern hotel in the heart of
Mandalay's downtown shopping
district. It offers clean, generous-
sized rooms and always
courteous service.

**MANDALAY CITY: Mandalay
City Hotel** $$
Conventional Road Map C3
26th St (82/83)
Tel *(02) 61700*
W mandalaycityhotel.com
Fish ponds and a pool make this
a relaxing retreat from the heat.

**MANDALAY CITY: Sedona
Mandalay** $$
Conventional Road Map C3
1, corner of 26th St and 66th St
Tel *(02) 36488*
W sedonahotels.com.sg
Grand five-star hotel in a choice
location opposite the palace
complex. It has great views, a
large pool, and cheerful service.

MANDALAY CITY: Smart $$
Conventional Road Map C3
167, 28th St (76/77)
Tel *(02) 32682*
W smarthotelmandalay.com
A top mid-range choice for its
spotless rooms, central location,
and efficient, smiling staff.

DK Choice

**MANDALAY CITY: Hotel by
the Red Canal** $$$
Boutique Road Map C3
417, corner of 63rd St & 22nd St
Tel *(02) 61177*
W hotelredcanal.com
Resembling a Burmese palace,
with carved wooden eaves and
rattan blinds on the windows,
this 26-room bolthole is the
city's most alluring place to stay.
It is hidden in the northeast
corner, away from the bustle,
but close to the main sights.

**MANDALAY CITY: Mandalay
Hill Resort** $$$
Resort Road Map C3
9, Kwin (416B), 10th St
Tel *(02) 35638*
W mandalayhillresorthotel.com
This lavish resort in landscaped
grounds at the foot of the hill is
among Myanmar's top hotels.

**MANDALAY CITY: Rupar
Mandalar** $$$
Boutique Road Map C3
A15, corner of 53rd & 30th St
Tel *(02) 61555*
W ruparmandalar.com
Beautifully designed boutique
hotel on the eastern outskirts of
Mandalay. Made mostly of
varnished teak, the place has all
the facilities of a five-star but a
lot more style.

MONYWA: Monywa Hotel $$
Resort Road Map C3
Yone Kyi Or, Bogyoke Rd
Tel *(071) 21581*
Motel-style place offering red-
tiled bungalows with hardwood
decks facing the lake and pool.
A relaxing, secure, and peaceful
base for visits to nearby sights.

**PYIN U LWIN: Aureum Palace
Governor's House** $$
Boutique Road Map D3
*Ward 6, Governor's Hill, Mandalay–
Lashio Highway*
W aureumpalacehotel.com
Luxury reconstruction of a grand,
colonial-era mansion, with rooms
in the main building and bunga-
lows in the grounds. Polished,
but a bit short on atmosphere.

PYIN U LWIN: Pyin Oo Lwin $$
Conventional Road Map D3
9, Nandar Rd, Kandawgyi Lakeside
Tel *(085) 21226*
W hotelpyinoolwin.com
This is the newest and best-value
option in town, with teak-lined
chalets in landscaped grounds
above the lake.

**PYIN U LWIN: Kandawgyi Hill
Resort** $$$
Resort Road Map D3
Kandawgyi Lakeside
W myanmartreasureresorts.com
Converted from an old British
colonial rest-house, the resort
offers accommodations in
spacious bungalows amid well-
tended, landscaped grounds
with pleasing lake views.

The colonial-style buildings of Pyin U Lwin's Kandawgyi Hill Resort

Eastern Myanmar

HSIPAW: Lily The Home $
B&B **Road Map** D3
108, Aung Tha Pyae Rd
Tel (082) 80318
W lilythehome.com
This popular Hsipaw guesthouse
is comfortable, friendly, and good
value. They also arrange treks and
guides for keen hikers.

**INLE LAKE: Paramount Inle
Resort** $$
Resort **Road Map** D4
Nga Phe Chaung
W paramountinleresort.com
Wood-lined rooms, the best ones
with decks jutting out over the
water. Not ideal for longer stays
as it is on the southwest shore,
an hour's boat ride from town.

DK Choice

**INLE LAKE: Aureum
Resort and Spa** $$$
Resort **Road Map** D4
Mine Thauk
Tel (081) 209866
W aureumpalacehotel.com
Luxurious stilt chalets in a
spectacular location facing the
lake. Private decks offer perfect
sunset views. The interiors contrast warm-toned hardwoods
with luminous local silks in fiery
colors. Currently the benchmark
among Inle's high-end resorts.

**INLE LAKE: Inle Lake View
Resort & Spa** $$$
Resort **Road Map** D4
Khaung Daing
Tel (0) 94936007
W inlelakeview.com
Set close to the shore in butterfly-
filled gardens, the hotel has a
heated infinity pool and beautiful
teak rooms with high ceilings,
canopied beds, and big windows.

INLE LAKE: Inle Princess $$$
Resort **Road Map** D4
Magyizin
Tel (081) 209055
W inle-princess.com
Gloriously peaceful setting down
a private water channel. The
huge chalets have kitsch boat-
shaped bath tubs.

INLE LAKE: Inle Resort $$$
Resort **Road Map** D4
Nyaungshwe
Tel (0) 95154444
W inleresort.com
This spectacular lakeside resort is
accessed via a stilt bridge across
beautiful lotus ponds, with
chalets on the water boasting

The spacious wood-panelled bedrooms
of the Paramount Resort at Inle Lake

traditional Burmese roofs. Guests
are offered high standards of
service and cuisine.

**INLE LAKE: Myanmar
Treasure Resort** $$$
Resort **Road Map** D4
Maing Thauk, Nyaungshwe
W myanmartreasureresorts.com
There are dreamy sunset views
from the front-row villas of this
resort on the northeast shore, set
up like an Intha stilt village.

INLE LAKE: Villa Inle $$$
Boutique **Road Map** D4
Mine Thauk
Tel (01) 242259
W hotelininle.com
Particularly beautiful teak villas
with floor-to-ceiling windows
and king-sized beds suspended
from high-vaulted ceilings.

**INLE LAKE (NYAUNGSHWE):
Aquarius Inn** $
B&B **Road Map** D4
2, Phaung Daw Pyan Rd,
Nam Pan Quarter
Tel (081) 209352
W aquariusinninlelake.com
Cozy little budget guesthouse
down a quiet street within walk-
ing distance of the bus station
and market. Friendly and clean.

**INLE LAKE (NYAUNGSHWE):
Amazing** $$
Boutique **Road Map** D4
Yone Gyi Rd
Tel (081) 209477
W hotelamazingnyaungshwe.com
Attractive boutique hotel close
to the boat jetty. Spacious rooms,
artful decor, and a great location
close to the local market.

KENGTUNG: Princess $
Conventional **Road Map** E3
Zay Dan Kalay St
Tel (084) 21319
The best base for exploring the
surrounding minority villages.
Unprepossessing looks, but very
clean. Central location in town.

Northern Myanmar

BHAMO: Friendship Hotel $
Conventional **Road Map** D2
Letwet Thondaya Rd
Tel (074) 50095
Large, well-maintained rooms
in a modern block within easy
reach of the market and river.
Free transfers to the boat jetty.

MYITKINA: United $
Conventional **Road Map** D2
38, Thitsat St
Tel (074) 22085
The town's cleanest option, this is
a basic, Chinese-style hotel popular with foreign aid workers.

DK Choice

PUTAO: Malikha Lodge $$$
Boutique **Road Map** D1
Mulashidi village
Tel (09) 860 0659
W malikhalodge.net
A beautiful boutique hideaway,
nestled between forest and rice
terraces south of Putao, this is
the only international-standard
hotel in the far north, and an
atmospheric springboard for
adventures in the nearby hills.
Each spacious bungalow is cen-
tered on a handmade teak bath-
tub with a fireplace next to it.

Southeastern
Myanmar

HPA-AN: Golden Sky $
Conventional **Road Map** D5
2, Thida St, West Thida Ward
Tel (058) 21510
Basic hotel on the north side of
town. Drab decor is redeemed by
the upper floor river views.

**KYAIKTIYO: Mountaintop
Hotel** $$
Conventional **Road Map** D5
Kyaiktiyo
Tel (01) 502479
W mountaintop-hotel.com
The most comfortable rooms on
the summit of Kyaiktiyo, only five
minutes from the shrine. Over-
priced, but worth it for sunrise.

**MAWLAMYINE: Mawlamyaing
Strand** $$
Conventional **Road Map** D5
Strand Rd, Phat Than Quarter
Tel (057) 25624
W mawlamyaingstrand.com
Mawlamyine's smartest hotel
surveys the riverfront. The rooms
are large and bright with com-
fortable beds, but lack views.

For more information on types of hotels see pages 198–201

WHERE TO EAT AND DRINK

The Burmese are deservedly proud of their cuisine which, while borrowing heavily from those of its neighbors, manages to remain totally distinctive. A wealth of spices and pungent seafood pastes combine to create curries with intense flavors, while dry-roasted nuts, pulses, and seeds sprinkled over the top add surprising textures. Noodles and tofu feature prominently in the cooking of the Shan Plateau, just one of several regional styles represented throughout the country. International food, such as pizza, pasta, and burgers, is also widely available in the big cities and tourist resorts, which offer a variety of dining options. The range extends from swish air-conditioned restaurants to relatively basic Burmese places where you can order a feast for a few dollars, and street stalls selling piping hot, tasty snacks for even less than that. Cafés range from American-style coffee-houses in the cities to traditional hole-in-the-wall teashops, while Chinese-style beer stations offer lively venues for watching soccer matches in the evenings.

Burmese Restaurants

The most authentic Burmese food is served in busy, no-frills restaurants around shopping districts and local neighbor-hoods, where the emphasis is definitely more on the cooking than the decor. It is best to ignore the strip lighting and plastic furniture, and head for the glass-topped buffet cabinet where dozens of different stews, curries, salads, and side dishes will be on display. Having selected one or two main courses, diners wait for them to be brought to their table, along with a host of accompa-niments, clear soup, and side dishes, ranging from bowls of steaming white rice to nose-tingling (dried shrimp relish), fermented tea-leaf salad, roughly chopped crudités, and green leaves.

Chinese influence is apparent in the open-air barbecue stalls, where customers pick a skewer of pork, chicken, mutton, or fish and wait for it to be flame-grilled and served up with deli-cious sauces. Shan restaurants also reveal Chinese inspiration in the different noodles they serve up in meaty broths, along with tofu made from chickpeas (garbanzo beans).

Tourist Restaurants

Until recently, foreign food was the exclusive preserve of restaurants in Myanmar's few five-star hotels, but since the revival of tourism, scores of places have opened in major

Muffins, cakes, and cookies at downtown Yangon's trendy Coffee Club bakery café

visitor destinations such as Nyaungshwe (Inle Lake), Bagan, and Ngapali (Western Myanmar) where visitors can enjoy pizza, burgers, and sushi.

In metropolitan cities such as Yangon and Mandalay, the appetite of the affluent elite for culinary novelties means that it is now possible to enjoy French patisserie and designer ice creams, and to surf the web over a muffin and a cappuccino.

Street Food

Some of the tastiest meals and snacks on offer in Myanmar are sold from street outlets. In larger cities, food stalls often cater for dozens of diners who sit at low tables on undersized plastic chairs while they eat. *Mohinga*, or noodle soup *(see p208),* is a favorite breakfast meal among local workers. In the evenings, Indian *chapati* and curry ven-dors spring up in downtown areas. Contrary to appearances, the food served in such places is usually safe and hygienic because turnover is brisk and everything freshly prepared each day. The same applies to fried snacks, such as the Indian *pakora*, cooked on hot griddles in the street, and the delicious *mont linmayar* (literally "husband and wife") – mini rice flour pancakes filled with quail eggs, yellow split peas, tomatoes, and spring onions. When crispy on the outside, two pancakes are flipped on top of each other to form a ball, said to resemble a loving couple, from where their Burmese name is derived. They are served in bags of 10 pairs with a tablespoon of sesame powder.'

Vegetarian Options

Myanmar presents no particular problems for vegetarians, and although the choice of dishes

A bowl of Shan-style noodles served with vegetables in a broth, Eastern Myanmar

will inevitably be more limited, most restaurants, whether Burmese or tourist-oriented, offer plenty of options. Stews made from chickpeas and other beans or pulses, which go well with rice and noodles, as well as Myanmar's delicious tomato salads are popular with vegetarians. Shan State is a region where vegetarians are particularly well served, thanks to the predominance of tofu, vegetable and noodle soups, and filling clay pot meals.

Feel Myanmar Food, a popular Burmese self-serve restaurant in Yangon

Teashops and Beer Stations

Traditional Burmese teashops are very much part of the culinary scene, particularly in Yangon, where a brew of strong, sweet tea (usually made with condensed milk) provides the accompaniment to a bowl of hot *mohinga*, steamed bun, *samosa*, or semolina cake. Teashops are where workers and senior citizens go to relax, chat, and read the newspaper.

Younger Burmese, however, tend to congregate more in Chinese-style beer stations, where soccer matches are shown on widescreen TVs and karaoke or other live entertainment is often laid on.

Alcohol

Beer is fast overtaking tea as the country's national drink. By far the most popular brand is Myanmar Beer, produced by a company jointly owned by the military and a conglomerate backed by Wa drug barons. Dagon and Mandalay, both refreshing lagers, are also owned either by the government or by military-linked conglomerates. In more high-end bars, Singaporean Tiger Beer may be on offer, along with boutique beers such as Spirulina (made with the eponymous algae) and ABC (a strong, dark beer rated at 8 per cent ABV).

Demand in tourist centers for wine has spawned two Burmese vineyards (*see p173*), Aythaya on the outskirts of Taunggyi, and Red Mountain on the shores of nearby Inle Lake. Both produce reds and whites, from mostly European vine stocks such as Shiraz, Cabernet Sauvignon, Tempranillo, and Dornfelder. Quality, while improving each year, is roughly comparable with mid-price New World wines.

Prices

As in any country, prices for meals vary greatly in Myanmar. While you can expect to pay no more than US$4 for an elaborate, filling meal in a traditional Burmese restaurant, a simple bowl of pasta with pesto could cost double that in a tourist café. Only in smart hotels and the odd gourmet restaurant are you likely to pay more than US$20 per head for a meal. Wine can dramatically increase your bill, with local bottles and New World imports costing US$15–25, or double that in upscale hotels.

Tipping

Service is nearly always included in the cost of your meal and tipping is not customary in ordinary Burmese places. In tourist restaurants, it is commonplace to leave the small change from the bill – up to 1,000–1,500 kyat – as a tip.

Tourists relaxing on the patio of a small Burmese teashop

Recommended Restaurants

The restaurants on the following pages have been carefully chosen from across the country to cover a range of possibilities, from fine dining and traditional to modern Burmese fusion cuisine and gourmet Thai. The more high-end places are often located in smart hotels, where the price you pay is as much for the ambience and showy service as the cooking. The DK Choice category draws attention to establishments that are exceptional in some way – either because they offer great value for money or because the food they serve stands out from the crowd.

The Flavors of Myanmar

Myanmar's cuisine is as varied and distinctive as the country itself. While sharing many of the culinary traditions of neighboring Thailand, it encompasses a wealth of dishes and flavors found nowhere else – a legacy of Myanmar's position at the cultural crossroads of Southeast Asia. Chinese influence is seen in the ubiquity of noodles and clear, sour soups, while the popularity of Indian curries, breads, and fried snacks dates from the period of British rule. Myanmar offers a veritable feast of flavors for the adventurous palate.

Balachaung shrimp and chili paste

Fresh produce being sold at one of the five-day markets around Inle Lake

Burmese Cuisine

The keynote flavors of Burmese cooking derive primarily from the extensive use of *ngapi* sauces, which are made using fermented seafood (shrimp, prawns, and fish) pounded with salt and fiery spices. Condiments and pastes, such as the ubiquitous *balachaung*, are based on *ngapi*. They are

the meal's *apu za* or "heating" component, which is always counterbalanced by *a-aye za* or "cooling" foods, including eggplant, cucumber, and dairy produce. The basic staples are rice or noodles, with protein provided by meat, poultry, or fish, but dozens of pulses, vegetables, fruits, spices, herbs, and pungent condiments are deployed to concoct even a

simple, everyday meal across Myanmar, many of them completely unfamiliar to Western taste buds.

A Typical Burmese Meal

Burmese meals are traditionally eaten on low tables, with diners seated cross-legged on straw mats, although small chairs are more common these

Garlic Kaffir limes Turmeric root Banana stems
Cumin seeds Dried shrimp Preserved ginger Peanuts
Chilies Cilantro

Selection of the many aromatics and flavorings found in Burmese cuisine

Regional Dishes and Specialties

Burmese tofu

The quintessential dish of Yangon and the Ayeyarwady Delta is *mohinga*. This reviving stew has a base of fish broth flavored with onions, garlic, ginger, and lemongrass. Rice vermicelli noodles and sliced banana stem give substance, and it is served with boiled eggs, *nga hpe* (fried fish cakes), and *akyaw* (chickpea fritters). It is most often eaten before work at street stalls, with diners seated on low plastic chairs. The equivalent in the Mandalay and Shan regions is *Shan kauk swe* (hot Shan noodles), prepared in a

broth with chunks of chicken, pork, or mutton, and steamed greens. Early morning markets are the best places to find authentic versions. A vegetarian variety uses tofu, in Myanmar made not with soy beans but with chickpeas and turmeric. These combine to give the tofu a rich yellow color and a firm, creamy consistency.

Mohinga, the national dish, is packed with definitively Burmese aromas and ingredients, such as tender banana stem core.

A typical Myanmar meal, consisting of dozens of different dishes and condiments

days. Among families, the first spoon of rice is always reserved for the elders, whether present or absent – a tradition known as *u cha*. While rice, curries, meat, and fish are eaten with the hands, chopsticks are used for noodles and spoons for salads. More than a dozen different preparations are served simultaneously, typically in small bowls, along with a pile of vegetables and raw salad, mint, radishes, watercress, and cucumber.

Salads and Street Foods

The Burmese are great lovers of *a-thoq*, or salads, which involve a wide range of ingredients blended with spices, oils, and a sprinkle of dry-roasted nuts. Perhaps the most distinctive of all is *lahpet thoq*, fermented tea-leaf salad, a pungent, slimy tangle of pickled tea leaves with many aromatic additions. On formal occasions it is served in special lacquerware boxes, divided into sections, and few meals are eaten without a taste-tingling portion on the side. The equally popular

Yangon street food vendor making *mohinga*, a substantial noodle soup

karyanchintheet thoq (tomato salad) is more likely to appeal to the Western palate. In Shan State, Burmese tofu is often used to make nourishing, filling salads featuring bean sprouts and raw green leaves.

Snacks and even full meals are served from street stalls. Workers frequently breakfast on *mohinga*, served from steaming cauldrons, while Indian deep-fried samosas and *pakoras* provide a boost before the commute home.

ON THE MENU

Myae oh myi shae Clay-pot meals, consisting of Chinese-inspired clear soups with vegetables and pork or chicken pieces.

Nangyi thoq A salad of thick rice noodles with spicy chicken, toasted chickpea flour, onions, chilies, lime, and sliced egg.

Htamin jin Dumplings from the Shan highlands, made with fermented rice, boiled fish, tomato paste, and mashed potato.

Mont lone ye bawn A typical Burmese dessert using coconut, jaggery (palm sap sugar), and rice, rolled into balls and steamed.

Shwe yin aye A dessert of agar jelly, tapioca, and sago, steeped in sweetened coconut milk.

Mont let saung Balls of sticky rice, tapioca, toasted sesame seeds, coconut milk, shredded coconut, and sugarcane syrup.

Shan noodles are wide and flat, and feature in the very popular spicy, tomato-based stew that takes their name.

Fermented tea-leaf salad also includes fried peas, garlic, chilies, tomatoes, crushed shrimp, lime, ginger, and peanut oil.

Burmese tomato salad is a deliciously refreshing amalgam of tomato and onion in a sweet and spicy peanut sauce.

Where to Eat and Drink

Yangon

999 Shan Noodle House $
Shan   **City Map** D4
130B, 34th St, Kyauktada Township
One of the best and most
conveniently located places in
the city to sample big bowls of
Shan noodles (rice, yellow, and
traditional) and crispy fried tofu.

Aung Thukha $
Burmese   **City Map** C1
17A, Dhammazedi Rd
Within walking distance of the
Shwedagon Pagoda, this dowdy
but clean – and very popular –
budget canteen serves a range of
salads and meaty curries.

Coffee Club $
Bakery Café   **City Map** C5
*Level 1, corner of Mahabandula Rd &
11th St, Lanmadaw Township*
Tel (0) 943207764
In the heart of downtown, this
trendy air-conditioned café has
free Wi-Fi, pleasant music, beautiful teak tables, and welcoming,
English-speaking staff. Great for
a light meal, sandwich, or latte.

Feel Myanmar Food $
Burmese   **City Map** C3
124, Pyidaungzu Yeiktha St
W feelrestaurant.com
Busy and crowded but a good
place to experiment with a wide
range of Burmese dishes from a
covered buffet. They are served
with a range of sides and sauces.

Khaing Khaing Kyaw $
Burmese
*671A, off 5.5 Miles Pyay Rd, Near Thu
Kha Kabar Clinic*
There is no better place in the
city than Khaing Khaing Kyaw to
initiate yourself into the joys of

A range of fresh vegetables ready to be
cooked at Khaing Khaing Kyaw

traditional Burmese cuisine, with
dozens of dishes prepared daily.
The restaurant offers great value
and is always scrupulously clean.

Kosan $
Burmese/Chinese   **City Map** C4
108, 19th St, Latha Township
Tel (0) 9428038032
W kosanmyanmar.com
"Beer Bar Street," as the brightly lit
19th St is known, is lined with
lively, Chinese-style barbecues
after dark; this tiny, open-fronted
restaurant is a good place to soak
up the atmosphere and cocktails.

Min Lan Rakhine $
Rakhine   **City Map** F2
*Min Lan St, Sayar San (South),
Sanpya Quarter, Bahan Township*
Succulent lobster, crab, squid,
and tiger prawns are sold to
customers by weight and
prepared Rakhine-style on an
open-flame grill. Although it
looks a bit down-at-heel from
the outside, the food is amazing.

Nilar Biryani $
Indian   **City Map** D4
*216, Anawrahta Rd, between
29 St & 30 St*
Yangon's best *biryani* restaurant,
where the rice is spooned from
huge vats on the terrace. Dishes
are full of flavor and the service is
brisk. Try banana *lassi* for dessert.

Sai's Tacos $
Mexican   **City Map** C1
*32A, Inya Myaing Rd, Bahan
Township*
Tel (01) 514950
For a break from Asian cooking,
try this down-to-earth Tex-Mex
joint offering tasty chicken bur-
ritos, black bean and vegetable
quesadillas, corn chips with gua-
camole, and great tortillas.

Green Elephant $$
Burmese
37, University Ave, Bahan Township
Tel (01) 537551
W greenelephant-restaurants.com
Quality Burmese home cooking
served in a large garden pavilion.
Popular with tour groups, with
dishes tailored to Western tastes,
and an attached crafts store.

House of Memories $$
Burmese   **City Map** B1
290, U Wisara Rd, Kamayut Tsp
Tel (01) 525195
W houseofmemoriesmyanmar.com
Proper Burmese food served in
a half-timbered, colonial-era
house with linen tablecloths,

Price Guide
Prices are based on an evening meal
for one person, including service tax
but no alcohol.

$ up to $7
$$ $7 to 20
$$$ above $20

historic photographs, and family
heirlooms as decor. Ask to sit on
the upstairs veranda. Brisk service.

Padonmar $$
Southeast Asian   **City Map** B3
105–107, Kha Yay Pin St, Dagon
Tel (0) 973029973
Delicious Burmese and Thai
curries and a tempting array of
fresh salads (including wonderful
grilled eggplant) served in the
garden or the loudly decorated
interior. Popular with tour groups.

Yangon Bakehouse $$
Bakery Café   **City Map** D1
*Pearl Condominium, Block C,
Kaba Aye Pagoda Rd*
Tel (0) 9250178879
Divine pastries, cookies, and
muffins freshly baked by female
workers trained as part of a
scheme to help disadvantaged
women. They also whip up great
salads and sandwiches, and the
best coffee in Myanmar.

L'Alchimiste $$$
French/Fusion
5, U Htun Nyein St
Tel (01) 660612
W lalchimisterestaurant.com
No one comes to Yangon to eat
gourmet French food but it is
hard to resist the romantic set-
ting and sumptuous cooking of
this fabulous restaurant sited in
an old colonial-era mansion on
the shores of Inya Lake. Reserve
ahead as it is popular with the
local elite and affluent expats.

Le Planteur $$$
Fusion
*80, University Ave, Bahan
Township*
Tel (01) 514230
Le Planteur pumps out plates of
gourmet, modern European
and Indo-Chinese fusion
cuisine, overseen by Swiss chef
Boris Granges. Fish and seafood
feature strongly, while the
service is snappy to the point of
ostentation. To experience the
full five-star experience, choose
from the à la carte menu, as the
set ones are not great value.

Mandalay $$$
International   **City Map** B3
*Belmond Governor's Residence Hotel,
35, Taw Win Rd*
Tel *(01) 229860*
One of Myanmar's finest restaurants, where you can dine on fragrant Burmese or Western cuisine seated on a veranda overlooking lotus ponds. Snappy service from liveried staff.

L'Opera $$$
Italian
*62D, U Htun Nyein St, Mayangone
Township*
Tel *(01) 665516*
Set in a garden on the leafy shores of Inya Lake, this top-notch Italian has a setting to match its wonderfully authentic food, although the service can be a bit pretentious. Advance booking is recommended.

Sharky's $$$
European   **City Map** C1
117, Dhammazedi Rd
Tel *(01) 524677*
This trendy deli-diner is hugely popular for pizza, artisan breads, cold meats, locally made cheeses, and delicious home-made ice cream. The restaurant upstairs is fancier, using state-of-the-art *sous-vide* cooking to ensure the Norwegian salmon, fresh Ngapali fish, and succulent local steaks are cooked to perfection. Imported wines are served.

Strand Café $$$
European   **City Map** E5
*Strand Hotel,
92, Strand Rd, Dagon Township*
Tel *(01) 243377*
A high tea of light sandwiches, scones, and pastries at the Strand Café has been de rigueur for visitors to the city since colonial times – although many now consider the experience to be a little overpriced.

Strand Grill $$$
International   **City Map** E5
Strand Hotel, 92, Strand Rd
Tel *(01) 243377*
Lobster thermidor at the Strand Grill has been a Yangon institution for decades, and the menu remains unashamedly gourmet, featuring lots of classic French-style dishes.

Thiripyitsaya Sky Bistro $$$
International   **City Map** D4
*Sakura Tower, 339, Bogyoke Aung
San Rd, Kyauktada Township*
Tel *(01) 255277*
The famous 360° view over the city and the nearby Sule Pagoda from the top of Yangon's highest

Htay Htay's Kitchen on Ngapali beach, one of the area's many seafood restaurants

skyscraper is a must-see, and the food is commendable if a little pricey. Come for coffee and cake if you're on a budget.

Café Sul $$$
International   **City Map** D4
Sule Shangri-La, 223, Sule Pagoda Rd
Tel *(01) 242828*
With gleaming modern decor, this café inside the Sule Shangri-La offers expansive international buffets for breakfast, lunch and dinner, plus an à la carte menu. Something for everyone, from curries and noodles to imported cheeses and European desserts.

Bago Region

BAGO: Hanthawaddy $$
Burmese/Chinese   **Road Map** D5
192, Hintha St, Shin Sawpu Quarter
By far the best of a generally poor bunch of restaurants in town, serving Burmese and Chinese dishes to visiting tour groups. Try the tasty grilled river prawns.

TAUNGOO: Mother's House $
International   **Road Map** D4
501–502, Yangon–Mandalay Hwy
Tel *(054) 24240*
A dependable hotel restaurant that is popular with tour groups as it serves delicious curries, rice, and noodle dishes in a large, clean dining room on the side of the main road. A handy stop on the journey north from Yangon.

Western Myanmar

MRAUK U: Moe Cherry $
International   **Road Map** B3
East of the palace walls
Tel *(043) 50177*
Tourist-oriented restaurant near the royal palace and museum that is the most popular place in town thanks to its eclectic menu and welcoming hosts.

NGAPALI: The Green Umbrella $$
Seafood   **Road Map** C4
Ngapali
One of many virtually identical seafood places on the beach, but with especially delightful owners. The fish steaks are fabulous, as are the cocktails and sunset views from the restaurant's sandy terrace.

DK Choice

NGAPALI: Htay Htay's Kitchen $$
Seafood   **Road Map** C4
*North end of beach, just past
the Bayview Hotel*
Htay Htay's Kitchen makes more effort than most to vary its menu, offering garlic butter tiger prawns, squid salad, and stuffed crab tempura in addition to the usual range of grilled fish steaks and curries – all melt-in-the-mouth fresh and served by cheerful staff. The friendly couple who run this restaurant also have a little souvenir store on site.

NGAPALI: Ngapali Kitchen $$
Seafood   **Road Map** C4
*Main Rd, behind the Aureum
Palace hotel*
Run by a fishing family from the village, this café offers a bit more variety than other places around, including Burmese, Chinese, and Thai food. They serve seared tuna fish, snapper, crab, and lobster fresh off the boat, beautifully cooked and presented.

NGWE SAUNG: The Royal Flower $$
Seafood   **Road Map** C5
Ngwe Saung village
Market-fresh local fish, prawns, crab, octopus, and lobster are all expertly grilled and served with spicy sauces. Fun atmosphere, cordial service, and only a short trishaw ride from the beach.

For more information on types of restaurants *see pages 206–7*

SITTWE: River Valley $$
Seafood   **Road Map** B4
5, Main St
Succulent Rakhine seafood at
good prices is on offer at River
Valley. The menu is extensive,
the service cordial, and the
dining room immaculate. The
restaurant is popular mainly with
foreign visitors and aid workers.

Bagan Archeological Zone

MYINKABA: San Thi Dar $
Pan-Asian   **Road Map** C3
*Myinkaba village, on New Bagan–
Old Bagan Rd*
Copious portions of fresh, honest,
tasty cooking from a warm local
family whose curries and salads
are the stuff of legend in this
tourist enclave. The food is
mostly vegetarian, but the
menu does have a page of
chicken and beef alternatives.

**NEW BAGAN: Green
Elephant** $$$
Pan-Asian   **Road Map** C3
Yamonar, Thiripyitsaya Quarter
Tel *(061) 65422*
The food served at this chain
restaurant is so-so and a bit
overpriced, but it is worth dining
here at sunset for the superb
riverside location and romantic
decor of antiques and candles.

NEW BAGAN: Si Thu $$$
Pan-Asian   **Road Map** C3
Yamonar, Thiripyitsaya Quarter
With a fabulous location looking
on to the river and views of the
distant Rakhine-Yoma Hills, this
café is perfect for sunset. The
Thai, Chinese, and Burmese food
is of consistently high quality.

**NEW BAGAN: Sunset
Garden** $$$
Chinese/Burmese   **Road Map** C3
Yamonar, Thiripyitsaya Quarter
Tel *(061) 65037*
Spellbinding views of the
Lawkananda Pagoda reflected
in the Ayeyarwady extend from
the terrace of this smart restaurant on the riverfront. It is usually
busy with large tour groups
during the day, but is recommended for sunset.

NYAUNG U: Aroma 2 $
Indian   **Road Map** C3
*Thiripyitsaya 4 St (Yarkin Thar
Hotel Rd)*
Tel *(0) 92042630*
"No Good, No Pay" is the motto of
this enduringly popular Indian
restaurant on Nyaung U's main

road. The vegetarian curries, *dals*,
butter chicken, rice, and *chapatis*
are more Burmese than Indian,
but they are tasty enough.

NYAUNG U: Queen $
International   **Road Map** C3
*Near Bagan-Umbra Hotel, Bagan–
Nyaung U Rd*
Tel *(061) 60176*
This popular roadside restaurant
on the outskirts of Nyaung U is
renowned for its superb river
prawn and butterfish curries,
served in traditional lacquerware
or clay pots, with local chicken-
soya bean paste and the full
range of condiments. They also
do tasty burgers, milkshakes, and
lassis throughout the day. A great
place to break a temple tour.

DK Choice

NYAUNG U: Black Bamboo $$
International   **Road Map** C3
Off Thiripyitsaya 4 St
Tel *(061) 60782*
Tucked away off Nyaung U's
main strip, this pretty, French-
run garden restaurant is a
relaxing haven. The menu of
international and Burmese
dishes is well thought-out, and
includes delicious tofu curry,
eggplant salad, and spaghetti
carbonara. The service is slow
or serene, depending on how
hungry you are. The resident
cats are a pleasant distraction.

OLD BAGAN: The Moon $
Vegetarian   **Road Map** C3
North of Ananda Temple
Guacamole *poppadoms* and
tamarind leaf curry are the
standout dishes on The Moon's
imaginative, though strictly
vegetarian, menu. The café's
roadside premises, north of the
Ananda Temple, are spotless, the
food freshly prepared, and the
service friendly, if a little slow.

OLD BAGAN: Yar Pyi $
Vegetarian   **Road Map** C3
North of Ananda Temple
An innovative home-cooked
menu is offered at this family-run
vegetarian café. Try the eggplant
or pumpkin curries, smoked tea-
leaf salad, and lassi. Great value.

OLD BAGAN: Sarabha II $$
Pan-Asian   **Road Map** C3
Tharabar Gate
Everyone staying at the nearby
Tharabar Gate Hotel eats here –
it is twice as good and half the
price. Tasty curries, salads, and
soups, and plenty of Chinese and
Thai options, served up in the
pretty, open-sided dining hall.

OLD BAGAN: Star Beam $$
Burmese/French   **Road Map** C3
North of Ananda Temple
Tel *(0) 9401523810*
Dine on carefully prepared
Myanmar specials, including
delicious Rakhine-style seafood
curry, and a range of popular
Western dishes, from avocado
salad to grilled fish fillet.

**POPA TAUNG KALAT: Popa
Mountain Resort** $$$
International   **Road Map** C3
Mount Popa
Tel *(02) 69168*
Even if you are not staying at this
hilltop resort, it is worth eating
here for the view of the Popa
Taung Kalat monastery on its
volcanic outcrop. Diners also get
to use the gorgeous infinity pool.

Mandalay Region

MANDALAY CITY: Aye Myit Tar $
Burmese   **Road Map** C3
530, 81st St
A great place to sample Burmese
cooking at its best, in a totally
authentic, hygienic environment.
Spotlessly clean (plates arrive

Deep-fried nibbles served at a Burmese street stall

shrink-wrapped), the little café is packed with local families in the evenings. Prices are a bit higher than in the canteen-style places, but the food is all freshly cooked, and delicious.

MANDALAY CITY: Lashio Lay $
Shan   **Road Map** C3
65, 23rd St (83/84)
Delicious Shan specialties cooked fresh each day for a mostly local clientele. Point out your main choice at the counter and they will serve it with all the usual trimmings. Cold beer is available.

MANDALAY CITY: Marie Min $
Indian/Vegetarian   **Road Map** C3
27th St (74/75)
Deservedly popular backpacker hangout serving healthy, delicious Indian vegetarian dishes. The pumpkin curry and samosas are particularly good, as is the strawberry *lassi* for dessert.

MANDALAY CITY: Minthiha $
Teahouse   **Road Map** C3
Corner of 72nd St and 28th St
Everyone comes to this famous traditional teahouse for the mutton puffs rustled up by waiters in matching burgundy shirts.

MANDALAY CITY: Nylon Ice Cream Bar $
Ice cream   **Road Map** C3
83rd St (25/26)
Wonderfully old-fashioned, quintessentially Burmese ice cream parlor – one of the few places in the world where you can order durian flavor ice cream. A pleasant spot in the evenings.

MANDALAY CITY: Pakokku Daw Lay May $
Burmese   **Road Map** C3
73rd St (27/28)
Scrupulously hygienic Burmese restaurant, with gleaming utensils, surfaces, and kitchen. The curries come at breakneck speed with a dozen side dishes.

MANDALAY CITY: Pan Cherry $
Indian   **Road Map** C3
81st St (26/27)
Tel *(02) 39924*
A bare-bones, open-fronted place with tiled floors and plastic chairs, which does a roaring trade with locals and backpackers. Simple but tasty Indian dishes are served up in double-quick time, and there are noodle dishes, too.

MANDALAY CITY: Rainforest $
Thai   **Road Map** C3
27th St (74/75)
Tel *(02) 36234*
This terrific little budget Thai

Spice Garden dining room, overlooking the pool of Hotel by the Red Canal

place is popular mainly with backpackers for its tasty Panang curry, fish bamboo, and salads. Come early for a balcony seat.

MANDALAY CITY: Super 81 $
Southeast Asian   **Road Map** C3
582, 81st St (38/39)
Super 81 is perfectly placed for a meal before a Moustache Brothers show, and ranks among the city's best-value restaurants. Among the dishes to try: soft-shell crab, delicious bean curd clay pot, and chicken with basil.

MANDALAY CITY: BBB $$
International   **Road Map** C3
292, 76th St (26/27), Chan Aye Thar Zan Township
Tel *(02) 73525*
An excellent option for those who've had their fill of curry and noodles, BBB offers club sandwiches, burgers, grills, pizza, and plenty of vegetarian options in a restaurant with a Swiss-chalet feel and ersatz American decor.

MANDALAY CITY: Café City $$
International   **Road Map** C3
66th St (East Moat Rd)
Vintage Burmese signs and plum-colored leather booths lend a retro edge to this hip diner opposite the palace in the heart of Mandalay city. Most foreign visitors come for the lobster, fish, or steak and chips – and the glacial airconditioning.

MANDALAY CITY: Green Elephant $$
Pan-Asian   **Road Map** C3
3H, Block 801, 27th St (64/65), Aung Daw Mu Quarter
Tel *(02) 61237*
🌐 greenelephant-restaurants.com
Housed in a colonial building with a pleasant garden space, the Mandalay branch of this popular chain does a roaring trade with tour groups. All the curries are freshly prepared and full of flavor.

MANDALAY CITY: Ko's Kitchen $$
Thai   **Road Map** C3
282, corner of 19th St & 80th St
Tel *(02) 69576*
Authentic, tasty northern Thai food served in a sparkling clean, air-conditioned dining hall just west of the Mandalay Palace complex. Try their scrumptious fried catfish salad with cashew nuts, or the spicy green chicken curry with rice.

MANDALAY CITY: Simplicity $$
Bakery Café   **Road Map** C3
35th St (91/92)
Located slightly away from the city's downtown core, this organic bakery café offers traditional Shan noodles, home-made dumplings, and other treats in addition to breads and scrumptious Chinese-style pastries.

MANDALAY CITY: The Golden Duck $$
Chinese   **Road Map** C3
192, corner of 80th St & 16th St
Tel *(02) 36808*
There is no better place in Mandalay to eat duck than this multistory Chinese joint in the city center. The meat is ordered by the half or whole, with a side helping of vegetables.

DK Choice

MANDALAY CITY: Koffee Korner $$$
International   **Road Map** C3
70th St (27/28)
Tel *(02) 68648*
Floodlit palm trees, funky Turkish lamps, and a large fish tank make this the most offbeat diner in town. The menu is as international as the clientele: Hungarian goulash, pizza, prawn thermidor, pasta pesto, and monster club sandwiches. Although far from the cheapest option in Mandalay, it is consistently good. Tiger Beer is available by the bottle.

MANDALAY CITY: Spice Garden $$$
Pan-Asian   **Road Map** C3
Hotel by the Red Canal
417, corner of 63rd St & 22nd St
Tel *(02) 68543*
Fine Indian and Pan-Asian cooking is served up by the poolside of Mandalay city's nicest hotel, the boutique Hotel by the Red Canal. Their good-value set menus comprise soup, salads, *tempura*, curry with sticky coconut rice, fruit, semolina cake, and tea-leaf salad with peanuts.

For more information on types of restaurants *see pages 206–7*

The charming courtyard of Monywa's Pleasant Island restaurant

MONYWA: Pleasant Island $$
Chinese/Thai   Road Map C3
Yone Kyi Or, Kan Thar Yar Lake,
Bogyoke Rd
Popular mainly because of its
position opposite the Win Unity
Resort, this tourist-friendly
restaurant sits on its own little
island. Serves pork, beef, chicken,
and fish in Burmese sauces.

PYIN U LWIN: Feel Café (Golf
Course) $$
Burmese/Thai   Road Map D3
Nandar Rd, near the Golf Club
Feel has two outlets in Pyin U
Lwin, and this one by the golf
course is the best, with bigger
portions, better food, and faster
service. Their smoky BBQ chicken
is the crowd puller.

PYIN U LWIN: Golden Triangle $$
Continental   Road Map D3
Mandalay–Lashio Rd
Settle into a wicker chair on the
pillared veranda of this lovely
bakery for a coffee and cinnamon
bun, or a more substantial pizza
or burger.

PYIN U LWIN: The Club
Terrace $$
Shan/European   Road Map D3
25, Club Road, Quarter No. 5
Tel *(085) 23311*
Wonderful food served in an
elegant colonial mansion, with a
delightful garden terrace for
drinks. The cooking – whether
Thai, Chinese, Shan or European
– is excellent, the service friendly,
and the atmosphere relaxing.

PYIN U LWIN: Woodland $$
European   Road Map D3
53, Circular Rd
This large garden restaurant
is the most animated place in
Pyin U Lwin, hosting live music
most evenings. They have an
extensive menu: try the pizza
or soft-shell crab. Cocktails are
available. Guests have access
to free Wi-Fi.

Eastern Myanmar

HSIPAW: Mrs Popcorn's Garden $
International   Road Map D3
Myauk Myo
Relaxed backpackers' restaurant
on the outskirts of town, serving
simple food made by the kindly,
eponymous owner herself,
including fried rice, juices, shakes,
fruit salad, and ginger lemon tea.

HSIPAW: Pontoon Coffee $
International   Road Map D3
Near Pontoon Bridge
Perfect chocolate-chip muffins
and espresso coffee, served by
welcoming Australian expat
Maureen, who has settled on
the leafy outskirts of Hsipaw. The
café is in a beautiful teak house
with a tranquil garden to the rear.
They also rustle up toasted sand-
wiches with real cheese and
home-made brown bread.

DK Choice

INLE LAKE: Inthar Heritage $$
Intha   Road Map D4
Inpawkhon village
Tel *(0) 95251232*
The most congenial stop for
lunch on the lake. Recipes from
Intha grandmothers are lovingly
prepared using home-grown,
organic produce, and served in
a warm, wood-lined dining hall
with wonderful views over the
rice fields. Everything is exquisitely presented, and the prices
are reasonable. Recommended
for cat lovers, who will enjoy
watching the gorgeous resident
Burmese cats.

KALAW: Paye Pyae $
Shan   Road Map D4
Union Highway, next to Thirigayha
Restaurant
This simple, unpretentious little
café in Kalaw is packed all day
with locals eating its tasty Shan

noodle clay pot meals containing
an exotic array of vegetables
and mushrooms.

KENGTUNG: Azure $
Chinese   Road Map E3
Naung Tung Lakeside
Reasonably priced Chinese
restaurant facing the lake,
with tables under a shady tree.
Chicken in cashew nut sauce
is their most popular dish, and
draft beer is available.

NYAUNGSHWE: Everest Nepali
Food Center $
Nepalese/Indian   Road Map D4
Kuaung Tau Anau St
Tel *(0) 9428322745*
Light, fragrant, and mostly
vegetarian curries, *dals*, and
chapatis served up in a cozy,
cool dining room down a quiet
back street. Great flavors and
charming service. Chilled bottled
beers are available.

NYAUNGSHWE: Lin Htett $
Burmese   Road Map D4
Southwest corner of Mingalar
Market, Yone Gyi Rd
Traditional Burmese place in the
town center where you can order
a range of meat and fish curries,
served with all the trimmings,
for just a few dollars.

NYAUNGSHWE: Live Dim Sum
House $
Chinese/Shan   Road Map D4
Yone Gyi Rd, near November Hotel
Tel *(0) 9428136964*
Delicious dim sum and Shan tofu
clay pot meals, prepared in an
open kitchen (hence "live") and
served in a clean, well-presented
restaurant by enthusiastic staff.

NYAUNGSHWE: Min Min $
International   Road Map D4
Yone Gyi Rd, Kan Thar Quarter
The friendliest of welcomes is
guaranteed at Min Min, a lively
little backpacker haunt where
you can enjoy tasty, mild local
curries, pancakes, pasta pesto,
and cheap cocktails.

A variety of dim sum on offer at
Nyaungshwe's Live Dim Sum House

NYAUNGSHWE: Sin Yaw $
Pan-Asian　　　**Road Map** D4
Yone Gyi Rd, Kan Thar Quarter
Tel *(0) 940351883*
This great-value place offers flavor-packed local dishes such as crispy fried lake fish, spiced Shan pork, and white seaweed salad, served in a cheerful diner by a friendly family.

NYAUNGSHWE: Thanakha Garden $
Burmese/Burgers　**Road Map** D4
43, Thar Zi Quarter, near the Paradise Hotel and Mingalar Market
Tel *(0) 9428371552*
Well-presented restaurant run with pride by a warm local family. Prawn and vegetable *tempura* and Inle fish curry are the standout dishes. Come early if you want a terrace table.

NYAUNGSHWE: Beyond Taste $$
Burmese/Western　**Road Map** D4
10, Phaung Daw Pyan St, Nant Pan Quarter
Tel *(0) 9428358111*
A restaurant that consistently generates superlative reviews, and with good reason. It serves local curries and Western food (great pizza), plus cocktails. The service is five-star.

NYAUNGSHWE: Green Chilli $$
Burmese/Thai　　**Road Map** D4
Hospital Rd, Mingalar Quarter
Tel *(081) 209132*
Varied and deliciously spicy curries are served in a beautiful Shan-style house with local art on the walls. The portions are generous, the house wine good, and the service attentive.

NYAUNGSHWE: Viewpoint Lodge $$$
Shan Fusion　　**Road Map** D4
Near Canal Bridge
Tel *(081) 209062*
The classiest place to eat in town. Go for the extravagant, tapas-style "Shan Discovery" menu, which comes in its own tabletop long-tailed boat. There are plenty of vegetarian options à la carte: try the sublime tofu and potato curry. The restaurant offers snappy service and a lovely setting, with views over rice fields. A bit pricey, but worth it.

PINDAYA: Green Tea $$
Burmese/Shan　**Road Map** D3
Shwe Umin Pagoda St
One of the loveliest places to eat in the region, both for its breezy waterfront location – which overlooks Pone Ta Lote Lake to the stupas of Pindaya village – and its fabulous, appealingly

presented Burmese and Shan cuisine. Be sure to ask for a table on the veranda.

TAUNGGYI: Sein Myanmar $
Shan　　　　**Road Map** D3
Bogyoke Aung San Rd
This is a busy Shan place, famous above all for its delicious *htamin jin* – a regional specialty that consists of balls of fermented rice kneaded with Inle Lake fish, tomato paste, and potatoes. The perfect stop for travelers heading back to Inle Lake after visiting the stupa complex at Kakku.

TAUNGGYI: Sunset Wine Garden $$$
International　　**Road Map** D3
Aythaya Vineyard, Htone Bo
Tel *(081) 208653*
Set amid rolling vineyards on the outskirts of the city, this smart restaurant serves dishes to complement its wines, including fish in banana leaves and mutton balls with bean sprouts.

Northern Myanmar

BHAMO: Shamie $
Indian　　　　**Road Map** D2
Tiyet Rd
Filling, flavorsome Indo-Muslim *biryanis*, kebabs, and meaty curries, as well as filled *parathas* and *chai* for breakfast. A handy choice if you're staying at the nearby Friendship Hotel.

KATHA: Shwe Sisa $
Chinese　　　　**Road Map** C2
Strand Rd
This beer station enjoys a prime spot on the riverside, and does grilled chicken and pork ribs to accompany your drinks. It is also one of the few places in town that screens live soccer.

MYITKYINA: Kiss Me $
Burmese　　　**Road Map** D2
Zaw John Rd
Fine river views and an extensive menu of mostly Burmese specialties, including a tasty tea-leaf salad, are on offer at this restaurant, a taxi ride north of the center of town, next to the Su Taung Pyi Pagoda complex.

MYITKYINA: River View $
Burmese　　　**Road Map** D2
Zaw John Rd
The dim sum served at this waterfront restaurant gets less enthusiastic reviews than the sunset vistas, which are sublime. A good spot for a leisurely evening drink of cold beer.

The unpretentious interior of the Mi Cho café, serving Indian food in Mawlamyine

MYITKYINA: Bamboo Field $$
Burmese　　　**Road Map** D2
313, Su Taung Pyi Rd (Union St)
Myitkyina's most upscale restaurant hosts weekend dance shows and karaoke. The menu is as diverse as the clientele – a mix of visiting businessmen and foreign aid workers.

Southeastern Myanmar

HPA-AN: San Ma Tau Myanmar $
Burmese　　　**Road Map** D5
290, Bogyoke St
Clean, friendly restaurant whose *smorgasbord* of fragrant curries and stir-fries draws crowds from across the town. You'll find it hard to spend more than a few dollars.

HPA-AN: White $
Burmese　　　**Road Map** D5
Thitsa St
Eat your fill of Shan noodle dishes and spicy mashed potato with tangy gravies, plus great *mohinga* and a variety of Myanmar snacks at this bustling Burmese all-day breakfast place.

MAWLAMYINE (MOULMEIN): Mi Cho $
Indian　　　　**Road Map** D5
North Bogyoke Rd
Great Indo-Muslim food in a tiny, cramped café. Get there early for the famous *biryani*. They also cook delicious *dal* and rice, and chicken curry with mango pickle.

MAWLAMYINE (MOULMEIN): Ykko $$
Pan-Asian　　　**Road Map** D5
Corner of Kannar St & Htarwai Bridge St
Tel *(0) 9041591212*
With a riverside setting, Ykko is a spruce, modern chain with reliable Wi-Fi and blissful air-conditioning offering a choice of a hundred different Asian dishes, iced coffees, and ice cream.

SHOPPING IN MYANMAR

Myanmar's traditional arts and crafts have experienced a sharp revival during the recent tourism boom. Lacquerware, carved wood, metalware, marionettes, brocade embroidery, and colorful cloth paintings fill stalls and shops around the country's main attractions, creating vibrant photo opportunities and a mouthwatering prospect for lovers of authentic Southeast Asian crafts. In the big cities, meanwhile, multistory malls are where the affluent middle classes shop for modern, imported consumer goods. For fresh produce, covered and street markets are still very much a staple throughout Myanmar, and provide an enthralling spectacle for foreign visitors more accustomed to supermarkets. The one common denominator, regardless of the size and kind of shop, is the politeness and good-natured demeanor of the vendors. Although haggling is very much the norm, it is unfailingly conducted in a relaxed spirit, often over a glass of tea and plate of nibbles.

Shoppers at Yangon's Bogyoke Aung San Zei, commonly known as Scott's Market

Opening Hours

Most city shops are open from 9am to 8 or 9pm. Yangon and Mandalay malls open by 10am and close around 10pm. It is worth keeping in mind that staff frequently begin closing well before the appointed hour if trade is slack. Traditional *zeis*, or markets, generally operate from sunrise to sunset. Some *zeis* also host busy night markets in the surrounding streets, which run until midnight, or later. Virtually all shops open seven days a week, except during the annual New Year festival of Thingyan (April), when they close for four or five days.

Bargaining

Apart from stores in shopping malls, high-end tourist shops, and food and drink outlets, where prices are by and large non-negotiable, the first sum quoted is almost always far higher than the final one the seller will accept. To reduce the amount, the buyer has to be ready to haggle. Effective negotiation requires three things: patience, persistence, and a sense of humor. Maintain a pleasant attitude throughout – remember that this is a social encounter as much as a commercial transaction. Don't rush the process – driving down a price may take 10 minutes or longer. And if all else fails, try walking away, which tends to prompt a drastic reduction.

How to Pay

Only a handful of the high-end boutiques and emporia in Myanmar accept credit or debit cards; the others accept payment only in cash, with mint condition, or nearly new, unfolded US dollar bills *(see pp232–3)*. For big-ticket items, such as objets d'art or pieces of quality lacquerware, paying with high-value bills will bring the price down a little as the rate of exchange offered will be more favorable. Change is always given in Myanmar's currency, the kyat. Kyat can be used to purchase low-priced or everyday items, such as cotton clothing and simple souvenirs. Receipts tend to be issued only in higher-end handicraft shops and modern malls, but they are available on request almost everywhere.

Rights and Refunds

As a rule, sales are final. Although modern shops in malls may have a returns policy, on the whole, once the money has changed hands, there's no going back. Guarantees tend only to apply to imported electrical goods, and cover replacements not refunds.

Open-air riverside market at Bhamo in Northern Myanmar

Shwedagon Pagoda's *zaungdan* shops with religious paraphernalia, textiles, and crafts

Packaging and Posting

When shopping in tourist souvenir emporia, visitors will commonly be offered export packaging. Goods will be wrapped very well for safe transport on a plane, with layers of newspaper and padding in the case of more expensive or fragile items. This service is always included in the price. With larger, valuable purchases, such as furniture or rugs, some kind of international shipping service may also be offered.

Crafts, Antiques, and Souvenir Emporia

The widest choice of traditional and antique Burmese items is offered in large emporia located at major tourist centers and in the big cities. Wonderful storehouses of hand-crafted woodwork, palm-leaf etchings, handwoven textiles, paintings, stone figurines, and Buddhas of bell-metal, bronze, and brass, these emporia tend to stock both antiques and recently made items – although it can be difficult to tell the two apart, as newer objects are often distressed or artfully worn. Lacquerware *(yun-de)*, in the form of round boxes, pedestal dishes *(kalat)*, stemmed rice bowls with spired lids *(hsun ok)*, tea trays, stackable tiffin carriers *(hsun gyaink)*, trunks, screens, and polygonal tables, dominates the showrooms, along with walls of colorfully attired string puppets and *kalagas*,

panels of velvet elaborately embroidered with gold and silver thread, showing Hindu or Buddhist mythological scenes.
In Yangon, one of the oldest established and best-stocked stores is **Nandawun**, on Baho Road, which also has a branch in the National Museum *(see p72)*. In a similar vein is **Elephant House**, run by the owners of the popular Green Elephant chain of restaurants, and **Augustine's Souvenir Shop** in Kamayut Township, one of Myanmar's foremost antique specialists. In Mandalay, **Aung Nan Myanmar Handicraft Workshop** is a great one-stop souvenir shop, as is **Shwe War Thein Handicrafts**, near the Tharabar Gate in Old Bagan, where visitors may watch teams of artisans at work. Most of the five-star hotels also have quality, on-site Burmese handicraft boutiques.
Many stores offer traditional Delta parasols for sale, but for the widest selection it is best to visit the workshops in Pathein *(see p105)* or, failing that, the delightful **Shwe Pathein** in Yangon, where handmade parasols are displayed in a wood-lined showroom.
Intricately decorated string puppets *(yok thei)*, depicting characters from Burmese mythology and folk history, make popular souvenirs. They may be seen on sale at emporia, shops, and stalls

across the country, and come in a range of different sizes and levels of detail. Most expensive of all are the large antique marionettes embellished with sequins and brocade. A huge selection is available at the shop attached to the **Mandalay Marionettes** theater in Mandalay.

Shopping Malls

Multistory shopping malls are springing up in all of Myanmar's major towns and cities, but particularly in Yangon and Mandalay. Air-conditioned and impeccably clean, with multiplex cinemas and Western-style food and drink outlets, they can be great places to recuperate from the heat of the streets, although the shops, which sell mostly imported consumer goods and modern fashion clothing, tend to appeal less to foreign visitors than the souvenir emporia. In Yangon, **Parkson FMI Center** on Bogyoke Aung San Road is the largest mall located downtown. **Blazon Shopping Center** offers brand-name stores. Farther north, the **Taw Win Center** *(see p221)* and **Dagon Center** are both more recent additions. Visitors to Mandalay are spoiled for choice when it comes to malls. The downtown **Mann Myanmar Plaza** and **Diamond Plaza** are among the largest in the country. **78 Mall** is also worth a browse.

Carved wooden statues at a handicrafts workshop in Mandalay

Markets

Burmese *zeis*, or markets, come in a variety of different forms, but the main ones, in big towns and cities, are nearly all covered, and divided into separate sections for fresh produce, clothes, hardware, and so on. Bordering on the scale of a mega mall, but with a distinctly old-fashioned Burmese feel, **Bogyoke Aung San Zei** (open 10am–5pm Tue–Sun) in down-town Yangon is Myanmar's largest covered market, with around 2,000 retailers packed on two floors of a huge, pink, colonial-era building. Cheaper than the emporia and tourist shops, its stores sell a full range of traditional Burmese arts, crafts, and antiques, in addition to regular local goods. The equivalent in Mandalay is the sprawling **Zegyo Market** *(see p143)*, ranged over four stories.

Each town also has municipal markets where everyday goods and fresh produce are sold from dawn onward. In Yangon, **Theingyi Zei** near Mahabandula Road is the largest, with an extensive covered section that spills into the surrounding streets. **Mani-Sithu Market** in Nyaung U (Bagan) offers a range of fresh vegetables and fruit, as well as clothing and collectibles.

In Shan State it is worth making time for one of the "five-day markets," held in specified towns every fifth day according to a rotating calendar. Local travel agents and guides will know the full schedule. In Inle Lake, the two main ones are at **Nyaungshwe** *(see p169)*, next to the main street, where a scaled-down version functions daily, and at **Inthein** *(see p167)*. Both attract large numbers of mino-rity people from the surround-ing hills, and are prime sources of authentic souvenirs, such as cheroots, hand-woven head-scarves, Shan jackets, Intha paja-mas, and other traditional attire.

Some streets after large *zei* also double as night markets. In Yangon, barbecue bars spring up after dark on **19th Street** in the heart of Chinatown (also known as Tayote Tan). Popularly called Beer Bar Street – or

Inle Lake flower seller with bunches of pink lotus, Eastern Myanmar

occasionally Myanmar Lan Kwai Fong – it attracts diners from across the city with grilled meat skewers, steaming bowls of dumplings, and exotic Chinese delicacies, including toasted grasshoppers. In Mandalay, a similar night market operates in the roads around Zegyo Market.

Pagodas

Zaungdan, the covered, stepped approaches to large pagodas, are usually lined with brightly lit, beautifully arranged market stalls specializing in religious paraphernalia such as incense, candles, floral offerings, and ritual utensils. These little shops are also good places to pick up Buddha figurines in wood, stone, and metal; sequin-encrusted ensembles worn by young boys at their *shin pyu* ceremonies; and various musical instruments, especially temple bells, drums, and wind chimes.

The largest such bazaars radiate from the **Shwedagon Pagoda** *(see pp74–7)* in Yangon, whose eastern entrance, spanned by sumptuously carved and decorated roof beams, is arguably the most attractive. In Mandalay, the **Mahamuni Temple's** *(see p142)* four entrances are also lined with stalls selling crafts, textiles, and clothing, as well as religious offerings. Two other noteworthy temple bazaars, both specifically aimed at foreign tourists, are those held on market day in the village of Inthein *(see p166)*, on Inle Lake, and at the **Ananda Temple** *(see pp124–5)* in Bagan.

Gemstones and Jewelry

Myanmar is the source of the world's finest jade and rubies, as well as many other precious and semiprecious gemstones, although buying them is probably best left to experts – jade is notoriously difficult to value accurately. That said, most of the jewelry shops in Yangon's Bogyoke Aung San Zei are reputable, as are the pieces of inlaid silver on sale at upscale hotel boutiques and emporia. Nearly all of the jade mined in Myanmar passes through the fascinating **Jade Market** in Mandalay *(see p142)*, where pieces both large and small are bought, sold, and polished.

Tiny carvings made from a variety of colored jade, Bogyoke Aung San Zei

Clothing and Textiles

Traditional Burmese *longyis* and *htameins* are sold at shops and market stalls around Myanmar, along with more contemporary fashions. For luxury versions in silk, worn for special occasions such as weddings, visit the large malls in Mandalay and Yangon, or Bogyoke Aung San Zei. Some of the finest Myanmar silk is woven in workshops on Inle Lake, where thread from the stems of lotus blooms is spun and transformed into shimmering garments, both pure and mixed with standard silk and cotton. The workshop most famous for lotus silk weaving is **Ko Than Hlaing Silk and Lotus Weaving**, in Inpawkhon village, where it is possible to watch the manufacturing process in action, and whose showroom is lined with *longyis*, blouses, shirts, and scarves in a variety of colors. The five-day markets held in towns and villages are also good places to find local clothes, especially the Thai fisherman-style pajamas traditionally worn by the Intha, and vivid yellow and red scarves favored by local Pa-O women. In

Mandalay, **Sut Ngai** is a famous source of traditional Kachin costume, including the button- and silver-adorned black velvet jackets, and the handwoven sequined hats worn at festivals.

Books and Art

Yangon is by far the best place in Myanmar to stock up on English-language books. **Bagan Book House** in the downtown area is a city institution that stocks an unrivaled selection of specialist guides and other titles on the country, as well as a great range of paperback fiction. **Myanmar Book Center** and **Monument Books** are two other excellent bookstores that cater mainly to students and expatriates, and have branches

Monument Books in Yangon, catering mainly to students and expatriates

in both Yangon and Mandalay. For an excellent selection of contemporary Burmese sculpture, painting, and photography, visit Yangon's **Pansodan Art Gallery**, **River Gallery**, or **Gallery Sixty Five**. Pansodan also has old advertisements, posters, and photographs.

DIRECTORY

Crafts, Antiques, and Souvenir Emporia

Augustine's Souvenir Shop
25, Thiri Mingalar Rd (Attia Rd), Kamayut Township, Yangon. **Tel** (01) 525359. W augustinesouvenir.com

Aung Nan Myanmar Handicraft Workshop
Road Map C3. 97–99, Mandalay-Sagaing Rd, Mandalay. **Tel** (02) 70145. W aungnan.com

Elephant House
Shopping Arcade, Inya Lake Hotel, 37, Kaba Aye Pagoda Rd, Yangon. **Tel** (01) 661887. W elephant-house.com

Mandalay Marionettes
Road Map C3. 66th St (26/27), Mandalay. **Tel** (02) 34446. W mandalaymarionettes.com

Nandawun
City Map B3. Baho Rd/ Ahlone Rd, Yangon. **Tel** (01) 221271. W myanmarhandicrafts.com

Shwe Pathein
City Map D5. 276, Strand Rd, Pabedan, Yangon. W myanmarhandmade.com

Shwe War Thein Handicrafts
Road Map C3. Tharabar Gate, Old Bagan. **Tel** (061) 67032.

Shopping Malls

78 Mall
Road Map C3. 38th St (78/80), Mandalay.

Blazon Shopping Center
City Map C1. U Wisara Rd/Chindwin Rd, Yangon.

Dagon Center
City Map B1. Pyay Rd/ Bagaya Rd, Yangon.

Diamond Plaza
Road Map C3. 34th St (77/78), Mandalay.

Mann Myanmar Plaza
Road Map C3. 28th St (84/85), Mandalay.

Parkson FMI Center
City Map D4. 380, Bogyoke Aung San Rd, Yangon.

Markets

19th Street
City Map C4. 19th St, Chinatown, Yangon.

Bogyoke Aung San Zei
City Map D4. Bogyoke Aung San Rd, Yangon.

Mani-Sithu Market
Road Map C3. Junction of Lanmadaw Rds 1 & 2, Nyaung U, Bagan.

Theingyi Zei
City Map C4. From 26th St to Shwedagon Pagoda Rd, between Anawrahta Rd and Mahabandula Rd, Yangon.

Clothing and Textiles

Ko Than Hlaing Silk and Lotus Weaving
Road Map D4. Inpawkhon, Inle Lake. **Tel** (0) 95211891. W silkandlotusweaving.biz

Sut Ngai
Road Map C3. 237, 33rd St (82/83), Mandalay. **Tel** (0) 92051707.

Books and Art

Bagan Book House
City Map E5. 100, 37th St, between Merchant Rd and Mahabandula Rd, Yangon. **Tel** (01) 377227.

Gallery Sixty Five
City Map D4. 65, Yaw Min Gyi St, Yangon. W gallerysixtyfive.com

Monument Books
City Map C1. Yangon: 150, Dhammazedi Rd. Road Map C3. Mandalay: 87/2, 77th St (26/27). W monumentbooks.com

Myanmar Book Center
City Map B3. Yangon: Baho Rd/Ahlone Rd. **Tel** (01) 212409. Road Map C3. Mandalay: Diamond Plaza Mall, 34th St (77/78). W myanmarbook.com

Pansodan Art Gallery
City Map E4. 286, Pansodan St, Yangon. **Tel** (0) 95130846.

River Gallery
City Map E5. Strand Hotel, 92, Strand Rd, Yangon. W rivergallerymyanmar.com

ENTERTAINMENT IN MYANMAR

Decades of military rule have had a stifling effect on Myanmar's entertainment industry. Visitors tend to spend evenings in hotels and restaurants, although the big cities also have a handful of venues that showcase traditional music, dance, and puppetry. The performers are mostly graduates of Mandalay's National School of Performing Arts, a crucible of talent for classical Burmese forms that now survive largely due to government support and income from tourism. The country's once thriving movie industry has fallen on hard times, and today its films tend to be low-budget romantic comedies on DVD; cinemas survive on Hollywood and Bollywood blockbusters, and Cantonese Kung Fu flicks. The club scene, although limited to a small number of upscale hotels, is developing fast with the rise of the Internet and a new generation of well-heeled youngsters in the big cities.

Performer in traditional costume at the Mintha Theater in Mandalay

Classical Burmese Music and Dance

Most of Myanmar's five-star hotels, and a few dedicated theaters in the big cities, host regular recitals of Burmese music and dance (see pp36–7).

Enlivened by striking traditional attire, the performances are as much of a feast for the eyes as the ears. They vividly underline how exotic and otherworldly Burma's classical culture must have appeared to foreign travelers in the 19th century, when the elegant forms currently staged were developed, refined, and codified in the court of the Konbaung Dynasty.

As in centuries past, Mandalay city is the place where visitors can most reliably expect to experience traditional music and dance presented in an authentic form. The **Mintha Theater**, near the palace complex, hosts a special tourist show from 8:30 to 9:30pm each evening, featuring top dancers in fabulous costumes accompanied by a five-piece classical orchestra. In Yangon, the equivalent venue is the impressive **Karaweik Palace**, floating on Kandawgyi Lake (see p79), where traditional songs and dances are presented against a sumptuous backdrop.

Pwe and A-nyeint

Apart from *nat* festivals, it is almost impossible to find traditional *pwe*, but performances of its folk theater form, *a-nyeint* (see p37), are staged daily by Mandalay's world-famous **Moustache Brothers**. Their notoriety derives from the fact that they spent years in detention for parodying the military government, and that their fate was publicized by Amnesty International. Ever since, crowds of foreign visitors have filled the makeshift theater in their home in downtown Mandalay to experience the show – a mix of slapstick, song, clowning, and satire, delivered in often incomprehensible English. Although Par Par Lay, the group leader, died in 2013, Lu Maw and Lu Zaw continue to perform. The rest of the company is made up of the wives and daughters-in-law of the trio, as well as members of the wider family. Many visitors complain that the show has become overcommercialized and has little entertainment value, but it is nevertheless a cultural institution in the city.

Marionettes

While most culture shows held at hotels and venues in the country usually include a short taste of traditional puppetry,

Colorfully dressed Kachin folk dancers at the Karaweik Palace, Yangon

A local cinema in Yangon displaying film posters

only **Mandalay Marionettes**, in a tiny theater near the palace complex, stage complete performances, with several different puppets and live music. Shows last an hour and could include a short introductory talk and buffet supper, as well as musical interludes on the Burmese harp, and a memorable candle dance.

Traditional Burmese marionettes used in *yok thei pwe* puppet theater productions

Cinemas

Myanmar's government censors are still wary of English-language movies, though things are starting to change, and mainstream Hollywood fare is increasingly common on the silver screen in Yangon and Mandalay. However, imported Indian, Cantonese, and South Korean movies still dominate. Since the onset of military rule in the 1960s, the country's own film industry has been in sharp decline. Only around 70 of the 244 grand cinema halls that used to exist in Myanmar survive. However, foreign investment has fueled the growth in

Yangon and Mandalay of new multiscreen cineplexes with state-of-the-art digital 3D projectors and surround sound. In Yangon, two of the most conveniently located include the one in the **Taw Win Center** on Pyay Road, near the National Museum, and in the **Junction Maw Tin** on Anawrahta Road.

Clubs and Bars

Yangon is the only place in the country with anything close to what foreign tourists would recognize as a nightlife. A handful of small, exclusive clubs and bars attached to the city's five-star hotels – patronized by a mix of youngsters from elite Myanmar families, aid workers, expatriates, and business travelers – host DJ gigs most weekends, and dancing until around midnight. The most consistently lively are the **Music Club** at the Park Royal, **DJ Bar** near the Inya Lake Hotel, and **GTR** on Kaba Aye Pagoda Road, the last being one of the few nightspots where the female clientele aren't predominantly sex workers. **BME2**, near the Summit Parkview Hotel, is similar to GTR, but tends to attract a slightly older crowd, and stays open the latest (usually until 3am). For local atmosphere, try **19th Street** *(see p219)* in Chinatown, which transforms into the Beer Bar Street (also called Myanmar Lan Kwai Fong) night market, where an alfresco meal of grilled meat and cold beers can be eaten at rows of Formica tables.

DIRECTORY

Classical Burmese Music and Dance

Karaweik Palace
City Map E2.
Kandawgyi Nature Park,
Kandawgyi Lake, Bahan Tsp,
Yangon. **Tel** (01) 295744.
ⓦ **karaweikpalace.com**

Mintha Theater
Road Map C3.
27th St (65/66), Mandalay.
Tel (0) 96803607.
ⓦ **minthatheater.com**

Pwe and A-nyeint

Moustache Brothers
Road Map C3.
39th St (80/81), Mandalay.
Tel (0) 943034220.

Marionettes

Mandalay Marionettes
Road Map C3.
66th St (26/27), Mandalay.
Tel (02) 34446.
ⓦ **mandalaymarionettes.com**

Cinemas

Junction Maw Tin
City Map C4. Junction Complex,
Anawrahta Rd, Yangon.
Tel (01) 218161.
ⓦ **junctioncentregroup.com/junction-mawtin.html**

Taw Win Center
City Map C3.
45, Pyay Rd, Yangon.
Tel (01) 8600111, ext. 3333.
ⓦ **tawwincentre.com/cinema**

Clubs and Bars

BME2
City Map C3. 350, Ahlone Rd
(next to the Summit Parkview
Hotel), Yangon.

DJ Bar
U Htun Nyein St,
near Inya Lake Hotel,
37, Kaba Aye Pagoda Rd, Yangon.
Tel (0) 95116767.

GTR
near Inya Lake Hotel, Yangon.
Tel (0) 9595135061.
ⓦ **facebook.com/GTRClub**

Music Club
City Map D4. Park Royal Yangon,
33, Alan Pya Pagoda St,
Yangon. **Tel** (01) 250388.
ⓦ **parkroyalhotels.com**

SPORTS AND OUTDOOR ACTIVITIES

The national pastime of *chinlone (see p40)* aside, participation in sport has been at low levels during the decades of military rule in Myanmar. With access to satellite TV, however, the country has seen a dramatic surge in the number of people watching and playing soccer. Among the elite, golf has also grown in popularity: Yangon has many international-standard courses, and there are numerous others farther afield. Swimming and cycling are likely to be the outdoor pursuits most often enjoyed by foreign visitors, although with enough of a budget, scuba diving in the Andaman Sea is another possibility.

Soccer

The Burmese are mad about soccer. This passionate, country-wide following for the sport is a relatively new phenomenon. Only about a decade ago, there were just a handful of semi-professional sides. Now, between 12 and 14 fully professional teams play in the Myanmar National League, inaugurated in 2009, whose three top sides are Mandalay's Yadanabon FC, Yangon United FC, and Kanbawza FC of Taunggyi. Fixtures are advertised on the teams' websites, and tickets (inexpensive by international standards) may be purchased at the gates.

If anything, support for European leagues, particularly the English Premiership, is even more enthusiastic than for domestic competitions, and foreign matches are routinely screened in bars. Manchester United enjoys the widest fan base across Myanmar.

Golf

A legacy of Burma's colonial heritage (and Scottish connections), golf enjoys a strong following among the country's upper classes, explaining why Yangon boasts one of the most impressive courses in Southeast Asia. Designed by Gary Player, the **Pun Hlaing Golf Club**, 8 miles (13 km) west of downtown across the river, is set amid a manicured tropical landscape, and kept in tournament condition year round. The same is true of the **Royal Mingalardon**, another prestigious course nearby. Yangon is also home to the **City Golf Resort**. For a more

historic feel, visit the grand **Yangon Golf Club**, founded in 1909 and Myanmar's oldest functioning golf club. Another vintage course is the one at **Pyin U Lwin**, the former British summer capital of Upper Burma. The **Yay Dagon Taung Golf Resort** in Mandalay, a half-hour drive from the town center, is the region's finest, with the **Shwe Man Taung Golf Resort** at the foot of Mandalay Hill a close second. A quality 18-hole course has been built at **Bagan**, and there is a nine-hole course at **Thandwe/Ngapali**.

Trekking

Kalaw is Myanmar's prime trekking destination *(see p173)*, thanks to its proximity to Inle Lake and several minority villages. **Ever Smile** and **A1 Information and Trekking Service** are among many Kalaw operators who organize day hikes and overnight stays. Less frequented alternatives, from where it is also possible to trek into ethnic minority areas, include Hsipaw, farther north, and Kengtung, to the east. In Hsipaw, local guesthouses such as **Lily The Home** or guides such as **Than Htike** can make all the necessary arrangements; in Kengtung the **Princess Hotel** can organize guides and treks.

In the far north, treks into the spectacular terrain around Hkakabo Razi, the country's highest mountain (19,294 ft/ 5,881 m), begin at Putao in Kachin State, where **Putao Trekking House** is the recommended operator. In the far west of Myanmar, routes up the highest peak in Chin State, Nat

Ma Taung, also known as Mount Victoria (10,016 ft/3,053 m), start on the massif's eastern side.

Cycling

Bicycles are widely available for rent at Inle Lake; at Bagan, where cycling offers a healthy alternative to the horse carts; and at Ngapali for leisurely tours of the fields and groves behind the beach. Most of the cycles are Chinese made, gearless, and usually in dubious states of repair. Test drive a few and check that the brakes work and that the steering column is sound. However, some companies have started renting out mountain bikes, which are more expensive but also sturdier and more comfortable.

In Yangon, **Bike World Explores Myanmar** is a Burmese-Australian outfit who run popular weekly guided city rides (6:30am on Sundays), as well as custom tours to most parts of the country. They run mountain-biking expeditions up Mount Victoria from Nyaung U and can arrange permits for the ascent.

The countryside around Inle Lake in Shan State, ideal for trekking and cycling

Swimming

Many mid-range and all five-star hotels in Myanmar have swimming pools, although few open their doors to nonresidents. One exception is the **Sedona** in Yangon, which has a huge, curviform pool with an island bar that is busy with expatriate families after school hours, but peaceful during the day.

While swimming in the country's rivers is not recommended, the waters of the Andaman Sea are blissfully warm, and safe, in Myanmar's top three resorts: **Chaungtha** *(see p105)*, **Ngwe Saung** *(see p105)*, and **Ngapali** *(see p106)*. The last has the clearest water.

Diving and Snorkeling

One of the world's last great tropical marine wildernesses, the Myeik Archipelago in the far south is among Southeast Asia's least explored diving destinations. The government maintains strict control over access to this ecologically fragile area,

Strolling next to the warm and clear waters off Ngapali beach

which offers no accredited diving schools or accommodations. Anyone wishing to dive here must join an expensive live-aboard diving tour, mostly based out of Phuket or Ranong in Thailand. To keep costs down, clients may arrange for the boat to pick them up in Kawthaung, Myanmar's southernmost town, two or three days into the tour, and drop them off in the same place. Recommended Thailand-based diving companies include **Nautica Diving** and **AIDC**. Permits to enter the Myeik Marine Reserve must be arranged in advance through

the Myanmar Travels and Tours office in Yangon *(see p229)*.

Good diving is also available in the relatively unexplored waters off Ngapali *(see p106)*, with most hotels offering trips to coral reefs, islets, wrecks, and caves. Contact diving specialists at **Ngapali Water Sports Center** at their office in the village, or via their website. A cheaper option would be to jump on a local fishing boat for a snorkeling tour in the crystal-clear waters just to the north of the resort; these leave every morning and afternoon from various sites on the beachfront.

DIRECTORY

Golf

Bagan Golf Course
Road Map C3. Anawrahta Rd, Nyaung U. **Tel** (0) 9402630885. **W** bagangolfresort.net

City Golf Resort
Thiri Mingalar Rd, Insein Township, Yangon. **Tel** (01) 641763. **W** citygolfresort.com

Pun Hlaing Golf Club
Pun Hlaing Golf Estate Ave, Yangon. **Tel** (01) 684021. **W** punhlaing-golfestate.com

Pyin U Lwin Golf Club
Road Map D3. Golf Club Rd, Pyin U Lwin. **Tel** (085) 22382.

Royal Mingalardon Golf Club
1, Mingalardon Garden City, Off NH 3, Yangon. **Tel** (0) 9449222222. **W** royalmingalardon-golf.com

Shwe Man Taung Golf Resort
Road Map C3. On the west side of Mandalay Hill, Mandalay. **Tel** (02) 60570.

Thandwe/Ngapali
Road Map C4. Off Ngapali beach, near Thandwe.

Yangon Golf Club
Kha Yae Pin St, Yangon. **Tel** (01) 635563. **W** yangongolfclub.com

Yay Dagon Taung Golf Resort
Road Map C3. Near Yay Tay Gun Hill, Mandalay. **Tel** (02) 88731.

Trekking

A1 Information and Trekking Service
Road Map D4. Merchant St, Kalaw. **Tel** (0) 949585199. **W** a1trekking. blogspot.co.uk

Ever Smile
Road Map D4. Yuzana St, Kalaw. **W** eversmile trekking.com

Lily The Home
Road Map D3. 108, Aung Tha Pyae Road, Hsipaw. **Tel** (082) 80318.

Princess Hotel
Road Map E3. 21, Zay Dan Kalay Rd, Kengtung. **Tel** (084) 21319.

Putao Trekking House
Road Map D1. Putao. **W** putaotrekking-house.com

Than Htike
Road Map D3. Hsipaw. **Tel** (0) 936186646.

Cycling

Bike World Explores Myanmar (BWEM)
10F, Khabaung Rd (Martin Avenue), 6 Miles Pyay Rd, Yangon. **W** myanmar-panorama.com

Swimming

Sedona Hotel
1, Kaba Aye Pagoda Rd, Yankin Township, Yangon. **Tel** (01) 860 5377. **W** sedonahotels.com.sg

Diving and Snorkeling

Andaman International Dive Center (AIDC)
97/21, Phet Kasem Rd, Moo 1, Ranong, 85000 Thailand. **Tel** (+66) (77) 834824. **W** aidcdive.com

Nautica Diving
via Dive Asia, 24, Karon Rd, Phuket, 83100 Thailand. **Tel** (+66) (76) 330598. **W** diveasia.com **W** nautica-diving.com

Ngapali Water Sport
Road Map C4. Ngapali. **Tel** (0) 9972230566. **W** ngapaliwatersport.com

SURVIVAL GUIDE

PRACTICAL INFORMATION

Since the tourism boycott was relaxed in 2010 and ended two years later, record numbers of travelers have visited Myanmar, whose infrastructure, however, has struggled to keep pace. Accommodations have been in short supply at all levels, although dozens of new hotels are under construction to help meet the spiraling demand. There has also been a boom in domestic air travel, a consequence of the generally poor state of the roads. That said, it is possible to get almost anywhere by public transport. Some regions remain off-limits to foreigners due to the ongoing insurgencies, but these are mostly peripheral areas, away from the tourist hubs. Given the complexities of travel, it is wise, at least for those not traveling on prearranged tours, to seek help from a Yangon-based travel agent.

When to Go

The tourist season starts in early October, once the monsoon rains have cleared, and peaks between December and February, when temperatures even in the central dry zone around Bagan and Mandalay are bearable during the day. From March onward, the heat builds steadily, regularly rising above 40° C (104° F) in Yangon and the Delta and to 45° C (113° F) in the Upper Ayeyarwady area, although Inle Lake remains pleasant. The southwest monsoon erupts in May, disrupting travel across the country for around five months, especially in the far south and southeast. While temperatures are lower at this time, humidity levels are considerably higher.

Advance Booking

The relatively short duration of the tourist season, from October to March, puts great pressure on hotels and other essential services in the main visitor destinations. This is especially true during peak season from December to mid-February, when it can be difficult to find any kind of accommodations in places like Bagan and Inle Lake. It is best to make hotel reservations for this period at least a couple of months in advance, and confirm your booking a few days before arrival. It is also a good idea to book any internal flights as far ahead as possible, as seats on more popular routes may be in short supply. A reliable travel agent *(see p229)* will be of invaluable help when trying to make advance bookings.

Visas and Passports

Visitors from all countries (except for those belonging to ASEAN, the Association of Southeast Asian Nations) require a visa, but most can now apply for an eVisa online through the official Ministry of Immigration and Population website. It is necessary to upload a color passport photo and to make a payment of $50 with a credit or debit card. Passports must be valid for at least six months after the intended date of arrival in Myanmar. Applications are usually processed within three days, and travelers receive notification of approval by email.

Currently eVisas are only valid for entry through one of the three main international airports: Yangon, Mandalay, and Nay Pyi Taw. Travelers arriving by land must apply for a visa from a Myanmar consulate in their home country, or in one of the neighboring states. Both Bangkok and Kuala Lumpur are popular places to apply for a visa in advance, with requirements and processing time usually similar to that for an eVisa.

Both eVisas and tourist visas issued by consulates are valid for entry into Myanmar for three months from the date of issue and last 28 days, extendable up to an additional 14 days for a fee of $3 a day, payable at the airport on departure.

Customs Information

Customs regulations are straightforward in Myanmar. Visitors are allowed to bring two liters of alcoholic beverage and 400 cigarettes with them. Any foreign currency exceeding US$2,000, along with valuable pieces of jewelry or gold, must be declared. Upon arrival, a Passenger's Declaration Form (PDF) should be completed, a copy of which will be handed to you. When leaving Myanmar,

Burmese villagers near the town of Monywa carrying local produce to market

◄ Young novices playing outside a monastery in the ancient city of Bagan gemstones (including jade), jewelry, and silverware bought in the country may only be exported on production of a cash memo compiled by an authorized retailer. A full list of customs regulations appears on the **Myanmar Customs** website.

Travel Safety Advice

Visitors can get up-to-date safety information from the UK **Foreign and Commonwealth Office**, the **State Department** in the US and the **Department of Foreign Affairs and Trade** in Australia.

What to Take

Travelers are advised to take with them everything they may require on their trip, especially medicines, toiletries, electronic gadgets, batteries, and chargers, all of which are either of inferior quality or in short supply in Myanmar. A flashlight or head torch will be useful when walking along unlit roads or uneven sidewalks at night. Luxury hotels go to some lengths to ensure guest rooms are free of mosquitos, but a mosquito net could be useful if staying in inexpensive hotels or in rural areas. Pale-colored, lightweight cotton clothing is best for Myanmar's intense tropical heat, as is a broad-brimmed hat. A robust and light water bottle will come in useful, and a packet of purification tablets, for those rare times when it may not be possible to find safe bottled water, is recommended. Travelers who wish to avoid generating unnecessary plastic waste might also consider purchasing a compact pump-action water filter.

Responsible Travel

During the tourism boycott led by the National League for Democracy (NLD), "responsible travel" in Myanmar meant avoiding the country altogether. That changed in 2010 when the ban was relaxed, but only a small percentage of the millions of foreign visitors since have followed NLD requests to travel

independently rather than with a tour operator, and to stay in small, family-run guesthouses rather than large hotels owned by supporters of the former military government. One reason for this has been government reluctance to issue permits to potential B&B and homestay owners, which has limited the availability of ethical alternatives. However, plenty of local accommodations exist, and have significantly less environmental impact than luxury hotels. Spending money with local people also ensures more of it ends up with the host community, an issue particularly relevant at Inle Lake, where the surge in visitors has not resulted in an improvement in the living standards of the locals. Few ordinary Burmese dare articulate opposition to development initiatives by powerful interests, but the proliferation of luxury lake resorts, and consequent inflation in the price of staples, has been far from welcome.

Vaccination

Proof of vaccination against yellow fever is required for anyone arriving from countries in the infected zone (most of Africa and South America), or for anyone who has visited these regions less than six days prior to arrival. The World Health Organization recommends that travelers are also immunized against diphtheria and tetanus; measles, mumps, and rubella (MMR); varicella (chickenpox); hepatitis A and B; and typhoid. While almost eradicated from Mandalay and Yangon, malaria is

Tourists on a locally hired canoe on a lake near Saddar Cave, Southeastern Myanmar

Universally recognized sign advertising a doctor's clinic in Myanmar

a problem in the rest of the country. Some strains recently identified in Myanmar are known to be resistant to Larium (Mefloquine), so Malarone or Doxycycline are recommended as prophylaxes.

DIRECTORY

eVisa Applications

Ministry of Immigration and Population
🆆 evisa.moip.gov.mm

Embassies

Australia
City Map E5. 88, Strand Rd, Yangon. **Tel** (01) 251810.
🆆 burma.embassy.gov.au

United Kingdom
City Map E5. 80, Strand Rd, Yangon. **Tel** (01) 370865.
🆆 ukinburma.fco.gov.uk

United States
110, University Avenue Rd, Kamayut Township. **Tel** (01) 536509.
🆆 burma.usembassy.gov

Travel Safety Advice

Australia
Department of Foreign Affairs and Trade 🆆 dfat.gov.au/
🆆 smartraveller.gov.au/
United Kingdom
Foreign and Commonwealth Office
🆆 gov.uk/foreign-travel-advice
United States
US Department of State
🆆 travel.state.gov/

Customs Information

Myanmar Customs
🆆 myanmarcustoms.gov.mm

Tourists looking at a site map at one of Myanmar's visitor attractions

Visitor Information

Official tourist information is available from the state-run travel agent, **Myanmar Travels and Tours** (MTT). MTT's Yangon office on Mahabandula Garden Street hands out free maps for destinations across the country, and there are other branches in Mandalay and Bagan. MTT agents can also help arrange permits to restricted regions, such as Hkakabo Razi in the far north and the Myeik (Mergui) Archipelago; however, privately run agencies generally offer much more useful information and assistance with planning an itinerary, and many can also help organize permits. **Go-Myanmar.com** is particularly helpful, with excellent online tourist information, and a Yangon office that can organize tours all over Myanmar.

Opening Hours

Shops in Myanmar open from 9:30am to 6 or 7pm Monday to Saturday, sometimes closing on Saturday afternoons. Markets start just before dawn and tend to close by 11am or noon. Banks work 10am to 3pm Monday to Friday, and government offices (including post offices) from 10am to 4:40pm. Opening times, however, are generally more flexible in tourist centers such as Nyaungshwe (Inle Lake) and Bagan, where businesses trade for as long as there are customers to service. This includes corner shops, Internet cafés, and bars, although travel agents tend to wind up by 7pm.

Admission Charges

Admission charges are levied at most major sites, including monuments, museums, and botanical gardens. In Bagan, the government issues tickets that have to be paid for in US dollars on arrival. Mandalay's combination ticket covers all the principal tourist locations and can be bought in kyat. Some important pagodas, including Yangon's Shwedagon and Botataung, charge foreign visitors for entry. Photographers should note that many places of worship demand an additional fee for the use of cameras.

Disabled Travelers

Facilities for the disabled are rare, although major pagodas and sites such as Mandalay Hill have elevators that bypass the stairways. Car access is generally good for most destinations, but wheelchair users will have to arrange a vehicle with sufficient trunk space. At Bagan and some other archeological sites, horse carts are on hand to aid access to the monuments. Throughout the country, sidewalks are uneven and present a major challenge, especially in the big cities with heavy traffic.

High-end hotels, by contrast, usually have luggage ramps and elevators. Mid-scale and budget places tend to be spread over several floors and may not always have functioning elevators. As yet, dedicated disabled toilets are nonexistent.

The websites of **Disability World**, **Mobility International USA**, **Society for Accessible Travel and Hospitality**, **Accessible Journeys**, and **Disability Rights UK** offer a range of useful resources for international travel.

Traveling with Children

Children are adored and welcomed almost everywhere in this family-oriented country. Parents traveling with offspring of all ages are a common sight at pagodas and other attractions. However, diapers, formula powder, baby food, wipes, and other childcare products are a rarity outside big city malls. Waste disposal facilities are also uncommon, so consider switching to reusables. All restaurants are welcoming to youngsters, although most do not offer any special menus, and much of the food may be too spicy for kids. Yogurt and ice cream, however, are widely available. Given the state of city sidewalks, strollers (pushchairs) are more trouble than they're worth, so bring a good carrier or backpack.

Families with children enjoying an evening on the beach in Myanmar

Language

With its tonal variations, Burmese can be a challenging language to learn. However, in tourist areas, most vendors, taxi drivers, and boatmen will speak and understand some English, albeit fractured and accented. By contrast, the English spoken in hotels, airline offices, and banks tends to be more fluent. When traveling in rural areas, especially the ethnic minority ones, it makes sense to employ an English-speaking guide.

Etiquette

The Burmese are exceptionally polite and considerate, and expect foreigners to behave in a similar way. Should you need to express frustration or complain about something, do so calmly and without raising your voice. As in any part of the world, losing your temper is likely to be counterproductive. When meeting people of the same sex, it is customary to shake hands. However, between people of different sexes it is not, except in a business context, where international norms apply. Men's names are prefixed by the honorific "U," women's by "Daw." Touching people's heads is considered highly disrespectful; avoid it even with children. Never point at or touch objects with your feet or sit with your legs outstretched, particularly when visiting pagodas. Bear in mind, too, that Myanmar is a highly conservative country and that local people may be offended by public displays of affection such as hugs or kisses.

Religious sites require sober dress. Keep arms and legs covered at all times (no shorts or crop tops), and be sure to leave footwear at the entrance to any pagoda; racks are usually provided for storage.

Finally, exercise great caution when discussing current affairs or politics. Although in recent times the regime has become nominally more democratic and transparent, and the press freer, criticism of the government in public can lead to trouble with the authorities for local people.

Photographing the sunset from atop a pagoda, Bagan Archeological Zone

Photography

The fabulously photogenic pagodas and landscapes of Myanmar can be freely photographed. People are generally happy to pose, but always seek permission first. It is never acceptable to take photographs of women bathing in the open. Photographing meditating monks is considered disrespectful. Some ethnic minorities dislike tourists taking pictures of pregnant women, and soldiers and police may also refuse to be snapped while on duty. Finally, never photograph a military installation or vehicle.

Time and Calendar

Myanmar Standard Time (MST) is six and a half hours ahead of GMT, 10.5 hours ahead of New York, 13.5 hours ahead of Los Angeles, an hour ahead of India, and an hour behind Thailand. Myanmar runs according to the standard seven-day week, but the Buddhist week has eight days, with Wednesday split into two halves. The traditional Burmese calendar also differs from the Gregorian one, being based on lunar months: Tabodwe (January/February); Tabaung (February/March); Tagu (March/April); Kason (April/May); Nayon (May/June); Waso (June/July); Wagaung (July/August); Tawthalin (August/September); Thadingyut (September/October); Tazaungmon (October/November); Nadaw (November/December); and Pyatho (December/January).

Electricity

Myanmar runs on 230 volts/50 Hz and uses two-pin plugs, for which a universal adapter is required when bringing devices from abroad. Electricity supplies are frequently interrupted, even in the big cities, and most hotels and business premises have diesel generator backup.

DIRECTORY

Visitor Information

Ayarwaddy Legend Travels & Tours
City Map E5. 104, 37th St (Lower Block), Kyauktada Township, Yangon. **Tel** (01) 252007.
Ⓦ ayarwaddylegend.com

Go-Myanmar.com
City Map E5. 90, Bogalay Zay St, Botahtaung Township, Yangon. **Tel** (0) 95973193410.
Ⓦ go-myanmar.com

Good News Travels
Room 18, Building 204, Yanshin Rd, Yangon. **Tel** (0) 9595116256.
Ⓦ myanmargoodnews-travel.com

Myanmar Travels and Tours
City Map E5. 118, Mahabandula Garden St, Yangon.
Tel (01) 371286.
Ⓦ myanmartourism.com

Tour Mandalay
City Map D1.
2/3, 3rd Floor, Pearl Condominium, Block A, Kaba Aye Pagoda Rd, Yangon.
Tel (01) 545850.
Ⓦ tourmandalay.travel

Disabled Travelers

Accessible Journeys
Ⓦ disabilitytravel.com

Disability Rights UK
Ⓦ disabilityrightsuk.org

Disability World
Ⓦ disabilityworld.com

Mobility International USA
Ⓦ miusa.org

Society for Accessible Travel and Hospitality
Ⓦ sath.org

Personal Security and Health

The combination of a highly authoritarian government and an exceptionally law-abiding population ensures that Myanmar is one of the world's safest destinations. Violent crime is rare and visitors can travel without undue fear of assault or robbery, even at night. That said, petty crime is on the rise in the big cities, especially around busy train and bus stations. Food in restaurants is generally safe to eat, although it's better to drink only bottled or purified water. Healthcare, however, lags behind that of Myanmar's neighbors. Seriously ill travelers have to be airlifted to Singapore or Bangkok, so it is essential to have insurance with adequate medical evacuation cover.

General Precautions

The main security risk for foreign travelers is petty theft, such as pickpocketing or bag snatching. Thieves know that foreigners have to pay for many things in US dollars and are likely to be carrying cash in their bags. It is therefore wise to keep money and valuables in a belt hidden inside your clothing when walking around crowded places. Secure your camera and purse when walking or riding on a bike, as motorcycle-mounted thieves have been known to grab items at intersections. Most high-end hotels have electronic safes in their rooms, or a large safe at the reception where passports, cash, tickets, and other valuables may be stored. Another basic tip is to take photocopies or scans of your passport, travel insurance, departure card, and other important documents, which will aid replacement in the event of theft or loss.

Police

Myanmar's police, distinguished by their grey uniforms, combat helmets, and yellow, blue, and red shoulder patches, have a high profile by the standards of Southeast Asia. They are rarely of help to foreign travelers, though, except in the event of a robbery, when they may issue a report for insurance purposes. Their demeanor on the whole tends to be forbidding; they do

Yangon traffic policeman with tricolored arm patches

not like to be photographed and few officers speak English. However, Yangon has recently set up a tourist police division with English-speaking officers specifically to assist visitors.

Medical Facilities

The government's expenditure on healthcare as a percentage of GDP is among the lowest in the world, and during the years of the NLD-led boycott, international donor organizations gave less to Myanmar per capita than to any other nation. As a consequence, healthcare standards are low, even in big cities. Wealthy locals or tourists requiring medical attention tend to seek it abroad. Local hospitals are crowded and poorly provisioned, medicines in short supply, and staff inadequately trained. The widespread reuse of unsterilized equipment and insufficient blood screening are other reasons to avoid them.

The country's best medical facility is Yangon's French-run **Myanmar International SOS Clinic**, which has a team of fully qualified international doctors. International-standard services are also available at the **Pun Hlaing Hospital** in the north of the city, with a smaller medical clinic located in the Parkson FMI Center.

Pharmacies

Basic drugs, such as painkillers and indigestion tablets, are available over the counter at local pharmacies, but foreign pharmaceuticals should not be purchased as they may be counterfeit or adulterated. Travelers are advised to bring sufficient medical supplies for the duration of their trip.

Travel Insurance

It is always a good idea to buy travel insurance before leaving home, but particularly so for a trip to Myanmar. Medical facilities being what they are, the policy should cover the potentially high price of emergency medical evacuation, plus theft, lost luggage, and costs run up by delays and cancellations.

Food- and Water-borne Diseases

The most common ailment that afflicts travelers to Myanmar is an upset stomach. Caused by unfamiliarity with otherwise harmless local bacteria in food, mild diarrhea is best left untreated; it will pass of its own accord after 24–36 hours. Drink plenty of fluids, supplemented

Yangon General Hospital, established in 1899 in a Victorian-style building

with rehydration salts (available locally) if necessary, and refrain from eating until the attack has passed. If it lasts for more than 48 hours, a more serious infection such as dysentery or giardiasis may be the cause, requiring a stool test and antibiotics.

Many stomach problems can, however, be avoided by taking some common-sense precautions: peel fruit before eating it; wash hands before meals; avoid food that has not been properly cooked, or which has obviously been reheated; stick to bottled water, or take along your own water purifier (which cuts down on plastic bottle waste); think twice before eating in an empty restaurant; and steer clear of meat or fish, unless you can be sure it is fresh and has been adequately cooked.

Narcotics

As one of the world's prime sources of methamphetamine and heroin, Myanmar suffers high levels of drug addiction. The country is the world's second largest producer of opium. The worst affected areas are the hills of the Golden Triangle border regions, where opium is grown *(see p177)* and crystal meth manufactured, and in Myitkyina, in Kachin State in Upper Burma, where the drug trade has financed the long-standing armed conflict with the state. Attempts to crack down on the trade are hampered by the complex political situation – the narcotics industry is controlled by ethnic minority syndicates with which the government needs to be on good terms to ensure the progress of its reforms.

Heat

Myanmar's heat and humidity can be intense, and to avoid sunstroke while on explorations of archeological sites, such as Bagan and Mrauk U, travelers should wear suitable sun hats, carry a Burmese paper parasol, or try *thanaka*, a

Burmese child wearing *thanaka* paste, a traditional natural sunscreen

natural plant-derived sunscreen used by the Burmese. Drink sufficient water as dehydration can cause headaches, dizziness, and more serious conditions such as kidney stones.

HIV-AIDS

Due largely to the prevalence of intravenous drug use in the country, as well as the illegality of prostitution, Myanmar suffers the third highest rate of HIV-AIDS in Asia, and the disease is on the increase. At least one third of the sex workers in the country are thought to be infected, and antiretroviral drugs are in short supply.

Women Travelers

Myanmar is, on the whole, a relaxing destination for women visitors, whether traveling alone or with friends. Harassment is rare – men will look away rather than be seen to be staring, and are courteous to the point of chivalrous on public transport. The chance to interact with other women is likely to be one of the most satisfying aspects of the trip. Many women travelers choose to fit in by adopting *htameins* – a great ice-breaker when meeting local women, elegant, and well suited to the climate. Women should be aware, though, that some pagodas prohibit them from climbing up to the upper terraces, entering the sanctum, or touching the deity.

Vendors wearing sun hats, Bodhi Tataung

Gay and Lesbian Travelers

Gay and lesbian sex is illegal in Myanmar, and although the law is seldom, if ever, enforced, attitudes remain highly conservative. There are very few openly LGBTQ public figures, and no gay bars, clubs, or pride marches, although cruising does go on in the trendier nightclubs of Yangon. Young people suspected of homosexuality tend to be sent to a monastery or nunnery in an attempt to straighten their sexual orientation. However, one indication that public opinion is slowly softening, at least in the pro-Western, affluent suburbs of Yangon, has been the creation of the group **Colors Rainbow**, which has organized gay pride forums and produced a cable TV show for the local LGBTQ community.

Public Toilets

Public toilets are few and far between. Travelers tend to rely on washrooms in restaurants, which will be well scrubbed and aired if in an upscale establishment, but very basic, with squat-style toilets in local cafés and teashops. Carry a good supply of toilet paper (routinely supplied by hotels), or adopt the local custom of using water.

Banking and Currency

Although Myanmar's banking system is fast catching up with the rest of the world, for the time being its undeveloped state means that many transactions by foreign visitors have to be made in US dollars. The kyat is accepted for small payments, but for larger ones (such as hotel bills), only mint, or near-mint, US dollar bills will do. Credit and debit cards are rarely accepted, and traveler's checks and VisaMoney are not taken anywhere. Currency exchange no longer has to be carried out on the black market, but even the banks require dollars – which means visitors have to carry enough US currency into the country to see them through their entire trip.

Security guards at the doors of a branch of KBZ Bank

US Dollars

It is essential that any dollar bills brought to Myanmar are in pristine condition. The Burmese will reject one if it has even a tiny fold, pen mark, blotch, or tear. When buying US currency prior to departure, check each bill front and back. Some travelers even resort to smoothing out potentially offensive wrinkles with a hot iron. Protect the bills from dirt and moisture inside a plastic bag if they are stored in a money belt.

An ATM (cash machine) operated by one of Myanmar's banks

Kyat

Myanmar's unit of currency is the kyat, pronounced "chaat" and abbreviated to "K" (or "MMK"). Although US dollars remain the currency of choice it is useful to keep some kyat handy for smaller expenses – taxi fares, admission, camera tickets for pagodas, and restaurants and street stalls. Bear in mind that the kyat cannot be converted outside Myanmar, and is not accepted in the transit areas of international airports.

Banks and Exchange

The stabilized exchange rate means that the black market is no longer the place to change money – banks now offer the best rates of exchange. US dollars are still the currency of choice, and while it is now sometimes also possible to exchange euros, and occasionally Singapore dollars, it is much better to bring cash in US dollars. Modern and efficient, private banks such as **CB Bank** and **KBZ Bank** are the quickest and easiest places to change currency. Some banks

have also started offering Western Union and Money-Gram money transfer services at selected branches. When checking your encashment make sure that a certificate or receipt has been issued, as it may later be demanded by customs officials.

Banking Hours

Banking hours are generally 10am–3pm Monday to Friday. Outside these times, currency can be changed at hotels, markets (such as Bogyoke Aung San Zei in Yangon), and large souvenir emporia, although the rates they offer may be lower than those of the banks. Note that better rates of exchange are given for higher denomination bills, so bring more hundreds than fifties and twenties.

ATM Services

Cash machines, or ATMs, have become far more common across Myanmar in recent years, but some do not dispense cash advances against foreign credit or debit cards. When they do, a large transaction fee (typically of around K5,000 or 4 per cent) is levied, and the money is dispensed in kyat. Large branches of both the CB and KBZ banks have ATMs in most of the main tourist destinations; they accept foreign-registered MasterCard, Visa, and Cirrus cards.

Credit and Debit Cards

Although an increasing number of airlines, restaurants, shops, and hotels accept cards, the overwhelming majority don't and visitors should never count on being able to use one. Places that do take cards usually charge a very large transaction fee for the privilege.

Traveler's Checks

Traveler's checks, and equivalent digital travel money, are useless in Myanmar, even if issued by major international agencies such as Thomas Cook, Visa, or American Express.

A donation box, commonly seen at pagodas and temples across Myanmar

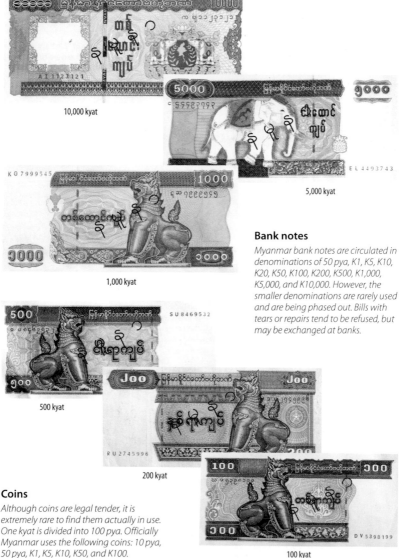

10,000 kyat

5,000 kyat

1,000 kyat

Bank notes

Myanmar bank notes are circulated in denominations of 50 pya, K1, K5, K10, K20, K50, K100, K200, K500, K1,000, K5,000, and K10,000. However, the smaller denominations are rarely used and are being phased out. Bills with tears or repairs tend to be refused, but may be exchanged at banks.

500 kyat

200 kyat

100 kyat

Coins

Although coins are legal tender, it is extremely rare to find them actually in use. One kyat is divided into 100 pya. Officially Myanmar uses the following coins: 10 pya, 50 pya, K1, K5, K10, K50, and K100.

Communications and Media

Myanmar's communication network is as archaic as its transport system, although both look set to change rapidly over the coming years as the country opens its doors to foreign investors. For the time being, however, cellphone use remains minimal, and the Internet slow, expensive, and partially censored. Press censorship has eased considerably since 2011, but choice is still severely limited, and criticism of the regime and its policies muted. The state-run postal system also falls well below international standards – it can be unreliable, and for sending souvenirs home, private couriers are still the safest option.

A street stall advertising a public telephone service in Yangon

Intha-style stilt structure housing the Ywama Post Office on Inle Lake

Post and Courier Services

There is no shortage of post offices in Myanmar, and while staff are smiling and helpful, postal services can be a bit undependable. Because there has never been a standardized way of transliterating Burmese into English, postal addresses in Myanmar are notoriously hit-and-miss – except in the city of Mandalay, whose grid plan system makes addresses easy to find. Foreign travelers typically report a success rate of 50 per cent or less for postcards. For sending souvenirs home, the only sensible option is to use a private courier such as **DHL** or **Express Mail Service International (EMS)**.

Telephone Calls

International calls can be made from most hotels and local sidewalk telephone centers, but are extremely expensive (several US

dollars per minute). Calls to trunk or local landline numbers are considerably cheaper, but still quite costly compared to other countries. Although Voice over Internet Protocol (VoIP) calls were banned for years – allegedly to protect revenue from international calls earned by the state-owned telecom company – it is now possible to cut costs by making web-based VoIP calls using applications such as Skype and GTalk.

Cellphones

The cell phone revolution has finally reached Myanmar, more than a decade after mobile telephony became the norm in the rest of Southeast Asia. Foreign telecom companies have been licensed to expand existing networks, and travelers can now buy local SIM cards for around $1.50. Major providers include Telenor and Ooredoo.

To buy a pay-as-you-go SIM card – available at the airport and all major towns – foreigners must provide a passport photo and photocopies of their passport and Myanmar visa. International roaming is also available for some foreign networks. General coverage is still patchy and mobile data provision unreliable, but the situation is rapidly improving.

Internet Facilities

Internet access – a rarity until very recently – is now fairly widespread in Myanmar, and getting more so every year. Many hotels, including those at the budget end of the spectrum, offer Wi-Fi to guests, and while not yet ubiquitous, public Wi-Fi connections are become more common in upscale cafés and restaurants. Connection speeds, however, still leave a lot to be desired, particularly in remote areas.

Installation costs and Internet subscription charges are high, so local users still mainly rely on Internet cafés. Most of these are cramped and crowded affairs, with old computers and keyboards, although some of the better ones do have air-conditioning and modern equipment. The government has now removed most of the previous restrictions on access to international news and social media websites. Twitter, Facebook, and the CNN and BBC websites can all now be accessed from within Myanmar.

A newspaper vendor sorting out his deliveries in Yangon

Newspapers and Magazines

A watershed moment in Myanmar's modern history took place in the spring of 2013, when four independent, privately owned newspapers hit the stands in Yangon – the first of more than a dozen similar publications to be published across the country in that year. Before this landmark relaxation of the formerly tight state control of Myanmar's press, the only papers available were held in check by threats of censorship, imprisonment, and torture for any journalist critical of the military regime. English-language editions are published by two newspapers. *The New Light of Myanmar* is essentially a propaganda tool for the government, favoring articles about the achievements of the military. The *Myanmar Times* is also close to the government, despite being partly foreign-owned. For a more impartial perspective on the nation's current affairs, *Irrawaddy* is a quality magazine produced by Burmese exiles living in Thailand. The *Democratic Voice of Burma (DVB)*, as its name suggests, is more overtly aligned with the pro-democracy movement. DVB is a banned organization and publishes only online on a website hosted on Norwegian servers. It also makes TV and radio broadcasts.

Television and Radio

As with the rest of the media in Myanmar, television and radio are tightly controlled by the state. The main channels are TV Myanmar and Myawaddy TV, which show a mix of soaps, entertainment, and news in Burmese. Satellite networks such as MRTV-4 also bundle local stations with foreign ones, many of them in English. CNN, BBC World, and National Geographic can be viewed on most hotel television sets.

Young novices enjoying a television show in an Inle Lake monastery

DIRECTORY

Post and Courier Services

DHL
City Map B4. 58, Wa Dan St, Lanmadaw Township, Yangon.
Tel (01) 215516. W dhl.com

Express Mail Service International (EMS)
City Map B1. 361, Pyay Rd, Yangon. **Tel** (01) 515151.
W ems.com.mm

Newspapers and Magazines

Democratic Voice of Burma
W dvb.no

Irrawaddy
W irrawaddy.org

Myanmar Times
W mmtimes.com

The New Light of Myanmar
W moi.gov.mm/npe/nlm

Useful Dialing Codes

- To call Myanmar from abroad, dial the international access code of the country you are in, followed by Myanmar's country code, 95, the city code, and finally the phone number.
- To make a domestic long-distance call in Myanmar, dial 0 followed by the city code and phone number.
- City codes: Yangon 1; Mandalay 2; Bagan 61; Bago 52; Hsipaw 82; Kalaw, Nyaungshwe, Taunggyi 81; Kawthaung 59; Kengtung 84; Mawlamyine 57; Meiktila 64; Myitkyina 74; Pathein 42; Pyay 53; Pyin U Lwin 85; Sagaing 72; Taungoo 54; Thandwe and Sittwe 43.
- Cellphone numbers usually have eight to 12 digits, including the cell phone prefix 9, while landline numbers have five to seven digits without the city codes.
- To make an international call from Myanmar, dial 00 followed by the country code, city code, and phone number.
- Country codes: UK 44; USA and Canada 1; Australia 61; New Zealand 64; France 33.

TRAVEL INFORMATION

Overland travel from neighboring states to Myanmar is gradually opening up, but the vast majority of international arrivals in the country are by air, at Yangon's Mingaladon Airport. From there, foreign tourists tend to take a domestic flight to one of several regional hubs. Hampered by poor infrastructure, travel by road and rail tends to be slower and more uncomfortable, although plenty of backpackers brave grueling overnight journeys to reach Inle Lake, Mandalay, and Bagan. Hired cars with drivers provide a less

arduous alternative. A more leisurely, and quintessentially Burmese, form of long-distance transport are the riverboats plying the Ayeyarwady, whether old government ferries or luxury cruisers. Whichever method of travel you opt for, however, bear in mind that pressure for tickets is particularly intense from December to February (the height of the winter tourist season) and that bookings should be made as far in advance as possible, either in person or with the help of a dependable local travel agent *(see p229)*.

Mandalay International Airport, with traditionally designed *pyatthat* roofs

Arriving by Air

Nearly every foreign visitor to Myanmar arrives by air at Yangon, although Mandalay International Airport also hosts flights from Singapore, Kunming in China and Bangkok and Chiang Mai in Thailand. The majority of Yangon flights originate in Singapore or Bangkok, but there are direct flights from Kolkata with **Air India**, Tokyo with **All Nippon**, Seoul with **Asiana**, Hong Kong with **Dragonair**, Hanoi with **Vietnam Airlines**, and Doha with **Qatar Airways**. Larger carriers such as **Malaysia Airlines**, **Singapore Airlines/Silk Air**, and **Thai Airways** generally rely on smaller subsidiaries to fly the connecting leg from their hub to Myanmar. The low-cost airline **Air Asia** also flies daily from Bangkok and Kuala Lumpur. This is the cheapest way to get to the country, but

may mean a long layover in Thailand or Malaysia. There are no direct flights from the US, the UK, or Europe, only from the Gulf and Southeast Asia.

Air Fares

The cost of flying to Myanmar varies with the season, the airline, and the travel agent. The busiest, most expensive period is from December to January and during the Thingyan festival

in April, when lots of Burmese workers travel home to their families. Discounted tickets are usually available during the monsoon (May to September). Usually, the most cost-effective route is to buy a late-availability charter flight to Bangkok from Europe or the US, then fly into Myanmar on a low-cost airline.

Arrival

Mingaladon International Airport lies on Yangon's outskirts, about 12 miles (20 km) north of downtown. Arrival, immigration, and customs formalities are conducted at a brisk pace by the standards of most of Asia, and the airport facilities are well maintained. Be sure to keep the duplicate customs slip handed back to you as it will be needed when leaving Myanmar. Note that luggage is often scanned prior to exiting the airport.

In the arrivals hall is a foreign-exchange facility where visitors can exchange US dollars and euros for kyat at reasonable rates. There is also a dependable ATM (cash machine) here.

Departures sign in Burmese and English at Thandwe Airport near Ngapali

Getting from Mingaladon Airport to Yangon

Visitors on prearranged tours are usually whisked away in air-conditioned buses or mini-buses, while independent travelers rely on local Toyota taxis – drivers wait outside the arrivals concourse. Although they are generally honest, it makes sense to check the correct fare in advance with your hotel manager or guesthouse owner when you book your accommodations as none of the taxis are metered. Note that the night rate is 30 per cent higher than the day fare. As yet, there are no dedicated shuttle buses in operation. The trip from the airport to downtown Yangon can take as little as 45 minutes on clear roads at night, or a couple of hours during rush hour in the daytime.

Cost-conscious travelers on tight budgets may wish to save a few

City taxi available at Yangon Mingaladon International Airport

dollars by catching a municipal bus, which costs less than US$1. To do this, turn right once out of the terminal and walk for 10 minutes until you reach Pyay Road. Bus no. 51 runs every 20 minutes from a stop there to downtown Yangon as far as Sule Pagoda from 7am to 10pm.

Overland Travel

It is sometimes possible to enter Myanmar overland at the Ruili–Muse entry point on the Chinese border in Yunnan. The necessary visas and paperwork may be arranged in Kunming. However, Burmese border officials have been known to refuse entry to foreigners, or restrict onward travel to Lashio, or insist that travelers leave the country via the same point afterward.

Four border crossings with Thailand are now open to foreigners, with no special permits required: Mae Sai–Tachileik; Ranong–Kawthaung; Mae Sot–Myawaddy; and Ban Phu Nam Ron–Htee Khee. From Tachileik, permit-free onward travel overland is allowed only as far as Kengtung, but visitors are permitted to fly onwards from there. The crossings at Kawthaung, Myawaddy, and Htee Khee are completely open. No special permits are needed and visitors can travel onward without any restrictions, other than the usual controls applicable to all tourists. Note, though, that overland travel from Kawthaung to Myeik is not possible; you must take a ferry.

Myanmar eVisas are not currently valid for entry at any of these border points; visas need to be arranged in advance, except the one-day permit for a visa run (Thai visas are available at all these crossings). There are no permitted points of entry by land or sea from Laos or Bangladesh. The remote crossing from India at Tamu is only open to those on special tour packages.

The spot where the borders of Myanmar, Laos, and Thailand meet, Golden Triangle region

Getting Around

With the exception of the new Yangon–Mandalay Expressway, road travel is slow and bumpy. Vehicles tend to be dilapidated and journeys long and uncomfortable. Rail travel is only a little more appealing, due to the lack of modern rolling stock and a very limited network. To cover long distances, travelers have to be prepared to either rough it, or else catch internal flights between the key sights and cities. Myanmar's domestic air services have expanded rapidly over the past few years, and with a degree of flexibility it is usually possible to get a seat when you need it. The same applies to traveling the Ayeyarwady by boat – an option for visitors with more time. But for those wishing to see much along the way, it is hard to beat renting a car and driver, which allows you the freedom to stop where you want and make the odd detour.

A locomotive of Myanmar Railways, which operates thousands of miles of track

Domestic Airlines

Myanmar's domestic air capacity has grown rapidly to cope with the sudden surge in demand since 2010. There are now several private carriers in addition to the state-run **Myanmar National Airlines**, including **Asian Wings Airways**, **Yangon Airways**, **Air Bagan**, **Air KBZ**, **Golden Myanmar Airlines**, and **Air Mandalay**. Foreign visitors have tended to avoid Myanmar National Airlines due to its poor safety record and all-round unreliability, but some of the new private firms have fared little better. Several of the serious incidents in recent years have involved private operators, including the December 2012 crash at Heho Airport (Inle Lake), in which two passengers were killed and 11 injured after an Air Bagan Fokker 100 landed in a field in thick fog. The good

news is that the old Fokkers are being phased out and replaced with modern aircraft.

Theoretically, online booking of flights is available through the websites of all the domestic airlines, although the process is far from seamless. Tickets are more easily purchased in advance at the airlines' offices in Yangon. Bear in mind, though, that by leaving reservations until only a day or two before your intended departure means that the seats may have sold out in busy periods. In Yangon, agents will make the booking on your behalf for the same price as the published fare, or sometimes a little less. Booking your domestic Myanmar flights through a tour operator in your home country is invariably the more expensive option, but is also the most secure way to ensure the dates and flights to suit your itinerary.

Trains

The British laid nearly 3,000 miles (4,800 km) of railroad in Burma and nearly all of it is still in use. Unfortunately, a lack of government investment over the past few decades has left the network and most of its rolling stock in a very run-down state. Although foreigners no longer have to pay officially inflated fares for train travel, tickets are still generally more expensive than the cost of a bus journey on the same route.

Despite the higher fares, some routes are popular with visitors, particularly the 388-mile (622-km) overnight haul from Yangon to Mandalay, which takes 15–16 hours. Other journeys worth considering are the five-hour trip to Kyaiktiyo for the Golden Rock Pagoda, which benefits from a state-of-the-art, comfortable new express train inaugurated in 2013; the rattling ride over the Gokteik Viaduct from Mandalay or Pyin U Lwin to Hsipaw and Lashio; the even more juddery ride along a branch line from Mandalay to Shwenyaung (near Inle Lake); and the night train from Yangon to Bagan. Whichever route you travel on, however, expect long delays, especially on branch lines and in the far north.

Express services are far quicker and more comfortable than local ones, and offer the choice between upper class, which has upholstered, reclining seats, and ordinary class, which

Small propeller aircraft at Thandwe Airport, the closest domestic airport to Ngapali

has upright ones. Some trains also have sleeper carriages with berths. Foreigners' fares are available for all these classes. The **Seat 61** train travel website has several useful resources on journeys in Myanmar.

Demand for tickets is high at all times of the year, but especially during the winter tourist season, when you should aim to book at least a couple of days in advance, or longer for a sleeper. The best place to do this in Yangon is at the **MTT office** on Mahabandula Garden Street (see p229), which has access to special tourist quotas. Or you can join the queues at the **Myanmar Railways Booking Office** (6–10am and 1–4pm daily). Reservations open three days prior to departure.

Buses

Buses are considerably faster, more comfortable, and cheaper than trains, although somewhat less characterful. Most long-distance services, such as the Yangon–Mandalay route, leave in the evening and travel over-night, stopping every hour or two at cafés along the route, so don't expect much sleep. The more luxurious coaches have airconditioning but it is rarely needed as temperatures tend to plummet in the small hours; take along a fleece or blanket for comfort. Tickets are sold from counters at the bus stations or through local travel agents, and should be bought two or three days in advance for popular routes such as Bagan–Inle Lake or Yangon–Mandalay.

Note that even if you only want to travel part of the way, you still have to pay the full fare.

Motorcycle and Car Rental

Most hotels, guesthouses, and travel agents in Yangon and the country's principal visitor destinations can arrange a car and driver for day trips or longer tours. Although far from being the cheapest way to travel, this is certainly the most flexible and least uncomfortable. Dedicated, air-conditioned tourist cars are the most expensive. They are hired out for 12 hours per day, and the fee will include gas, tolls, and the driver's expenses. You can also find cheaper "private drivers" with older, non-air-conditioned cars, who will typically charge 30 per cent less. Self-drive is extremely rare, costly, and difficult to arrange, which is probably just as well given the driving conditions in Myanmar. Motorcycles, a handy way of getting around, are available for rent in many visitor destinations, including Mandalay, where **Mr Jerry** has Chinese-made 125cc bikes in various states of repair.

Ferries

At any given time, thousands of Burmese, and around half the country's freight, will be travel-ing on Myanmar's rivers, the majority of them in dilapidated government ferries run by the Inland Water Transport (IWT). Tickets may be purchased in advance from any IWT jetty.

While this is the slowest way to travel in Myanmar – it takes four days to reach Mandalay from Yangon by river, a route covered in two hours by plane – it affords memorable glimpses of local life. The most popular route among foreign visitors is the one between Mandalay and Bagan, which is also covered by a fleet of small private boats.

DIRECTORY

Domestic Airlines

Air Bagan
City Map C1. 56, Shwe Taung Gyar St, Bahan, Yangon. **Tel** (01) 513322. W airbagan.com

Air KBZ
City Map D5. 33–49, corner of Bank St & Mahabandula Garden St, Yangon. **Tel** (01) 372977. W airkbz.com

Air Mandalay
1, Pyay Rd, Hlaing Township W airmandalay.com

Asian Wings Airways
City Map C1. 34 (A1), Shwe Taung Gyar St, Bahan, Yangon. **Tel** (01) 515261. W asianwings-airways.com

Golden Myanmar Airlines
1st Flr, Sayar San Plaza, University Avenue Rd, Yangon. **Tel** (01) 8604035. W gmairlines.com

Myanmar National Airlines
City Map E5. 104, Kannar Rd (Strand Rd), Yangon. W flymna.com

Yangon Airways
City Map E3. 166, Level 5, MMB Tower, Upper Pansodan St, Yangon. **Tel** (01) 383100. W yangonair.com

Trains

Myanmar Railways Booking Office
City Map E4. Bogyoke Aung San Road, opposite Sakura Tower, Yangon.

Seat 61
W seat61.com/Burma.htm

Motorcycle and Car Rental

Mr Jerry
Road Map C3. 83rd St (25/26), nr Mandalay City Hotel, Mandalay.

Riverboat cruising down the Ayeyarwady near Mingun, Mandalay Region

Local Transport

Public transport in Myanmar is, like most of the country's infrastructure, poorly resourced and in need of upgrading. Buses are overcrowded, airless, hot, and falling apart, and the only suburban train line – in Yangon – supports a slow skeleton service. As a consequence, both locals and visitors tend to be reliant on taxis, which are ubiquitous and relatively inexpensive, and come in a variety of shapes and sizes, from shiny new Japanese imported cars to rickety trishaws. To cover short distances, horse carts can be a useful alternative, especially for exploring archeological sites. For market runs, however, pickup trucks, which cram dozens of people on wooden boards placed over the rear flatbed, are the favorite local option. In the cities, plenty of private companies also run sightseeing tours and short excursions to local and regional places of interest and these frequently offer good value.

agree a fare and ride with the windows open. Taxis are plentiful, except in the evenings, when there may be a somewhat longer wait. Drivers will also be reluctant to take on longer trips to the suburbs at this time, preferring to remain downtown. If you are staying in a guesthouse or hotel, it might be best to ask the manager or owner to arrange a taxi on your behalf; they'll fix the fare and ensure the driver knows where you want to go.

In Mandalay and some other towns, motorcycle taxis are a popular alternative to cars – they are cheaper and faster at congested times.

Buses and Minibuses

Fleets of buses grind through the streets of all the main towns and cities in Myanmar, although few foreigners ever use them. Packed solid with passengers, they are horrendously uncomfortable and poorly maintained. The absence of numbers in English, and route maps, also make the systems hard to navigate.

The same applies to the smaller minibuses that work the routes mainly to and from markets, stopping for passengers whenever they are hailed from the roadside. Taxis are a more convenient option than minibuses and buses as fares are low and they are easy to come by (except during the evening rush hour).

Sign advertising taxis and bicycles for rent

Motorcycle Taxis and Taxis

The past few years have seen a gradual phasing out of the old taxis that used to serve the cities of Myanmar and a proliferation of more reliable, spacious new Japanese Toyotas. The best of the new taxis are metered and air-conditioned, but most are not. After flagging one down,

Suburban Railroad

Only Yangon has a suburban rail line. Because trains travel at an average of only 10 mph (17 kph), and don't loop through the commercial district, the suburban rail is not of much use to the city's commuters, most of whom make the journey to work by road. Passing through the loop does, however, offer a novel sightseeing opportunity for visiting foreigners. Trains run from 3:45am to 10:15pm, starting and ending at Yangon Train Station on Bogyoke Aung San Road, and take three hours to complete the 28-mile (46-km) circuit, with 39 stops en route.

A Myanmar Railways train passing a lush field in the countryside

The quirky trishaw, a mode of transport popular in Myanmar

Trishaws and Horse Carts

In smaller towns where bus services are limited, trishaws or *sei-kar* (a corruption of the English word "sidecar") are the most convenient option. Invented in Mandalay in the 1930s, these quirky little vehicles are popular in Myanmar. They are essentially bicycles with a passenger seat attached to the side that can accommodate two people, one facing forward, the other to the rear. Compact, easy to ride, and environmentally friendly, they are perfect for navigating narrow side streets and lanes. Fares are also very low.

Horse carts or *myint hlei* still operate widely in the rural areas of Myanmar, particularly on market days. Visitors will come across them in large numbers at archeological sites such as Bagan, Inwa (Ava), and Mrauk U, where they provide a gentle way to get around the sandy lanes leading to the monuments. At these tourist sites, the horse cart drivers generally speak a little English and act as guides. They usually charge per day of sightseeing. The fee rises if booked through a hotel or travel agent.

Pickup Trucks

Pickup trucks or *lein ka* (from "line car") often run alongside buses in cities, covering similar routes to the outlying suburbs from market districts, and also operate between towns and villages. Passengers ride in the usually covered flatbed section to the rear, sitting on planks of wood, makeshift seats attached to the sides, or simply squashed in on top of sacks of provisions. Young men and boys also ride on the roof if there's no room inside. Foreigners tend to avoid traveling this way unless desperate as the lack of legroom can be excruciating after a few miles. However, in some places, *lein ka* are unavoidable. One example is the Golden Rock Pagoda at Kyaiktiyo, which can only be reached in a crowded pickup. Fares are comparable with local buses. For an extra 50 per cent fee, it is sometimes possible to secure a more comfortable seat in the cab up front.

Tours

Several companies in Yangon and Mandalay offer half- and full-day trips to sights in and around the cities, usually in air-conditioned minibuses or cars. As a rule, you will be picked up and dropped off at your hotel.

The price may or may not include meals. Shop around as costs vary dramatically. Tried-and-tested operators include **Asian Trails**, who offer city tours of Yangon as well as trips to Bago and other towns, and **Diethelm Travel**, who offer cycling trips around Inwa's ruins and walking tours of Yangon's old colonial enclave. In addition to city sightseeing tours, **Shan Yoma Travel and Tours** and **Green Myanmar Travels and Tours** also offer guided trips around Bagan and Inle Lake.

A tour group shelters under umbrellas at the massive stupa at Mingun

General Index

Acknowledgments

Dorling Kindersley would like to thank the following people whose help and assistance contributed to the preparation of this book.

Author

Born and raised in Wales and the Middle East, David Abram began travel writing after answering an advertisement for writers for a new guide to India. The subsequent Rough Guide was called "the Bible for any visitor" by *Condé Nast Traveler* and is still in print. He returned to Asia in 2010 to overhaul the Insight Guides Myanmar book, and now divides his time between updating trips, writing travel features, photographic assignments, and tour company consultancy. David lives in Somerset, UK, with his partner and two children. davidabram.co.uk; Twitter @DavidRAbram.

Fact Checker John Oates
Proofreader Debra Wolter
Indexer Ankita Awasthi Tröger
Phrase Book Andiamo! Language Services Ltd
Editorial Consultant Anna Streiffert
Editorial Assistance Fay Franklin, Scarlett O'Hara
Additional Illustrations Sunita Gahir
Additional Photography Philip Blenkinsop, Ian O'Leary

Revisions Team Emma Brady, Samantha Cook, Tim Hannigan, Rahul Kumar, Erin Richards, Ankita Sharma, Rituraj Singh

Picture Credits

a = above; b = below/bottom; c = center; f = far; l = left; r = right; t = top

The publishers would like to thank the following individuals, companies, and picture libraries for their permission to reproduce their photographs:

123RF.com: Stefan Ember 160b.
4Corners: Richard Taylor 173br.
David Abram: 40cr, 175cra.
Alamy Images: 19th era 57bl; AF archive 40tr; age fotostock/Erich Häfele 191cr; age fotostock/Ignacio Palacios 104t; Rex Allen 176tl; Steve Bly 195br; epa european press photo agency b.v. 232cla; F1online digitale Bildagentur GmbH 132tr; GM Photo Images 123cr; Chris Hellier 37cra; hemis.fr/ Franck Guiziou 39br, 43cr; Imagestate Media Partners Limited/Impact Photos/Alain Evrard 59bl; Maurice Joseph 43tl, 44cr; JTB Media Creation, Inc. 37br; Frans Lemmens 96bl; Yadid Levy 33br, 166cl; Scott Mallon 41tr; National Geographic Image Collection/Alex Treadway 182b; Pictorial Press Ltd 57br; Graham Prentice 29br; Robert Harding Picture Library/James Strachan 128tr; V&A Images 36tr; Wim Wiskerke 190br; Xinhua 40cl.

Amara Group Myanmar: amaragroupmyanmar.com 28cl.
AWL Images: Michele Falzone 121cr; Katie Garrod 21br, 51bc, 178; Christian Kober 42–3; Nigel Pavitt 39bl, 44bl, 101b; Jane Sweeney 177tl.
The Bridgeman Art Library: Luca Tettoni 8–9.
Corbis: epa/Law Eh Soe 161t, 161crb; Flame/Angelo Cavalli 5t; Hulton-Deutsch Collection 51cb; Ocean 182t.
CPA Media: 38tr, 38c, 38cr, 41b, 49crb, 49bc, 50bc, 52cb, 52br, 53tr, 53bc, 53br, 54tr, 55clb, 55br, 56tl, 56bl, 57crb, 58c, 77bc, 92cb, 98tr, 99crb, 115tc, 145tl, 185br.
Dreamstime: Steve Allen 100, 124cla, 129bl, 170–71, 196–7; Chirawan 31bl; Stefano Ember 167cra, Steve Estvanik 176b; Fischer0182 25cl; Abdul Sami Haqqani 58br; Hamsterman 38bl; Song Heming 25bc; Jackmalipan 12t; Jasmina 124cb; Kjersti Joergensen 23tr; Anthony Aneese Totah Jr 24clb; Kkg1 25cr; Georgios Kollidas 58bl; Martin Lehmann 60–61; Markwaters 59tr; Hugo Maes 168bl; Mathes 25tr; Danilo Mongiello 42cla; Jerzy Opoka 33bl; Ornthariga 54bc; Panuruangjan 24cl; Poomapat Putongtirapisita 81br; Rgbe 25cb; Seqoya 152bl; Witchu Sermsawadsri 1; Benjawan Sittidech 166bl; Valery Shanin 240b; Szefei 224–5, 235bl; Timurk 32tr; Tiverylucky 30–31; Wing Ho Tsang 237c; Voraorn 2–3; Wilczon 25crb; Zzvet 4br, 36cr, 36–7c, 37cl, 220cl, 220bl.
FLPA: Biosphoto/Michel Gunther 24bc; Imagebroker 25bl, 237bl; Imagebroker/Egmont Strigl 25cla; Photo Researchers 24crb.
Getty Images: Flickr/John Seaton Callahan 187b; Hulton Archive/ Print Collector 36br; Keystone 58bc; National Geographic/Steve Winter 27cla; Oxford Scientific/Gerard Soury 24bl; Universal Images Group 24cra.
Green Hill Valley Elephant Camp: 172tr.
Himalaya Trekking and Culture Travels and Tours Co. Ltd./S'Nyein Lwin: snyeinlwin@gmail.com 62tr, 185tl.
iStock: garth11 107br; Craig Lovell 177br.
Aung Myo Chit: nkgmaymyo@gmail.com 183br.
NASA: Earth Observatory 27br.
Nature Picture Library: Inaki Relanzon 37tc.
Paukan Cruises: 28tr, 28–9c.
Photoshot: U Aung 43br; Mel Longhurst 136cl, 234cla; Picture Alliance/P. Wegner 24c; Ezequiel Scagnetti 59br, 105bl; Xinhua/U Aung 46b, 47cra.
Robert Harding Picture Library: Jean-Pierre de Mann 36cl; Richard Maschmeyer 127bc; Luca Tettoni 37bl, 129tl. **Spice Garden:** 213tc.
Front Endpaper: All images © Dorling Kindersley except **AWL Images:** Katie Garrod Rtl; **Dreamstime:** Steve Allen Lclb.
Jacket Images: Front: 4Corners: Richard Taylor; DK Images: James Tye bl; **Spine:** 4Corners: Richard Taylor.
All other images © Dorling Kindersley
For further information see: www.dkimages.com

Special Editions of DK Travel Guides

DK Travel Guides can be purchased in bulk quantities at discounted prices for use in promotions or as premiums. We are also able to offer special editions and personalized jackets, corporate imprints, and excerpts from all of our books, tailored specifically to meet your own needs.

To find out more, please contact:
in the United States **specialsales@dk.com**
in the UK **travelguides@uk.dk.com**
in Canada DK Special Sales at **specialmarkets@dk.com**
in Australia **penguincorporatesales@penguinrandomhouse.com.au**

Phrase Book

Burmese is the official language of Myanmar, and the first language of 32 million people, with a further 10 million speaking it as their second language. Although Myanmar has about 135 minor ethnic groups, each with their own language, Burmese is used throughout the country. It is a part of the Tibeto-Burman subgroup of the Sino-Tibetan family of languages. Spoken Burmese is a tonal, pitch-register, and syllable-timed language, meaning that phonemic contrasts can be made on the basis of the tone of a vowel. Pitch, phonation, intensity, duration, and vowel quality are included in these contrasts. Burmese is an analytic, mainly monosyllabic language with a subject-object-verb word order, unlike English, which has a subject-verb-object order. Pronouns vary according to the gender and status of the audience. The written form uses the Burmese script, which was derived either from the Mon or the Pyu script, both of which stemmed from the ancient Brahmi script of the Indian sub-continent. The Burmese alphabet consists of 33 letters and 12 vowels. It is written from left to right and does not require spaces between words; single syllables are joined together to make sentences which, as a whole, carry meaning. However, modern writing generally contains spaces to improve readability. Most Burmese loanwords are in the form of nouns and adopted from Pali (the liturgical language of Theravada Buddhism), Mon, and English, and, to a lesser degree, from Sanskrit, Hindi, and Chinese.

Guidelines for Pronunciation

When speaking Burmese the tone used is significant as the wrong tone can not only change the meaning of the sentence but make it sound impolite or discourteous.

The three basic tones are:

Rising tone (long)	*Marr*, which means "fault"
Low tone (normal)	*Mar*, which means "hard"
High tone (sharp)	*Ma*, which means "from"

Basic Burmese words are pronounced in a similar way to English words. For example, *May*, which means "mother," is pronounced the same way that an English speaker would say "May" when referring to the fifth month of the year.

Burmese has 33 consonants, and some of them have the same phonetic sounds. Consonants are both aspirated and unaspirated, but as a uniform system of transliteration does not exist, they are romanized variably. The chart below shows the pronunciation of some frequently used consonants.

Guide Symbol	English Example
B	**b**oss, **b**all
Ch	**ch**art, tea**ch**
D	**d**og
F	**ph**one
G	**g**o, be**g**in
H	**h**and, **h**ouse
J	lou**ng**e
K	s**k**y, chi**ck**en
Kha	as in the name **Kha**n
Ky	**j**eep, or like the Chinese **ky**in
L	**l**ane
M	**m**an
N	**n**atio**n**
Ng	si**ng**ing, thi**ng**
Ny	o**ni**on, mi**ni**on, or like the Malay **nya**-**nyi**
P	s**p**ot, pur**p**le
Ph	**p**ot
S	**s**ing, **s**ee
Shw	**sh**ed
Hs	**s**ound
T	**st**op
Th	**t**ongue
W	**w**ind, **w**alk
Y	**y**es
Z	**z**oo

Spoken Burmese emphasizes different consonants than English. For example, in English, the final consonant of the following words would be pronounced:

Bac**k**
Ca**t**
Ru**de**

In Burmese, however, final consonants in many syllables become glottal stops or are nasalized, and are therefore rarely emphasized or pronounced. For example:

K as in Kyai**k**tiyo, which is pronounced *Chaih-Tee-Ou*
Ne as in Mawlamyi**ne**, which is pronounced *Mau-La-Myain*
Ng as in Saga**ing**, which is pronounced *Za-Gainh*
R as in Myanma**r**, which is pronounced *Myan-Ma*
T as in Thatbyinny**u**, which is pronounced *Thah-Byin-Nyu*

In an Emergency

Help!	*Ku-Nyi-Par*
Fire!	*Mee*
Where is the nearest hospital?	*A-**Nee**-Sone-Say-Yone-Bae-Mar-Lal?*
Call an ambulance!	*Lu-Nar-Tin-Car-Ko-Khaw-Par*
Call the police!	*Ye-Ko-Khaw-Par*
Call a doctor!	*Sa-**Yar**-Win-Ko-Khaw-Par*

Communication Essentials

Hello	***Min**-Ga-Lar-Par*
Goodbye	*Note-Sat-Par-Tal*
Yes	*Hote-Par-Tal*
No	*Ma-**Hote**-Par*
Please	*Kyay-Zuu-**Pyu**-Pe*
Thank you	*Kyay-Zuu-Tin-Par-Tal*
I don't understand	*Kya-**Note**-Narr-Ma-**Lal**-Par*
I don't know	*Kya-**Note**-Ma-**Thi**-Par*
Sorry	*Taung-Pan-Par-Tal*
Excuse me	*Kya-**Note**-Ko-Khwint-Pyu-Par*
What?	*Bar-Lal?*
Why?	*Bar-**Kyaut**-Lal?*
Where?	*Bal-Mar-Lal?*
When?	*Bal-A-**Chain**-Lal?*
How?	*Bal-Lo-Lal?*

Useful Phrases

How are you?	*Tin-Nay-Kaung-Par-Ta-**Lar**?*
Very well, thank you	*Kaung-Par-Tal, Tint-Ko-Kyay-Zuu-Tin-Par-Tal*
Not very well	*Tate-**Ma**-**Kaung**-Par*
What is this?	*Dar-Ka-Bar-Lal?*
How do I get to…?	*…Ko-Kya-**Note**-Ba-Lo-Twar-Ya-Ma-Lal?*
Where is the…	*…Ka-Bal-Mar-Shi-Lal?*
Where is the restroom/toilet?	***Tant**-Sin-Khann-Lar?*
Do you speak English?	*Tin-Englate-Lo-Pyaw-Par-Ta-**Lar**?*
I can't speak Burmese	*Kya-**Note**-Myanmar-Lo-Ma-**Pyaw**-Tat-Par*

Useful Words

woman/women	*A-**Myo**-Ta-**Mee** / A-**Myo**-Ta-**Mee**-Myar*
man/men	*A-**Myo**-Tar / A-**Myo**-Tar-Myar*
child/children	*Ka-**Lay** / Ka-**Lay**-Myar*
family	*Mi-Tar-Su*
hot	*Puu-Tal*
cold	*Aye-Tal*
good	*Kaung-Tal*
bad	*Soe-Tal*
open	*Phwint-Par*
closed	*Pate-Htar-Tal*
left	*Bal-**Phat***
right	*Nyar-**Phat***
straight ahead	*Tae-Tae-Twer-Par*
near	*Nee-Tal*
far	*Way-Tal*
entrance	*Win-Paut*
exit	*Htwet-Paut*
toilet	*Tant-Sin-Khann*

Money

I want to change US$100 into Burmese currency	*Kya-**Note**-Dola-Tit-**Yar**-Ko-Myanmar-Kyat-Ngwe-To Pyaung-Lal-Lo-Par-Tal*
I'd like to cash these traveler's checks	*D-Kha-**Yee**-Twer-Check-Lat-Mat Myar-Ko-Kya-**Note**-Ngwe-Tar-Ya Lo-Par-Tal*

exchange rate	Ngwe-Lal-Lal-Nome
bank	Ban
money/cash	Pite-San
credit card	Credit Card

Keeping in Touch

I'd like to make a telephone call	Kya-**Note**-Telephone-Sat-Lo-Par-Tal
I'd like to make an international phone call	Kya-**Note**-Naing-Gan-Charr-To Telephone-Sat-Lo-Par-Tal
cellphone	Mobile Phone
telephone enquiries	Telephone-Nint-Pat-Tat-Ywe-Sone-Sann-May-Myann-Chinn
public phone box	**Amyarr**-Tone-Phone-Yone
area code	Day-**Ta**-Nan-Pat
post office	Sar-**Dite**
letter	Sar
registered letter	Mat-Pone-Tin-Hter-Taw-Sar
address	Late-Sar
street	Lann
town	Myo
village	Ywar
Internet café	Internet-Sine
email	Email

Shopping

Where can I buy…?	…Ko-Bal-Mar-Wel-Naing-Par-Ta-**Lal**?
How much does this cost?	Di-**Yar**-Ka-Zay-Bae-Laut-Lal?
May I try this on?	Kya-**Note**-Dar -Ko-Sann-Kyi-Naing-Par-Ta-Lar?
I would like…	Kya-**Note**… Chin-Par-Tal
Do you have…?	Tint-Twin… Shi-Par-Ta-**Lar**?
Do you take credit cards?	Tin-Credit-Card-Myar-Lat-Khan-Par-Ta-**Lar**?
What time do you open/close?	Tin-Bal-A-**Chain**-Twin-Phwint / Pate-Par-Ta-**Lal**?
How much?	Bal-Lout-Lal?
expensive	Zay-Kyi-Tal
cheap	Zay-Cho-Tal
to bargain	Zay-Sit-Yan
size	A-**Yawe**-A-**Sarr**
color	A-**Yaung**
black	A-**Net**-Yaung
white	A-**Phyu**-Yaung
red	A-**Ne**-Yaung
blue	A-**Pyar**-Yaung
green	A-**Sane**-Yaung
yellow	A-**War**-Yaung
bookstore	Sar-Oat-Saing
department store	Kone-Sone-Saing
market	Zei (Zayy)
pharmacy	Say-Saing
supermarket	Supermarket
souvenir shop	A-**Mat**-Ta-Ya-Pyit-See-Saing
souvenirs	A-**Mat**-Ta-Ya-Pyit-See-Myar
lacquer painting	Yoon-Pa-**Chi**
painting on silk	Poe-Htae-Pa-**Chi**
wooden statue	Pa-Pu-**Yote**-Htu
silk scarf	Poe-Pa-**War**

Sightseeing

bay	Pin-Lal-Aww
beach	Kann-Chay
cave	Umin
countryside	Kyay-Latt-Day-Ta
covered stairway	Zaungdan
festival	Pwal-Daw
forest	Tit-Taw
island	Kyunn
lake	Yay-Kan
monastery	Kyaung
mountain	Taung
museum	Pya-Tite
nature spirit	Nat
ordination hall	Thein
pagoda	Pha-**Yarr** / Zay-Di
pavilion	Tazaung
river	Myit
temple	Pha-**Yarr**-Kyaung
tourist office	Naing-Gan-Char-Kha-**Yee**-Tal-Yone
travel agent	Kha-**Yee**-Twar-Ko-**Sar-Lal**

Getting Around

When does the train for… leave?	…Ya-**Htar**-Bal-A-**Chain**-Twin-Htwet-Khwar-Ma-**Lal**?
A ticket to… please	Kyay-Zuu-Pyu-Ywe… To-Lat-Mat-Tit-**Saung**-Pay-Par
How long does it take to get to… ?	… To-Yaut-Yan-Bal-Laut-Kyar-Ta-**Lal**?
I'd like to reserve a seat, please	Kyay-Zuu-Pyu-Ywe-Kya-**Note**-A-**Twet**-Htaing-Khone-Tit-**Nay**-Yar-Mar-Yu-Lo-Par-Tal
Which platform for the… train?	…Ya-**Htar**-A-**Twet**-Sinn-Kyan-Ka-Bal-Har-Lal?
Where is the bus stop/station?	Car-Mat-Tine / Car-Sate-Bal-Mar-Lal?
airport	Lay-Sate
arrivals	Site-Yaut-Mu-Myar
bus	Bus
bus station	Car-Kyi-win
bicycle	Sat-Bee
car	Car
car rental	Car-A-**Ngar**-Htar-Na
ferry	Kyo-Po-Yin
motorbike	Cycle
one-way ticket	Kha-Yee-Tit-**Kyaung**-Sar-Lat-Mat
plane	Lay-Yin
plane ticket	Lay-Yin-Lat-Mat
return ticket	A-**Pyan**-Lat-Mat
taxi	Taxi
ticket	Lat-Mat
train	Ya-**Htar**
train station	Bu-Tar-Yone

Accommodations

Do you have a vacant room?	Tin-Do-C-Twin-A-**Khan**-Loot-Shi-Par-Ta-**Lar**?
Room	A-**Khan**
Double/twin room	Na-**Yaut**-Khan
Single room	Tit-**Yaut**-Khan
I have a reservation	Kya-**Note**-Kyo-Tin-Mar-Hter-Par-Tal
hotel	Hotel
guesthouse	Tae-Kho-Khan
airconditioning	Lay-Aye-Pay-Chin
bathroom	Yay-Choe-Khan
passport number	Naing-Gan-Kuu-Lat-Mat-Nan-Pat

Eating Out

A table for two, please	Kyay-Zuu-Pyu-Pe-Na-**Yaut**-A-**Twet**-Sa-**Pwal**-Pay-Par
May I see the menu?	Kya-**Note**-Menu-Ko-Kyi-Ywe-Ya-Par-Ta-**Lar**?
I am a vegetarian	Kya-**Note**-Di-Tat-Tat-Loot-Sarr-Tu-Pyit-Par-Tal
Do you have any special dishes today?	Tint-Twin-Ya-**Nay**-A-**Twet**-A-**Htoo**-Hinn-Lyar-Myar-Shi-Par-Ta-**Lar**?
Can I have the bill, please?	Kyay-Zuu-Pyu-Ywe-Kya-Tint-Ngwe-Shinn-Pa-Ya-Say?
bitter	Khar-Tal
breakfast	Na-**Nat**-Sar
Burmese specialties	Myanmar-A-**Htoo**-Pyu-A-**Sarr**-A-**Sar**-Myar
chopsticks	Tu
fork	Kha-**Yinn**
knife	Darr
restaurant	Sarr-Taut-Saing
sour	Chin-Tal
spicy (hot)	Sat-Tal
spoon	Zoon
sweet	Cho-Tal
to drink	Taut-Yan
to eat	Sarr-Yan
Western food	A-**Naut**-Tine-A-**Sarr**-A-**Sar**

Menu Decoder

apple	Pann-Tee
baguette	Pyin-Tit-Paung-Mote-Lone
bamboo shoots	Myit
banana	Nga-**Pyaw**-Tee
bean sprouts	Pal-Pin-Paut
beer	Bee-Yar
beef	A-**Mal**-Tar
bottle	Pa-**Linn**
bread	Paung-Mote
butter	Htaw-Pat
chicken	Kyat-Tar
chili	Nga-**Yote**-Tee
coconut	Own-Tee
coffee	Coffee
coriander	Nan-Nan-Pin
crab	Ga-**Nann**
dessert	A-**Cho**-Pwal
drinks	Taut-Sa-Yar-Myar
duck	Bal-Tar
egg	Oo
fish	Ngar

fish sauce	*Ngar Ngan Pyar Yay*
fruit	*Tit-Tee*
fruit juice	*Tit-Tee-Phyaw-Yay*
garlic	*Kyat-Ton-Phyu*
ginger	*Ginn*
glass	*Phan-Khwat*
ice	*Yay-Khae*
ice cream	*Yay-Khae-Mote*
lamb	*Toe-Tar*
lemon	*Tan-**Pa**-**Yo**-Tee*
lemongrass	*Sa-**Par**-Lin*
lime	*Tan-**Pa**-**Yar**-Tee*
lobster	*Kyaut-Pa-**Zon***
mandarin orange	*Lain-Maw-Tee*
mango	*Ta-**Yat**-Tee*
meat	*A-**Tar***
menu	*Menu*
milk	*Nwar-No*
mineral water	*Taut-Yay-Tant*
mushrooms	*Mo*
noodles	*Khaut-Swal*
noodle soup	*Mohinga*
onion	*Kyat-Ton-Ne*
papaya	*Tin-Baw-Tee*
paté	*A-**Tarr**-Nit*
peach	*Mat-Mon-Tee*
pepper	*Nga-**Yote**-Kaung*
pork	*Wat-Tar*
potato (sweet potato)	*Arr-Luu (Ka-Soon-Oo)*
prawn	*Pa-Zon*
rice	*Hta-**Min***
salad	*A-**Tote***
salt	*Sarr*
soft drinks	*A-**Cho**-Yay-Myar*
soup	*Hinn-Yay*
soy sauce	*Pal-Ngan-Pyar-Yay*
spring rolls	*Kaw-Pyant-Myar*
stir-fried	*Mwe-Kyaw-Hter-Taw*
sugar	*Ta-**Kyarr***
tea	*Lat-**Phat**-Yay*
vegetables	*Hinn-Tee-Hinn-Ywat-Myar*
water	*Yay*
wine	*Wine*

Health

What's the matter with you?	*Tin-Bar-Pyit-Ter-Lal?*
I do not feel well	*Kya-**Note**-Nay-Ma-Kaung-Par*
It hurts here	*Di-Nay-Yar-Mar-Nar-Tal*
I have a fever	*Kya-**Note**-Twin-A-**Phyar**-Shi-Tal*
I am allergic to…	*Kya-**Note**-Di… Nint-Ma-Tae-Par*
accident (traffic)	*Ma-**Taw**-Ta-**Sa**-Mhu (Yin)*
allergy	*Ma-**Tae**-Chinn*
ambulance	*Lu-Nar-Tin-Yin*
antibiotics	*Poe-Tat-Say-Myar*
bandage	*Pat-Tee*
blood	*Tway*
blood pressure (high/low)	*Tway-Paung-Chain (Myint-Di / Nal-Di)*
cough	*Chaung-Soe-Tal*
diabetes	*See-Cho / Tway-Cho*
diarrhea	*Wann-Shaw-Tal*
dizzy	*Muu-Tal*
doctor	*Sa-**Yar**-Win*
ear	*Narr*
flu	*Tote-Kway*
food poisoning	*A-**Sar**-A-**Sate**-Tint-Tal*
headache	*Khaung-Kite-Tal*
heart	*Na-Lone*
hospital	*Say-Yone*
hygiene	*Tant-Shinn-Mhu*
illness	*Phyarr-Nar-Chin*
injection	*Htoe-Say*
malaria	*Ngat-Phyar*
medicine	*Say*
operate	*Khwal-Sate-Tal*
prescription	*Say-Sar*
sore throat	*Lal-Pinn-Nar-Tal*
temperature	*A-**Pu**-Chain*
toothache	*Twar-Nar-Tal*

Time, Days, and Seasons

minute	*Mi-Nit*
hour	*Nar-Ye*
day	*Nay-Yat*
week	*A-**Pat***
month	*La*
year	*Nit*
Monday	*Ta-**Ninn**-Lar-Nay*

Tuesday	*In-Gar-Nay*
Wednesday	*Bote-Da-Huu-Nay*
Thursday	*Kyar-Tar-Pa-**Tay**-Nay*
Friday	*Taut-Kyar-Nay*
Saturday	*Sa-**Nay**-Nay*
Sunday	*Ta-**Ninn**-Ga-**Nway**-Nay*
season	*Yar-Tee*
spring	*Nway-Oo-Yar-Tee*
summer	*Nway-Yar-Tee*
fall	*Saung-Oo-Yar-Tee*
winter	*Saung-Yar-Tee*
dry season	*Chaut-Tway-Yar-Tee*
rainy season	*Moe-Yar-Tee*
rain (it is raining)	*Moe (Moe-Nway-Nar-Di)*
wind	*Lay*
sunny	*Nay-Tar-Di*
weather	*Yar-Tee-Oo-Tu*
warm/cold	*Nway-Tal / Aye-Tal*
morning	*Na-**Nat***
midday	*Nay-Lal*
afternoon	*Nay-Khinn*
evening	*Nya-Nay-Khinn*
night	*Nya*
What time is it?	*Bal-A-**Chain**-Shi-P-Lal?*

Numbers

1	*Tit*
2	*Nit*
3	*Tone*
4	*Lay*
5	*Ngar*
6	*Chaut*
7	*Khun*
8	*Shit*
9	*Koe*
10	*Tit-**Sal***
11	*Ta-**Sat**-Tit*
12	*Ta-**Sat**-Nit*
13	*Ta-**Sat**-Tone*
14	*Ta-**Sat**-Lay*
15	*Ta-**Sat**-Ngar*
20	*Na-**Sal***
21	*Na-**Sal**-Tit*
22	*Na-**Sal**-Nit*
23	*Na-Sal-Tone*
24	*Na-**Sal**-Lay*
25	*Na-**Sal**-Ngar*
30	*Tone-Sal*
40	*Lay-Sal*
50	*Ngar-Sal*
60	*Chaut-Sal*
70	*Khun-Na-**Sal***
80	*Shit-Sal*
90	*Koe-Sal*
100	*Ta-**Yar***
200	*Na-**Yar***
1,000	*Ta-**Htaung***
10,000	*Ta-**Taung***
100,000	*Ta-**Tane***
1,000,000	*Ta-**Tan** / Sal-**Tane***

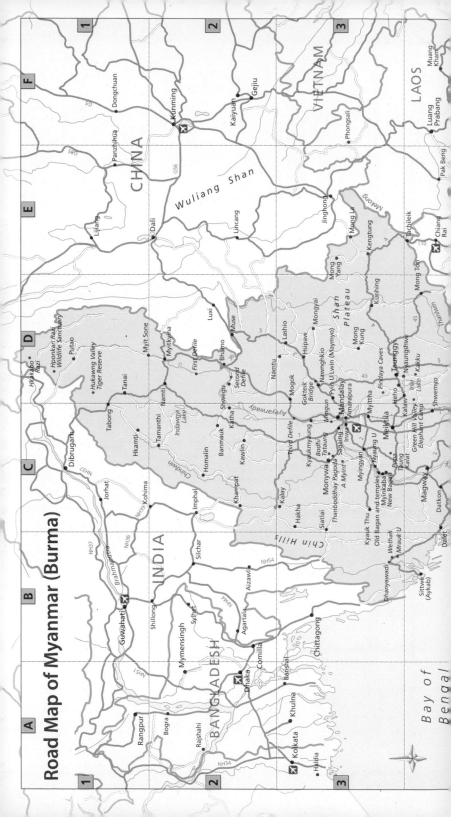

Road Map of Myanmar (Burma)